SWIM

*Going Nowhere in
Particular on
the English Waterways*

STEVE
HAYWOOD

summersdale

TOO NARROW TO SWING A CAT

Copyright © Steve Haywood, 2011

Map by Robert Littleford

All rights reserved.

No part of this book may be reproduced by any means, nor transmitted, nor translated into a machine language, without the written permission of the publishers.

The right of Steve Haywood to be identified as the author of this work has been asserted in accordance with sections 77 and 78 of the Copyright, Designs and Patents Act 1988.

Summersdale Publishers Ltd
46 West Street
Chichester
West Sussex
PO19 1RP
UK

www.summersdale.com

Printed and bound in Great Britain

ISBN: 978-1-84953-065-1

Substantial discounts on bulk quantities of Summersdale books are available to corporations, professional associations and other organisations. For details contact Summersdale Publishers by telephone: +44 (0) 1243 771107, fax: +44 (0) 1243 786300 or email: nicky@summersdale.com.

To Dave Watkin, a precious and much-loved friend

About the Author

Steve Haywood is an award-winning TV producer, a former editor of BBC1's *Rough Justice* who has worked for programmes as varied as *Nationwide* and *Panorama*. Based in London, he writes a lively, provocative waterways column for *Canal Boat* magazine.

CONTENTS

WINTER

ONE
London and Banbury

When I got her, she was very different to how I imagined she'd be. She wasn't the sleek and glossy red setter I'd pictured myself owning. Neither was she the wide-eyed spaniel I'd dreamed about. Or the fluffy Labrador pup I'd always coveted. She hadn't got great floppy ears; she didn't put both paws on my shoulders and lick me to death. She didn't have that warm and reassuring doggy smell about her. In fact, she wasn't a dog at all.

She was a cat. Well, a kitten to be more precise. A ragged, long-haired ball of fur of indeterminate genealogy, black with a messy smudge of white down her back and with the hairiest, most pointed ears I'd seen on any living creature. They were like the ears of a lynx, sharpened to a paintbrush tip with hairs that seemed to be rooted inside her head. If this wasn't unusual enough for a domestic cat, she had a tail so long and bushy it suggested that among the varied strands of DNA that comprised her make-up a squirrel's had somehow managed to get in there at some stage.

She sat in the palm of my hand, looking at the world with curiosity through her wide, yellow eyes. She was especially interested in that bit of the world called Em. She had already decided she did not like Em. Hardly surprising really, since it was evident that Em was hardly over the moon about her either. Which was understandable, I guess. It had taken Em long enough to dissuade me from getting a dog; she was hardly going to be enthusiastic about a smaller version of the same which would scratch the living room upholstery to shreds and dig up the garden bedding plants for a toilet.

'What on earth is that?' she asked eventually – though this, as I should have realised, was more of a demand for an explanation than a simple question. After all, Em is a woman who knows a thing or two about the world. Among the things she knows is what a cat is.

So it didn't help when I said, 'It's a cat.'

'I know it's a sodding cat,' she snapped. 'What I want to know is how it got here. And what are you doing with it?'

This one was a bit trickier. The truth is I wasn't certain how it had happened either. The last I knew I was lying in bed planning another of the canal boat journeys I take when I become bored, or when life in London becomes too stressful. I was staring at the ceiling wondering how Em would handle the idea of me being away from home for most of the summer while she'd have to go to work, mixing it on the tube twice a day in the rush hour. I wondered how I'd handle it myself, too. We've had a narrowboat for years but it's not all long, lazy days basking in the sunshine, I can tell you. Especially if you're boating on your own. Travelling week after week through lost parts of the English countryside so beautiful it makes you want to weep can be an exhausting business. Drinking on your own in pubs every night can get you down too, believe me. A man needs company when he's on the move. What was I supposed to do if I couldn't get a dog?

I must have mentioned the problem to my mate Dave. The idea of a cat must have come up. One way or another, I found myself not long afterwards knocking on the door of a suburban house in Eltham, a few miles from where we live in south-east London. There, a fearsome Irish woman from Cats Protection started firing so many searching questions at me I wondered if I'd stumbled into social services and she was vetting me for adoption.

Eventually, after she'd given me the third-degree on my living arrangements, my domestic status and my annual income, I managed to change the subject by talking about the trip I was thinking of making. For some reason this seemed to irritate her.

'What do you mean, "lost parts of England"?' she snapped. 'The land we now know as England is a country that's been settled for 35,000 years; it's been a unified state since 927. It's been plotted, mapped and charted since time immemorial. How can any of it be "lost"? It is a part of a small, overcrowded island given to building roads as a hobby and dropping rubbish on them as an expression of its national identity. Countryside, you say? There isn't any countryside in England. At the rate they're widening the M1 it's only a matter of time before the whole place turns into a single strip of tarmac...'

'No, no, it's not like that at all,' I protested. 'That's just a trick of the maps. If you judged England by an atlas you'd be right in thinking that it was made up entirely of roads, given the amount of them which seem to snake around all over the place. But it looks worse than it is because they're completely out of scale. On an average atlas, a motorway's 8 miles wide. It makes us look as if there's nothing but roads. On a narrowboat, you realise that isn't true. From the canals you see a different England.'

She looked unconvinced. She may have known more about the history of England than was good for any sane person, but she was from Ireland, remember. Where Donegal is. And Galway. Where they know what countryside really is.

She pushed a small, untidy bundle in my direction and made me sign a large cheque. The bundle was the cat; the cheque was described as a voluntary donation to funds.

'She didn't even give me a choice,' I complained to Dave later.

'What? About whether you gave her any money?'

'No, about which cat I had. It was either that one or nothing, take it or leave it.'

'You can't fault her, though,' Dave said. 'She has a reputation for matching the right cat to the right owners. It's uncanny how she does it, a magic she has…'

A magic, eh? What sort of magic would that be, I wondered. Magic like Tommy Cooper's where the trick always goes wrong? Whatever it was, it clearly hadn't worked with Em. I realised this standing in front of her that day trying to justify why I'd got a cat without consulting her. She looked at me and then looked at the cat; then she looked at the cat a bit more before looking back at me. I felt like I'd been discovered having an affair. I felt like I'd just been caught in bed in the act.

'This isn't part of a plan to go off on one of your trips on the boat again, is it?' she asked eventually.

'A trip? What trip would that be? How did you know about it anyhow?'

'I know everything that happens in this house,' she said. 'I even know what you're thinking before you do. I knew about the cat months ago. I could see it in your eyes.' She swept away into another room. 'Just make sure it does its business in a litter tray. And if it falls in the canal and drowns, or if it runs away, don't come crying to me. Cats and boats just don't go together. You should know that by now.'

Em and I have had canal boats of one sort or another for more than thirty years and for most of that time we've had cats too. She was right: they didn't go together. We had a cat once which we inherited with a flat we bought. That summer we took it to the boat, but no sooner did it step on board than it stepped off, never to be seen again. We had more luck later with other cats, but it was never love at first sight with them and the waterways. One was forever climbing towpath trees and getting stuck so that I was constantly having to rescue it from the end of some precarious branch or another – once in the middle of the night when it was impossible to sleep with the noise it was making. Another was always going walkabout. On one occasion near Branston in Staffordshire, where the pickle comes from, it disappeared for three days, ruining what until then had been a perfectly good holiday.

So why did I expect that it would be any different with a new cat? Why was I so hopeful? Well, for starters I knew more about cats. When I had my first I was naïve enough to think that cats were domesticated creatures with wild genes. Several cats down the line, I realised that they were wild animals which had allowed themselves to be seduced into domestication because of their unaccountable weakness for soft furnishings and central heating. You'd be mistaken, however, to think they were really like that. That they were totally domesticated. That they were just fluffy and cuddly, like toys with a mind. I mean, you only have to look at them. You only have to examine their spooky eyes and that capability they have of narrowing their pupils to a diabolical slit so they can see as well in pitch black as bright sunshine. You only have to look at their claws and their teeth, and how wide they can open their mouths when they yawn. You only have to ponder on the infinite patience cats possess, which allows them to wait forever when they're stalking prey.

Now put all that together with their lithe bodies, their lightning reactions and their ability to leap what for us would be the equivalent of a six-storey building. What you have are creatures designed for the sole purpose of efficient killing. It makes you wonder why we trust them. Why we have them in our houses. What makes us so confident that if we've upset one we won't wake up in the night with one round our throat, kicking at us with its hind legs in the way they do which you know from just playing with them is capable of reducing flesh to bloody ribbons in seconds?

I reasoned that since I understood cats more, I could better understand the way a cat thought. My rationale was that this would allow me to relate to a cat on its own terms. In this I was reassured by the fact that I knew a lot more than I used to about canals too. I figured that if I took a trip with a cat as company I could moor in places a cat would like – and if I couldn't, I'd at least know the risky places and be able to take precautions. If I could move from one happy hunting ground to the next, and keep the cushions on the boat plumped, and make sure the feeding bowl was full, then I reckoned I could construct the equivalent of a feline heaven from which no intelligent cat would even think of straying.

I thought I'd try it out by taking the new cat to the boat while she was still a kitten. On this initial induction I had no intention of cruising: the idea was to establish the boat as the home it would become for us both during the summer.

It worked at first. Well, it worked for about an hour.

Justice was in her winter mooring in Banbury – up a cul-de-sac off the Oxford Canal, underneath Kraft Foods and adjacent to a Citroën garage. At first blush this may not seem to be the ideal environment for a human, let alone a cat, and in some senses this is true. It is next to busy roads. It is noisy and dirty. But a boatyard – any boatyard – is a fascinating place for a creature as curious as a cat. It is filled with old engines and piles of discarded wood and sheds wherein lie untold places to hide and innumerable little furry creatures which cannot wait to be tortured to death.

Smudge – for I had christened her Smudge out of deference to the smear of white fur that besmirched her otherwise glossy black back – walked around as if to the manor born. She was particularly taken with the small narrow ledges that ran along either side of *Justice* which allowed her access to the back cabin and engine room at the rear, and to the lounge, galley and master bedroom nearly 60 feet in front at the bow. These gunnels, as they're called, could have been designed for cats. Four inches or so wide, they are made to accommodate a human foot, but for us walking up them is an uncertain, hazardous exercise. They are narrow and we are top-heavy. They get wet and we slip.

But for a cat, 4 inches is an airport runway. In 4 inches a cat could dance a moonwalk on its two hind legs juggling the heads of mice at the same time. On a 4-inch ledge a cat can sleep as soundly as it would in the middle of a king-sized bed, unfazed by the water below. Smudge was particularly taken with the gunnel on the right side because she soon discovered that though most of the portholes on the boat didn't open, there was one on this side that did, allowing her direct access to the bathroom and the opportunity to lick any dripping tap – a filthy habit she'd brought with her from London.

In no time at all she seemed completely comfortable around the water and I relaxed as a result. This was a bad mistake; I should have known better. I'd been putting away food or lighting fires or something, I forget what. Suddenly I became aware that she'd disappeared, and though I looked high and low I couldn't find her. At first I concentrated my efforts inside the boat; but when that didn't work I cast my net wider and began searching the rest of the yard, spending the afternoon probing every little nook and cranny until finally night fell and there was nothing more I could do except stop.

When I spoke to Em I was frantic. 'I can't understand it,' I said, almost in tears. 'Why has she abandoned me like this? I loved that cat, you know. OK, I know I'd not had her long but there was something between us, there really was. We had a special relationship; it was the meeting of minds across different species...'

I'd have probably gone on in this maudlin tone for longer, except Em interrupted with one of her idiotic questions. She wanted to know what the temperature was in Banbury. The temperature? What had the temperature got to do with anything? Didn't she realise that I'd lost my cat? That I was heartbroken?

'Yes, yes, yes...' she said, 'but is it cold up there?'

'Inside or out?'

'Both.'

'Freezing outside – there's a frost. Inside it's about seventy now the fire's burnt through.'

'Then it's a no-brainer,' she announced. 'This is a cat we're talking about, not a polar bear. It's inside, it's bound to be. Where it's warmest.'

'But I've searched the boat...'

'Like you searched the airing cupboard for that towel last week? Like you're always searching for underwear, claiming you haven't got any clean when you've got half the stock of M&S secreted away in various drawers?'

'OK, OK,' I said, 'I take your point.'

Of course, I located her within minutes. She was under the sink, curled up in the vegetable rack, her head cushioned on a large potato. She opened one eye and looked at me lazily.

I was furious. I jabbed my finger at her. 'Don't you ever do that to me again. EVER!' I shouted. 'I have been worried sick about you and I've wasted the whole afternoon looking for you. You need to understand, I am the boss round here. ME! And I'm not having it.'

But she was a cat; she could pretend not to understand me. Worse, she was a London cat, a 'Sarf Lunnun' cat at that. She was like those punks you see with their skirts hitched up to make them shorter, fagging it behind Lewisham Station after school. Confident. Defiant. In yer face, Mister. Up yours.

She turned to me and yawned.

This was no good, no good at all. We couldn't go on like this; we'd have to reach an understanding.

I'd have to understand that the cat would do what it wanted.

TWO
An Expedition to Napton

There remained now only one question, though it was a rather fundamental one. It's great fun embarking on a journey – any journey – but as a starting point it's useful to know where you're going. This is a problem on canals. It's a problem because when it comes down to it, you're never actually going anywhere. Of course, you go places in the sense that you pass through them. Through pretty villages tucked away in the middle of nowhere; through gracious market towns dotted around the shires; through our teeming, overwhelming, overbearing cities. But that said, you've no real destination. You're not going anywhere. Or not with any particular purpose, which is generally why people move from A to B.

On narrowboats it's that philosophical thing about the journey being more important than the arrival.

I had some idea I might just take off and wander the waterways at random; but I've done too much of that sort of thing in the past, and while it may feed the free spirit and provide succour to the soul, it doesn't encourage much of a sense of purpose in a bloke like me who needs to be focused as he gets older and realises time's running out on him. I began to consider more challenging options. One night, during one of our Merlot moments, I paused in the middle of my fourteenth unit that week to announce to Em that I was thinking about taking *Justice* around the coast of Britain. Or maybe I would cruise her across the Atlantic to America. Or down the Congo.

It was just after Christmas and it was snowing deep and crisp and even, so the patio outside was a foot deep in the stuff – as bad as I've ever known it in London. She looked at me blankly the way she does on occasions, wondering how she ever got involved with someone like me in the first place; wondering whether the alcohol would get me before she got the pension.

'No, you won't,' she said. 'That would be silly. That sort of thing kills you.'

'You're right,' I conceded, 'I guess I'll have to take the festivals option instead.'

This idea – travelling from one waterways festival to the next – had been my fall-back position. OK, it was a bit tame compared to some of the other expeditions I'd been considering, but it's no use pretending otherwise: tame is what I am. I'm also a very proud man. I've had too much experience of coming up with Big Ideas when I've got half a bottle of Bulgaria's best coursing through my veins, only to have to do some humiliating backtracking when the implications of what I'd been proposing strike me the following day.

In truth, a bit of gentle cruising between waterways festivals was a far more attractive proposition than any sort of adventuring – especially to someone who was on the verge of achieving his life's ambition of a free bus pass and didn't want to blow it on the last lap. There are waterways festivals all over the place nowadays; you can't move without stumbling across one. In July and August you can barely moor your boat without finding yourself next to a hoopla stall, overwhelmed by a towpath-ful of morris dancers and folkies clutching guitars. But where there's a waterways festival there's always a beer tent too – which is no bad thing. Far from it. Waterways festivals and their beer tents could comfortably become the focus of my summer.

Whatever my overall plan turned out to be, it would have to incorporate at least one festival which I'd already committed myself to attending. This was Canalway Cavalcade which is held annually over the May Day bank holiday in London's Little Venice, and which signals the start of the narrowboat cruising season. Don't press me on the details, but some years back I found myself conscripted onto the organising committee. It started when I let Libby buy me a drink. Then she locked the door and wouldn't let me out. One way or another, I'd agreed this year to take *Justice* there and so I was obliged to make an early journey south. It was probably too early in the year for Em's liking. The implications of me being away were beginning to dawn on her. She sat at the kitchen table in a sulk, staring out of the window at the snow which had begun to fall again. The cat sat next to her, intrigued by all the white fluffy stuff.

'I don't see why you're taking this so badly,' I said. 'You knew I'd be going off sooner or later. You can hardly throw a hissy fit just because I'm firming up plans.'

'I feel I'm being abandoned,' she said. 'You're leaving me and taking the boat and our cat.'

'But it's not our cat,' I said. 'It's my cat. And you don't even like it, anyhow.'

'That's not the point. What's yours is mine, isn't it? Do we have to label everything now? Besides, I wouldn't mind going cruising. It'll be ages before I can get away from London.'

To spare you more of this poignant domestic vignette, let me just say that it resolved itself when the two of us determined there and then to leave for the boat. It may have been the back end of December and driving conditions may have been vile. Even so, we decided to go away, and damn the consequences. We would celebrate New Year on the water. We would welcome in what for me was going to be a long period of cruising, by going on a cruise. It took no time at all to pack for our departure, but it was only after we'd dug out the cat basket from the cellar that we noticed we'd lost the cat we were going to put into it.

We found her on the patio in the snow. But not gingerly padding through the stuff, not feeling her way around it tentatively, cautiously, the way you'd expect of a cat. No, she was lying on her back in the middle of it, her rear legs indelicately splayed out and her front ones flicking up pawfuls of the stuff, biting them as they fell around her as if they'd been butterflies frolicking around a cabbage patch. We both watched her in silence for a while. By anyone's standards, this was unusual behaviour for a cat. Cats are supposed to curl up in front of fires in bad weather, not be out playing in it.

Em turned to me, shaking her head in disbelief as if she had just witnessed a freak show.

'That is some weird creature, your cat,' she said. 'It's bonkers.'

If anyone ever says to me once more how cold it must be on a canal boat in winter, I shall strip them down to their underwear and take them onto *Justice* in December when it snows in the day, and at night the canal freezes over, and temperatures reach those of the Siberian tundra. And do you know what? They'll still be uncomfortably warm. Even with the doors and the windows wide open. Even with an icy gale blowing in from outside. Even with Tomasz Shafernaker banging on every night on the BBC about Arctic cold fronts and severe weather warnings.

Narrowboats are not cold, and that's an end of it. On the contrary, they are too warm. This is because they're insulated better than houses, and stuffed with all manner of heating devices installed by inexperienced skippers who have swallowed those apocryphal stories boatbuilders tell about people being found in the middle of winter frozen to death in their beds. Mind you, I shouldn't be sniffy about inexperienced skippers. I was one once, and when Em and I had *Justice* built I insisted on doing exactly the same thing. *Justice* is about 58 feet long, approximately 50 feet of which is cabin. This is approximately 7 feet wide and 6 feet high. If you work all this out, it means that we have about 2,000 cubic feet of living area to heat – about half the size of an average UK kitchen.

Yet in this small space we have a central heating boiler and four radiators, as well as two solid-fuel stoves which will burn wood or coal or the local postman if we felt like stuffing him in there. We also have a great lump of an engine which only runs efficiently when it's too hot to touch. It means that the engine room is so blistering it could double as the Palm House at Kew if we weren't always having to open the doors to stop the place spontaneously combusting.

Narrowboats, cold? You might as well say that Ferraris are slow.

Out of London, the temperatures seemed too low for it to snow, but from a distance the countryside looked as if it were covered in it. Cruising north out of Banbury towards Warwickshire the winter fields were a dazzling white, the hedges and the damp trees frost-covered, so that every branch and every stem and twig was rimed with its own delicate covering of ice as if each had been carefully dipped into liquid nitrogen. We moored that night just up from Forge Farm, where in the shifting shadows of the fading evening, an eerie tangle of scarecrows leaning against the wall of one of the barns suggested an apocalyptic vision of the dead waiting for Judgment Day.

The next morning it was bright again, the winter's sun as vivid as a Mediterranean summer, though the light was hard and brittle and so sharp it needled your eyes. The fields were glacial; the surrounding woods, copses and hedges glistening so much that you had to squint to look at them. We worked up the five Claydon locks which carry the canal more than 30 feet up this section of the Thames valley, our boots scrunching the frosted grass with a sound like gravel underfoot. Later in the day, as the morning turned to afternoon and the light gradually dimmed, we negotiated the 11 snaking miles of the canal summit, eventually dropping towards the village of Napton by another flight of locks which we negotiated in darkness, the settling frost on the cast-iron paddle gear sticking to our fingers as we worked through.

By now it was bitterly cold and as we made our way downhill it became colder and blacker still, the village lights sprinkled across the hill beyond, our only point of reference, shimmering in the distance so that you couldn't tell where the shadowy earth ended and the indistinct, star-speckled sky began.

Once we'd moored up, and the engine had fallen silent, Smudge came out onto the deck to examine where we were. She had done the same the previous night, only then she had turned tail immediately and gone back into the warmth of the cabin. This time she hopped off onto the towpath, slithering precariously before leaping from the gunnel. She glanced behind her for a moment before disappearing through a gap in the hedgerow. We knew that sooner or later she would do this, but it was still a shock when she did.

Later we sat in The Folly hugging pints of Hook Norton in front of a red hot stove crackling with fragrant wood. There was hardly anyone else in the place. But there was hardly anyone else on the canal either. Since Banbury we'd barely encountered another moving boat.

'She'll be OK,' Em said to me, squeezing my hand. 'You've said it before yourself: cats are only a whisker away from the wild. But she'll come back, once she gets hungry for food or affection. That's the way it is with cats. You have to train them…'

I wasn't convinced. Train cats? You'd have more luck training house flies.

I called Smudge when we got back to the boat. I suppose I half expected she'd be there waiting for us, curled up on the rug or splayed out across the radiator. My voice seemed very thin in the immensity of the silent night, the only other sound apart from the creaking ice thickening on the canal; the only respite to the darkness the occasional, probing beam of a car headlight herding shadows on some distant country lane.

'It's the fact she's a rescue cat that worries me most,' I said. 'She's walked off once before. Who's to say she won't do it again?'

'Well it's no use worrying, it's too late for that,' Em said. 'You knew there were risks bringing her with us. Either she'll come back or she won't.'

And of course, she did come back. She came back at just past 4.14 a.m., a time I can attest to with some accuracy seeing as how I'd been tossing and turning all night, listening out for her so intently that I was aware of the slightest change in tone of Em's breathing or the most insignificant movement of the boat. She bounded aboard and through the bedroom door which I'd left open, leaping straight onto my chest and butting my chin affectionately with the side of her head. Her fur was brittle; underneath where she was beginning to warm she was damp and clammy.

I was half asleep, I guess. I could have sworn I heard her voice which was becoming familiar now: that discordant estuary whine like an old pushbike with worn brakes.

'Fell for that one eh, Sunshine? Same as you did last time,' she seemed to say. 'Now, about this name of mine... '

Yes, this name of hers. Smudge. It wouldn't do, would it? Shouting for her in the night-time at Napton had demonstrated how unsuitable it was. It had no poetry, no spirit, no soul. A smudge is what you leave behind after you've finished cleaning the mirror. It's what you deposit on the window when you've been nosey. Smudge was the sort of name an eleven-year-old girl might choose for a cat, not the sort of name which a post-war baby boomer should have come up with. Or at least not someone who'd lived through the sixties and bought Sgt. Pepper on its release.

The Victorian novelist Samuel Butler said that the test of literary skill wasn't writing great books but naming a kitten, and I was beginning to see what he meant. One of our friends came up with the idea of calling her Nutkins, out of deference to her splendid squirrel-like tail which, like the rest of her, was growing by the week. For a while, as the New Year got underway and January turned into February, I quite took to the name until I began to think it even more girlie than Smudge. There then followed a phase when I called her Nutkins-Smudge, but this double-barrelled combination of the two names compounded their awfulness. Nutkins-Smudge would have been a good name for a blimpish colonel not long returned from the colonies in those days when we had colonies. Or for a flat-chested debutante down from the country in the days when we had them too.

This was the problem: it was too old fashioned for a beautiful cat like her living in the computer age. She was an i-cat and an i-catching one too. During March Em took unilateral action and started calling her Bella, which was just about acceptable in these Italy-obsessed times when the merest hint of association with a *caffè* in Rome or a Tuscan sunset confers glamour on the most commonplace of objects. But it was all getting silly. The poet T. S. Eliot had talked only about the need to give a cat three names, and here we were on the fourth and still counting...

Eventually, the problem resolved itself in that spontaneous way problems sometimes do when you're on a roll, and when life and everything about it seems to fall into place effortlessly. It happened because the cat developed a regular routine. Back in London, she'd taken to going out at night after we'd gone to bed, coming back about 3 or 4 a.m. as she'd done on the boat during the Christmas trip. Except that sometimes, if whatever party she was at went on too long, she wouldn't be back at all by the time I got up three or four hours later. When that happened I'd start worrying about her as I always seemed to be doing. I'd stand on the edge of the flower beds near the patio wall and call her, yelling out the word 'cat' with the inflection on the vowel like some demented Australian teenager in a lunchtime soap.

Most times she'd come back immediately, bounding over the wall with untrammelled enthusiasm which I knew was nothing to do with me and everything to do with the biscuits I was feeding her. Other times, though, she wouldn't appear at all, and my early fears about her well-being would resurface. I was becoming neurotic about her – and I knew it.

'Cat! Cat! Cat!' I'd scream, until the neighbours thought it was me who was demented, not the Australian teenager.

'Cat! Cat! Cat!' I'd shriek, my voice getting hysterically higher and my emphasis on the vowel getting more pronounced, until 'cat' eventually came out sounding like 'kit'.

Now this wasn't a bad idea, was it? Kit? Kit the cat. Geddit?

Despite its association with chocolate bars, this wasn't a bad name for a female canal cat as anyone familiar with waterways history would know. Kit was the nickname of Eily Gayford, an iconic boatwoman who was recruited at the beginning of World War Two by the Ministry of War Transport to train young women as crew for narrowboats, in order to free up men for the front line.

If I was going to have a female canal cat on board, then Kit was as good a name as any.

SPRING

THREE
Banbury to Cropredy

It's April, early morning, and although it's so cold outside it blisters your lungs to breathe, the sun is blazing in a cloudless sky. Driving up the M40 to the boat at Banbury, it's blindingly bright, though as the day wears on it becomes warmer – warmer than you might think possible after such a cold start. Through the windscreen I can feel the heat under my shirt, though this may just be my soul smouldering with the happiness of getting away from London. I pass High Wycombe and soon afterwards drive through the deep chalk cutting, beyond which the chequered fields of Oxfordshire stretch out like a patchwork quilt, signalling my escape to the countryside. As soon as I see it I feel a surge of joy.

This is the first day of my trip. For weeks I've been coming up from home preparing for it. I have drilled and screwed and hammered and scraped; I have given *Justice* so many licks of paint I've become like a cow with a salt block. Everything that was loose, I've tightened; everything that was missing, I've replaced; everything that was broken, I've repaired. I have done so much to the boat I've even been reduced to cleaning out the bilge – which is about as low as you can get on a boat, seeing as how the bilge is in the very bottom: the stagnant repository of every drip of sludgy oil oozing from the engine and every drop of rainwater leaking in from outside.

I was going to bail it out by hand, but Jim who also moors at the yard shakes his head as if I am something which has wandered in from the primeval swamp, unaware of the advantages of new technology. 'Don't be daft,' he says. 'Use The Gulper instead. The Gulper will clear it in no time.'

The Gulper turns out to be a grimy vacuum cleaner. It is black and thick with accretions of grease but it has a GT engine that makes it worth its Capital Letters.

'It only holds about a gallon, though,' Jim cautions me. 'Make sure you don't overfill it.'

This warning goes straight over my head; I'm convinced there can't be anything like a gallon of water in the bilge.

One minute and two gallons later I discover just how wrong I was. The Gulper, it is true, sucks up bilge water with formidable efficiency. The trouble is, when it's sucked up as much it can handle it sprays it out at the back. And the front, too. And the sides as well, for that matter. My engine room is covered in a filthy black residue. It drips off the walls and the roof. It drips off me.

Jim chuckles when he sees what has happened. 'It don't care what it eats for breakfast, that thing,' he says in a tone of voice that makes me think this is what passes for consolation in his world.

This episode with The Gulper, along with my procrastination, has made me a standing joke in the yard. Every morning Graham and Linda, who live on a boat there, go off to work; and every morning they ask me when I'll be leaving and I tell them it'll be later in the day. Then they come back that night and I'm still there, skulking in the cabin hiding from them so I won't look stupid because I've found something else that needs attention before I go.

This just can't go on, I know. OK, so I haven't finished half the jobs I wanted to finish. But so what? On a narrowboat you never do finish half the jobs you want to. That's because if you look hard enough you can always find more jobs to keep you occupied. That's all some boat owners ever do. They are creatures of the marina and their craft are meticulous floating cottages, lustrous testimonies to the painter's art, finished to coachwork standards with their brasses polished to perfection. But boats like this never go anywhere except to the local pub on a bank holiday. And they don't even go there if it's too busy – which it generally is on a bank holiday.

I am not like that. Many years ago I identified the essential characteristic of the narrowboat – the primary feature of its design that distinguishes it from a cottage, floating or otherwise. You may have noticed it yourself. The fact is, narrowboats move: they were designed as a means of transport. I can't speak for other people, but me, I can't understand why you'd want a narrowboat if you weren't intending to go somewhere in it. I'm never happier than when *Justice* is underway, feathering the canal with her bow.

Today, arriving at Banbury, I am in a state of high excitement, all keyed up to get off. My time for departure has finally come. I have shopping in the boot. I have clean clothes. I have a cat lying quietly in a basket on the back seat, though her serenity troubles me. It is peculiar behaviour for a cat in a car, but then everything this cat does is peculiar. Our previous cats hated cars and anything to do with them. Even seeing Jeremy Clarkson on the telly made them restless. Try and actually put them inside a car and they went crazy. They'd attempt to claw their way out, even if this meant ripping through you to do it. By comparison, Kit seems serenely happy travelling. She has been asleep most of the journey. Now she sits waiting to see where I have brought her, 'purrfectly contented', you might say.

I unlock the boat, unpack the car and busy myself with the many jobs that the start of a cruise entails. My neighbours in the yard, however, are not convinced by my resolution to leave that day. They have seen it all before.

'No, you've got to believe me this time,' I protest to Graham and Linda when they stop for a chat on their way to work. 'This time it's for real. I've got one or two things to clear up and then I'm off, there'll be no stopping me.'

'See you tonight, then,' they say with a knowing smile.

And they are right. When they get back I still haven't gone. Instead, I am lying stretched out on the towpath giving *Justice*'s hull one last coat of paint. 'Once I finish this, I'll be away,' I explain. 'Well... after I've been to Tesco's, that is. I've run out of matches...'

It's probably just pity on their part, but they give me matches. In case matches aren't enough they give me a gas lighter and a tin of fuel too; and when I start mumbling that I have to go to B&Q because I need a new hosepipe for my water tank, they give me one of those as well. The way it's shaping up, I reckon that if I say I'm short of company Linda will probably pack her bags and offer to crew for me. I get the sense it really is time to move. I get the sense that they wouldn't mind getting rid of me.

So I go. I start the engine and Kit and I slip out of the yard into an evening that has suddenly turned bitterly cold now the sun has set. This has a profound effect on my mood. I don't feel as cheerful as I did; I don't feel as happy. It will be dark soon and I don't even know where I'm going to moor. I might end up having to sleep opposite the Alcan factory or under the railway bridge near the motorway. But I can't delay any longer. Graham and Linda are standing on the bank waving goodbye to me, wishing me good luck. Or maybe they are just making sure I leave.

One way or another, I wave back and head off into the thickening gloom. Why should I care where I'm going? This is supposed to be an adventure after all.

I'll say one thing about Banbury: leaving it, the air's a lot better. The town has got problems, you see. One of them is that it stinks. True, it sometimes only barely stinks, so you can hardly tell it's stinking. But other times it stinks to high heaven, and you'd have to be a blob without a nose not to notice it. The smell comes from Kraft Foods, just up from where we moor. Kraft is the second largest food and drinks company in the world, and since it's an American company, its Banbury factory is described as 'one of the world's largest soluble coffee facilities.' If it was UK-based it would be described as 'a very big factory making lots of instant coffee.' Even so, it would still stink. It's bound to stink: they make 11 billion cups of coffee a year there. It's bad enough when they're brewing the stuff, but when they start burning the leftover grounds, it makes you want to throw up.

The funny thing is that over the years I've got used to it, and after a day or two I hardly notice that it's there. But when I go away and come back, I smell it as intensely as I ever did. And, bizarrely, I realise that I'm rather fond of it. This is because over the years I've come to associate the smell of burning coffee grounds with the canals. It conjures up memories of trips I've made from Banbury in the past and evokes that sense of excitement I always get when I start a journey. I suppose the smell's got into the wrong part of my brain. Once that happens there's no way you can get it out.

It's the same with diesel fumes. I can be standing in the middle of Oxford Street on a busy Saturday when the crowds are washing over me in a putrid wave, yet a lungful of exhaust from an old Routemaster is all I need to take me back to some sylvan waterway glade, where a leaking lock drips out a melody and kingfishers flash between the willows. You can understand it, I guess. Narrowboats nearly always have diesel engines and I've smelt them in so many idyllic places I'm bound to associate the two.

There are sounds I connect with the waterways too; one of the most common is the noise of trains which you hear all the time on a boat, because railways often follow the routes of waterways. Even if you can't see a railway most times you can be sure you're never far from one. You'll frequently moor up at the end of the day thinking you're in the middle of nowhere, only to find trains trespassing on your dreams as faraway engines echo through the night.

I find trains strangely reassuring, especially when I'm cruising late into the night as I was that day I left Banbury. North of the town, the Chiltern line between Birmingham and London runs close to the cut, and the trains rattling up the track with their carriage lights flashing like a strobe were a comfort to me in the overwhelming immensity of the darkness in which I found myself. Darkness like that is unnerving, take it from me. Especially on overcast nights when you can't see the stars, or much else either, save for a dull, red glow on the horizon which is a city somewhere far away. You don't experience night like that very often in this country, and when you do it makes you feel inconsequential, a speck in the great universe. If you're cruising alone, trains are at least company; otherwise you'd get spooked and stop for the night. Or start doing silly things to make yourself feel better. Which is what I did.

I got out my iPod and started listening to Abba. Then I joined in, singing a chorus or two of 'Dancing Queen' and doing a Meryl Streep on the deck as I was steering, bopping about like she did in *Mamma Mia!*

You can do things like that on a boat at night in the countryside because there's no one there to see you. The people passing in the train won't notice you, you can be sure of that. They sit silhouetted by their glowing windows in their heated carriages, staring out with so much on their minds they wouldn't see E.T.'s spaceship landing on the track, let alone you cavorting around like a lunatic. Even if they did happen to become aware of you in the distance – maybe just at that moment you were leaping about like Meryl did on her way down to the quayside with half the population of Skopelos following her – they wouldn't care. As far as they're concerned, you're a weirdo being on a boat at night anyhow. A bit of dancing's not going to make you any more of a weirdo.

I went through the lock at Bourton, which I'll always think of as Irene's lock after a friend who lived there until her death a year or two back. Next up was Slat Mill. It was dark by now and a ghostly flock of sheep were sheltering behind the wall of a field coughing like consumptives. That didn't make me feel any better either.

Even so, I was in my stride now; I could have gone on all night, except that for some reason when I got to Cropredy the day suddenly caught up with me and I was overwhelmed by intense tiredness. Luckily, in the cutting below the shop there was a convenient mooring available and I slipped into it without a second thought. I was so exhausted by now that I barely had the energy to clean my teeth before dropping into bed. Even Kit was shattered. Too shattered to want to go out, certainly. She curled up at my feet at the foot of the bed until we were both woken by the church clock the next morning.

FOUR

To Braunston and down the Grand Union

When Em stepped into the cabin, Kit looked up at her with an expression that seemed to say, 'Where the hell has that come from? Jeez, I thought we were well rid of her.' Em glowered back at her with a similar level of antagonism. It was clear from her face that she, Em, thought that she should be the one cruising on the boat through the picturesque Midlands countryside, not the useless ball of fur lying in front of the fire in her chair, looking for all the world as if it owned the place.

The cat yawned and settled itself down more comfortably. Em swept it onto the floor with her handbag and sat down in its place. She is not an overly sentimental woman, Em.

'Well,' she demanded, 'what are the plans?'

We were in Braunston, Britain's 'canal capital' – although this title makes it sound rather more grandiose than it is, for it's little more than a smallish Northamptonshire village splayed out along a hillside with a church at one end and a council estate at the other. It's in a key position, though: 50 miles from Birmingham and on the axis of four major canal routes, two south and two north, making it unique on the waterways system.

In the golden days of canal-carrying it was a bustling inland port and its busy towpath was thick with boatyards, dry docks and chandlers servicing the needs of a transport industry which underpinned the Industrial Revolution. Today, 250 years later, the action's moved elsewhere and Braunston's been left as a quiet backwater, geared to the leisure boat market, for which it's particularly well suited. It's near the M1, close to the Watford Gap, and its accessibility makes it a popular spot to moor boats in one of the many marinas which have sprung up in the area. So many marinas, in fact, that parts of Braunston are like one big marina. Imagine a waterside caravan park. In fact, imagine about half a dozen waterside caravan parks strung together.

Kit and I travelled there along the Oxford Canal, retracing the route across the summit as far as Napton which Em and I had followed on our Christmas cruise. From there I pressed on into Northamptonshire across a landscape scarred with the ridge and furrow remnants of medieval strip farming. There was no more traffic on the canal than in December, and astonishingly I only passed one boat all day. Steering it was a bearded academic type with a pinched face and fewer clothes than the weather demanded. I nodded to him the way you do on canals, probably mumbling a courteous word or two, something about the conditions or how cold it was. The strength of his response threw me. He looked at me over the top of his half-moon spectacles and delivered a meteorological discourse on isobars, adiabatics and gradient winds. This was followed by another on the loneliness of the Oxford summit at this time of the year, about how shallow it was and how tortuously twisty. About how it was 'just so reassuring' to see another boat and 'feel that one wasn't entirely alone'.

All this in about twenty seconds. Delivered at breakneck speed.

Blimey! I know we like to be polite on canals, but this was all a bit much even for me. This sort of camaraderie might have been OK if we'd been two tramp steamers crossing in the Channel during a force 12, but it was a bit over the top for a couple of old geezers gently pottering past each other on narrowboats in the Midlands.

Mind you, at least he acknowledged me. A lot of the new skippers on the cut nowadays have taken to blanking you out, staring ahead as if they hadn't seen you; or looking in the opposite direction as if something had just caught their attention so that, oh no, they can't hear a thing you say, however loudly you're shouting. I put it down to the intimacy of the canal community, which makes a lot of them feel uncomfortable. They pay lip service to it, but they're not used to being sociable. Maybe I'm being too kind though. Maybe they're just being rude. Some of them at least recognise their social awkwardness. They give you a wan smile, so watery that if it wasn't part of their face it would drip into the canal. Then they raise a limp, embarrassed hand as if to say, 'I come from the town and I'm really not comfortable with this social interaction thingy, but here goes...'

In one respect my passage up the Oxford was different to Christmas because it attracted more attention than it had before from people moored on the towpath in residential boats – the 'liveaboards'. As I went by they'd press their noses against their windows and follow my progress until I'd disappeared from view. They always looked worried. I guess this was because my presence was one of the first signs that winter was over, and that the canals were emerging from their hibernation. On the one hand this was good news for them: the nights were drawing out, it would soon get warmer and they could emerge from their cocoons onto the towpath for barbies, evening drinks and parties into the night. The downside was there'd be more boats around to speed past and send them lurching across their cabins at just the moment they were shaving or pouring water from a boiling kettle. You couldn't help but sympathise with them. They lived in Shangri-La. Soon it would be under siege from fleets of hooligan holidaymakers with their raucous children and uncontrollable dogs. At the moment there was just me and the odd underdressed academic; soon there would be flotillas of boat owners on the move, a veritable Dunkirk of evacuees from the city gagging to reacquaint themselves with cows – if only to eat them burnt over charcoal.

For the moment, however, the waterways lay serene and tranquil, the summer another world away. It was still as chilly as midwinter and every occupied boat had a fire on the go so that comforting plumes of smoke curled gently from their chimneys, hanging over the water in a delicate haze. Some boats were burning logs in their stoves and the smell of the wood seemed perfumed, almost sweet; in other places the acrid odour of coal was predominant, like railway stations long ago.

Em was spending a week with me and had come up from London by train and taxi, bad-tempered from her journey. Unfortunately my trip from Napton hadn't been trouble-free either. I'd been attempting to multitask by cleaning the brasses as I went – which is what the old boatmen used to do. Sadly, I hadn't got the same level of skill as they had and I'd run *Justice* up the bank a couple of times before I gave up on the idea as a bad job. It had put me in a bad mood.

We went for a drink in a pub we've used for years, only they'd made Friday 'Concert Night' and we couldn't hear ourselves talk. This was a mercy since at least it stopped us bickering –

although I guessed from the movements around Em's mouth that this wasn't entirely putting her off. Back at the boat, the casserole I'd prepared had burnt, which added to the general pessimism of the evening. Eventually we gave up the struggle to be sociable and went to bed early. OK, so it hadn't been the best start to a week together, but at least it meant that we got a good night's rest and could get up early the next morning refreshed for our trip.

We might have been more enthusiastic about it had the weather been better; but the following day turned out to be dismal: windy, wet and cold – the sort of conditions that make you realise why most sane people wouldn't go near a canal outside of the summer months. We slowly worked up the flight of six locks that take the Grand Union east to where it passes through a tunnel more than a mile long. Soon afterwards there's a junction near the small village of Long Buckby, and from there it veers sharply southwards down seven more locks towards London and the Cavalcade festival that was our destination.

The locks are big here – twice the width of those on the Oxford: great lumbering things with heavy gates that you have to get your back behind to move. They're no more complicated than smaller locks, though. Locks of any sort aren't exactly cutting-edge technology or else they wouldn't let hirers loose on them five minutes after they've picked up a boat. Operating them is only a matter of winding up a few ratchets in the right order. True, death and chaos will ensue if you wind the ratchets in the wrong order but, hey, nothing in life is a complete pushover.

Em and I soon got into our locking routine which we've been doing for so long it's second nature. There's something reassuring about the repetition of familiar activities like this; something comforting when both of you are acting in concert, scarcely conscious of what you're doing, but each knowing automatically what has to be done and what the other person expects of you. Hours can pass as minutes when you get into this sort of groove, working single-mindedly towards the same goal. You can get into a hypnotic trance in which your actions don't seem to be yours, and even your place in the physical world seems indeterminate, as if you're wandering about in a dream.

When you get into this mindset, anything outside of yourself is a distraction, an imposition on your state of mind. For us the spell was broken when we realised we were catching up another boat travelling up the locks in the same direction. We both saw it about the same time. Stopping what we were doing, we stared at it, outraged. What was another boat doing on our canal? What did it think it was playing at?

It turned out to be another narrowboat about the same size as *Justice*, steered by a fifty-something bloke in a boiler suit and flat cap, who I guessed from his florid complexion was fond of a drink or two of an evening. He was transporting it professionally from a marina to a boatyard where it was scheduled to come out of the water for maintenance. He'd made a dozen similar trips in the previous month in as many different boats, he told us in an irascible tone of voice which made it patently obvious that he wasn't happy about this situation. But then, he wasn't a very happy man generally.

'I've had enough of it, you better believe me,' he said. 'I don't know why I'm still doing the bloody job. I know every lock in this flight like the back of my hand, and take it from me they're all bastards.'

Personally, I couldn't see what he was getting himself all het up about. Steering canal boats around the countryside and getting paid for it would be a dream job for a lot of people. Besides, what did he expect? That the owners of the boats should get them repaired at other yards in order to give him the opportunity of more varied cruising? That the marina should somehow relocate to make his work more interesting?

We began sharing locks together which is the protocol in these situations. This should have made it easier for us all, since there were more of us to do the work. But it didn't shape up that way. We'd arrive at a lock and start to do something, only to find that he'd hopped off his boat and wanted to do it differently. So at the next lock we'd do it his way, but still he wasn't happy. He wanted to do it all. He'd rush to get to locks before us or worse, when we got there before him, he'd muscle us out of the way.

And all the while his whinge-o-meter was creeping up the scale. He could whinge for England, this guy. Potentially he was a world whinging champion. He whinged about the weather. He whinged about the state of the canals. He whinged about how exhausting all this travelling was for a bloke his age who should be doing a lot more with his life than humping poncey canal boats up and down the cut for bloody people who'd got more money than sense…

OK, I could go along with him as far as the weather and the state of the canals. I could even sympathise at how exhausting he found his work. He lost me at the poncey boat bit, though. Call me oversensitive, but I was reasonably confident he was getting at us with this one. It was clear he thought we were stupid, which may be true. But he thought we were rich too, which certainly isn't. I'd had enough of him anyhow and suggested to Em that we might take an early lunch to give him the chance to get ahead of us again.

So we moored up and had a cheese sandwich. We drank tea. We ate biscuits. When we looked out of the boat again, he was thankfully nowhere to be seen, though just to make sure I went for a walk up the towpath. I didn't want to find him moored up around the next bend waiting to pounce on us. Mind you, I needn't have bothered going to all the trouble. Almost immediately after we'd set off again, we ran into another working boater, this one a younger bloke. He was steering a 'flat' – a sort of pontoon with a crane on the back – and he was just as bad in his own way. Worse really, because he got racist. We hadn't been with him for more than a few minutes before he started having a go at Lithuanian plumbers for no other reason than that they were Lithuanian. Why he'd got a downer on Lithuanian plumbers rather than, say, Latvian plumbers, or the more common or garden Polish plumber, he never made entirely clear.

Perhaps his wife had run off with a Lithuanian plumber. Perhaps she was a Lithuanian plumber.

It was still early enough for another lunch, so we stopped again.

'You get a lot of opportunities to eat on canals,' I remarked to Em.

'You get tempted a lot to kill people too,' she replied. 'Do you think anyone would notice if we quietly bumped off one or two people along the way?'

That afternoon we moored in Stoke Bruerne, just past another long tunnel which passes under Blisworth Hill. Whether it was because we were sheltered there, or because there'd been some subtle change in the millibars on which the underdressed academic might have been able to shed some light, I don't know. Perhaps it was because we were closer to the equator. One way or another, the weather changed for the better very suddenly. Where before it was dull and overcast, the sky was now clear; where it had rained, the sun now shone, so crystal clear it lit up the late afternoon until it was luminous. The colours seemed lucid, the surface of the canal about as far away from its usual turgid brown as you could imagine. That day it was pale green like ancient glass, and the hedges and trees stretching down to the water's edge were the same, soft and muted with the light diffusing through their new spring leaf growth.

Kit was soon outside and cavorting on the towpath, hunting flies or chasing leaves.

Stoke Bruerne is described in the guidebooks as one of the best examples there is of a classic canal village, and it deserves the accolade. With its thatched pub and honeystone cottages, and the canal and locks passing right through the centre, it's about as English as Elgar. It's chocolate-box England, the type of place they used to put on chocolate boxes when they did that sort of thing. Now they make jigsaws of it, and put pictures of it in glossy coffee-table books about England, and feature it on tourist websites. In its own small way it's perfect, like a well-cut tennis court or a well-tended rose garden. What's not to like about it except you sometimes feel you're messing the place up by just being there? What's not to rave about except that occasionally you feel it's a place designed more to look at than to be in?

I rolled up my sleeves and had another go at polishing the boat brasses. I kept getting disturbed by people passing on the towpath, though. Even so early in the year with the waterways themselves so empty, Stoke Bruerne was busy with a constant stream of sightseers who treated me as one of the sights they'd come to see. Not unreasonably, I suppose. Stoke Bruerne's a canal centre; I was on a canal boat and part of the scene. They wanted to know where I'd come from and where I was going. They wanted to know how old the boat was and whether we lived on it. They asked if I minded them taking a picture of *Justice*. They asked if I'd object to taking a picture of them against it. Inevitably, among the questions I was plied with was the one everyone on a narrowboat gets asked sooner or later.

So let's get this over with once and for all, even though the subject is always a little distasteful for us English who never feel altogether comfortable talking about grubby subjects like money. A narrowboat used to cost £1000 a foot to have built; now you can say goodbye to twice that, more if you go for posh options on engines or internal fittings. However, if you're very lucky and know what you're doing, you might be able to pick up something for as little as £15,000, sometimes even less – though for that price anything you buy will be a wreck and need a lot of work doing to it. Most of the boats you see on the canals lie between these two extremes and will have cost their owners in the region of £30,000–60,000. For that they get the equivalent of a mid-range family car, rather than an old banger or a Porsche.

Look no further for the recent growth of popularity of the canals than evenings like this at places like Stoke Bruerne where, after conversations of this sort, couples retire to the pub where they nurture their dreams over beer and wine and talk about 'lump sums' and 'downsizing' and 'final pay-offs.'

But beware, dreams can sometimes turn sour. A few days later as we passed through Hemel Hempstead in Hertfordshire we met a couple at the lock side who recounted a heartbreaking tale of the problems they'd had with their new boat. They had seen life afloat as a cheap housing option, and rather than disabuse them, they'd been encouraged to indulge their fantasies by an unscrupulous builder who'd sold them a craft entirely unfitted to their needs. The electrics had never worked properly, the heating and plumbing were a constant worry, and now – a nightmare – the holding tank of their lavatory had begun to leak and was filling the bilges.

Winter too, had proved harder than they could cope with, so now they were selling up, hoping to recoup at least a small proportion of their precious life savings which they'd invested in the venture.

They started talking to me because they recognised me from a column I write in a waterways magazine. But there was nothing I could do to help them. There was nothing anyone could do to help them.

I could have wept.

FIVE
A Few Days in Denham

Kit was missing. We woke up and she wasn't there. We couldn't understand it; there didn't seem to be any explanation for her disappearance.

Every day since departing from Cropredy she'd left the boat in the evening between eight and nine o'clock as soon as it began to get dark, and she'd come back sometime before the morning when we'd find her curled underneath the coffee table, waiting patiently for her food bowl to be replenished. She was as regular as clockwork. She did it at Cosgrove where we moored close to the elegant Solomon's Bridge with its decorative pillars on either side carved from sandstone. And at Marsworth – Maffers as the old boatpeople used to call the place – near the daffodil-covered summit of the canal. She'd done it too when we stopped overnight in Cassiobury Park near Watford, a place which for 250 years was the estate of the Earls of Essex and which you'd have thought more than anywhere else would tempt a courtly cat like her to do a runner. But no.

Wherever we moored, she'd come back with a routine which never varied.

Not this morning, though. Not the morning we woke at Denham adjacent to the River Colne on the edge of London.

At first we were sure she was hiding on the boat, and we searched the place high and low, peering under beds, into the darkest corners of cupboards and even the backs of drawers, convinced that she had to be somewhere close. We turned the place upside down looking for her until it finally began to dawn on us that she wasn't on board, and that she hadn't come back. The landscape round this part of the world is characterised by an intricate network of lakes formed by old gravel pits which are so thick with wildfowl it's like being on the Severn Estuary or in North Norfolk. We began to comb the area in the immediate vicinity of the boat, but without any success. What could we do after that? We couldn't just up sticks and abandon her.

We began to hunt further afield, around the banks of the lakes and the pastureland surrounding them. Morning melted away into the afternoon. We had lunch and afterwards extended the search wider still, until day became evening and the shadows of the birch trees in the wood next to the canal lengthened and we went back to the boat. I took the opportunity to put my feet up and dozed off – although even then I wasn't free of her and she haunted my dreams. I kept waking fitfully, convinced I could hear her scratching about outside, or meowing in the distance.

She wasn't there, of course; there was no sign of her anywhere. Night fell and I took a walk up the towpath with a torch, flashing the beam into the wood and shouting out her name until I was hoarse. I was certain she could hear me, certain she was just playing hard to get as usual. I knew she'd be back by the following morning.

And yet at the same time I couldn't be sure something hadn't happened to her. The minks around the lakes are savage. I couldn't help wondering if there'd been a stand-off. Perhaps she was hurt, maybe even dead? I felt sick in the pit of my stomach just thinking about it.

The next morning she still hadn't shown and we prepared for another anxious day of searching. By now I'd persuaded myself that all this was happening because we'd moored near lakes. Isn't there something about water that triggers cats to walk on their wild side? Everyone knows that, don't they? So why hadn't I moored somewhere else, somewhere that wouldn't have attracted her so much, somewhere... somewhere... well, just somewhere else without all this water around.

'It's no use us worrying like this. It's futile,' Em said. 'She'll find her way back; we'll have to trust her.'

'Us' worrying? 'We' having to trust her? If nothing else, at least as a result of this crisis I was seeing a new side of Em; a different, more gentle aspect of her relationship with the cat. This wasn't altogether a surprise, I have to confess. A couple of days before I'd seen Kit discreetly rubbing against Em's ankle, and I saw Em – I'm not inventing this – bend down surreptitiously and tickle her behind her ears. Neither of them thought I'd seen the incident, and it would have been imprudent to bring up the topic with either of them later, so it went unmentioned. Even so, I'd logged it and filed it. You never know when information like this might be useful.

We went out looking for her again. It felt like we were wasting our time, but at least I had time. My only commitment was getting to the Cavalcade festival in Little Venice. Em was on holiday, though it wasn't much of a holiday waiting around for a cat. We agreed that if Kit hadn't showed by the following day I'd hold the fort while she returned to London to see if she could salvage some holiday entitlement by going back to work early.

In the interim we decided to call off the search and spend what might be our last holiday afternoon together exploring the village of Denham a mile or so from the canal. Denham's a place with a reputation. It's said to be one of the prettiest villages in the Home Counties and the guide books make it sound idyllic. One speaks of a 'peaceful and unspoiled village'; another talks of its 'great charm'. The place must have something going for it: a list of its former and current residents reads like a list of the top table at a BAFTA awards ceremony. The actor Sir John Mills lived here for many years until his death; former James Bond star Roger Moore still does, supplementing his pension by occasionally raising his eyebrow in ads for the Post Office. Shane Richie – Alfie Moon from *EastEnders* – lived in Denham, and Robert Lindsay and Cilla Black still do, although she's not supposed to be popular with the neighbours – something to do with her trees blocking out light, apparently. Other former Denhamians include the composer Mike 'Tubular Bells' Oldfield, Mr Tomorrow's World, Raymond Baxter and pop star Jess Conrad – though you'd have to be a hundred years old to remember him. Frankly, you wonder why they all bothered. I mean, this is supposed to be a country village. Country villages are supposed to be havens of peace and quiet. But Denham's a hellhole jammed between the North Orbital and the M40. No sooner had Em and I left the boat and walked beyond the shelter of the woodland bordering the canal than we were overwhelmed with the noise of traffic thundering in and out of London. The din of it hangs over Denham like a dark cloud. It gets inside your head. It gets in your bones. It's a shame really because, visually, the village is as lovely as everyone says.

From the canal you approach it across a country park which leads to a village road and a building which I guess had once been a simple mill cottage but which, over the years, has swollen into an immense Dutch gable-ended chateau. It stands next to the mill race at the end of a gravelled drive, each of its windows sporting a louvred shutter on either side which gives it a classy look, like something transposed from the south of France.

It was wisteria time and wherever you looked Denham was draped with hanging fronds of pale violet flowers. The chateau near the mill had a line of it at first floor level like a tight belt trying to contain any more excessive growth; and John Mills' former house, marked with a blue plaque, was covered too. It's another massive Dutch gable-ended building – although it impressed me less for its architecture than for the fact that his daughter Hayley was brought up in the house. Hayley's about my age, and as a child she was a movie star herself for Walt Disney. Like every other testosterone-charged teenage boy in the country I had a painful crush on her. My wispy prepubescent self, minus the beer belly which was later to weigh it down, was entranced by her wide eyes, her luscious lips, her long blonde hair, and well… let's just leave it there, shall we?

I didn't feel comfortable in Denham; I'm surprised anyone could. There are alarms on every house, CCTV cameras all over the place and Neighbourhood Watch signs wherever you look. On ugly blue posters attached to lamp-posts the Thames Valley Police advise you not to leave valuables in your car. On the fence surrounding the flint and stone tower of St Mary's Church there are other police placards in garish purple telling you the same thing just in case you missed the message the first time round. Next to them – literally – the point is made for a third time on a flysheet from Crimestoppers printed in a fetching shade of Day-Glo yellow.

And this isn't the half of it. Around the church perimeters there are brash blue hoardings warning potential thieves of a system in operation to protect the roof lead. Further on in the village more notices announce that certain houses are protected by private security firms. One has the picture of an Alsatian dog with the warning 'I can make it to the fence in 2.8 seconds. CAN YOU?' You can find signs similar to this on every council estate in the country.

But hang on a second – this isn't a council estate. It's a posh village in Buckinghamshire where you wouldn't get the sniff of a two-bedroomed terrace for under six figures. What is with these people? They seem to be in the midst of a paranoid crisis about crime. OK, they may have more cause to worry about crime than the rest of us because I guess they've got a lot more than the rest of us to steal. Cilla lost a 'lorra' jewellery in a raid a few years back – more than £1 million of it according to the papers. And there's thieving still happening now. As we wandered around we saw posters offering a reward for information about the theft of a couple of horses which had recently gone missing. Even so, it doesn't explain Denham's obsession with crime or the ugliness of all the signs around aimed at countering it. Don't these people ever walk around their own village? Don't they see it? Or do they just live entombed in their big houses, so separated from the rest of their community that they're unaware they're living under conditions of near siege?

We had intended going for a drink at one of the local pubs, but we made the mistake of taking a circular route around the village first. This led us back through the churchyard again where signs we hadn't seen before warned us not to let our dog foul the grass. At length we came out onto the village green where another sign requested us not to park our car in a certain place because it was a private house and the gates were in constant use. Close by was a third sign which had presumably been erected by a resident familiar with the discomfort faced by dogs who've been on a long walk and who haven't been allowed to relieve themselves in the churchyard. This cautioned us against allowing them to dump on their drive. There was even a sign outside the pub telling us not to go inside in muddy boots. Having neither dog, nor car, nor soiled footwear, all this officiousness was beginning to get us down a bit so we decided to give the drink a miss and go back to the boat.

It'd have been better if we'd gone straight there, but instead we returned by way of a circuit around the country park. Believe me, if the concentration of signs in Denham village was bad, it was as nothing compared with the amount of them in Denham Country Park. They were all over the place like graffiti: massive billboards all along the riverbank like something you'd see on a freeway in the United States. They prohibited us from swimming, from diving, from jumping in the water, from boating, fishing or barbecuing. Other similarly unsightly notices on the pathways cautioned us against deep water and strong currents. One extraordinary one even warned us of the danger of overhead power lines – which might have been a useful thing to know had the cables been trailing just above our heads rather than on pylons so high they represented more of a risk to planes landing at Heathrow than to anyone walking underneath.

The overall effect of all this overbearing signage is to make Denham Country Park unlike anything you'd ever see in the real countryside. Every last tree is exactly positioned, every hedge and blade of grass carefully planted so that it's about as genuinely rural as the Venetian Hotel in Las Vegas is genuinely Venetian. It's artificial – an idea of what the countryside should be rather than what the countryside actually is.

The same criticism is often levelled at the canals today. It's said that because they're not part of a functioning transport system any more, they're too twee, more of a theme park now and not even the adventure they used to be just a few years back when they were hidden secret places canopied by trees, threading through a forgotten England which had lain virtually unchanged for centuries.

But then it's only old blokes like me who say that, and we're just grumpy old sods.

Anyhow, what do we know about anything at our age?

Back on board, Em and I prepared for what was looking increasingly likely to be the last night of our holiday. We made dinner, both of us – for the moment, at least – instinctively avoiding mentioning the cat and the fact that it would be her third night away. Both of us knew without having to say it that with every hour that passed there was less and less chance of her ever coming back. We laid the table and as the cabin began to darken we lit candles and sat sipping wine. Conversation was muted, desultory. Outside a gentle wind had blown up; water lapped rhythmically against the hull of the boat.

Then just as we were beginning to brace ourselves to address the topic which had been hanging over us, we heard the soft thud of paws landing on the front deck. We glanced at each other and immediately afterwards we felt a sharp gust of chilly air as she levered open the front door and pulled aside the covering curtain. Without so much as a by-your-leave, she sauntered into the cabin and rolled over onto her back inviting us to tickle her tummy. At the same time she mewed in the way that cats do when they're ingratiating themselves. It's the nearest they ever get to guilt.

Eventually she got up and walked over to her food bowl where she started nibbling in a detached, disinterested way as if this eating lark was a job which had to be done, but from which you didn't necessarily have to derive pleasure. Clearly, among the privations she'd suffered during her absence from us, lack of sustenance didn't figure highly. She hadn't been yearning for human company either, since she'd have walked straight out of the boat again afterwards if I hadn't dashed for the door and slammed it shut in her face.

'You ungrateful little bastard,' I found myself shouting through gritted teeth. 'Where on earth have you been? Do you realise you've ruined our sodding holiday...'

Cats, of course, don't smile. They don't have the facial muscles for it, let alone the sense of humour. Even so, I could swear her mouth turned up at the corners and that she looked at me with a certain amusement in her eyes, eyes which suddenly seemed narrower than normal, and craftier than I'd ever noticed before. She rolled over on the rug again and squirmed about on her back with her legs in the air, the way you or I might do if we'd heard some particularly amusing joke which left us helpless with laughter.

If I hadn't been so relieved she wasn't dead I'd have killed her.

Over the ensuing months when she was back to her normal routine and had gone out and come back a hundred times, I couldn't help but be curious as to where she'd been the nights in Denham when she hadn't returned. I couldn't help conjecturing on what had kept her out. She didn't seem to have suffered any harm by the excursion. It hadn't scarred her mentally or physically. Had she just slept wild, eaten what she could catch? Or had she tarted up to some other poor unsuspecting sucker like me, promising love and undying affection for a handful of dry biscuits?

We'd often sit together companionably in the cabin in the evenings and I'd stare at her until she became aware that she was being watched and stare back at me, making eye contact in a way that I didn't think cats were comfortable doing.

I wondered then if she was trying to find a way of telling me what had happened to her, whether she was searching around for some method of communicating to me the adventures she'd had. Once, sitting on my lap, she began to chirrup unusually in a way which could have been her attempt at trying to talk. It sounded to me as if she was saying I was a mug or something like that, although when cats are purring, the noise they make can sound like anything. Besides, I was nodding off to sleep, too lost in my own world to be sure of anything in hers.

SIX

Fun and Games
in Little Venice

As soon as we'd turned the corner at Bulls Bridge junction and begun the long, lock-free stretch which takes you 10 miles through the drab, outlying reaches of western Metroland into the centre of London, it started to feel like a waterways festival. Suddenly, from out of nowhere, a canal which had been all but deserted was busy with a stream of boats. Where they'd come from was difficult to say. A few had approached the junction from the other direction to us, from Brentford where the Grand Union meets the River Thames. Some, I suppose, had been following us as we'd travelled south. Most, I guess, had come from London itself, for as you might expect there's a massive population of boats in the capital, squeezed into every half-yard of available space; and the Canalway Cavalcade festival (to give it its full name) is as much a celebration of the new season for them as for outsiders.

Some of the boats were already bedecked with livery and had flags and bunting draped across their roofs flapping noisily in the wind; others had already started celebrating and their crews were cradling glasses of wine and cans of beer. The weather was still holding up, and although it was blustery, the sun was sharp and bright. It was the Friday before the May Day bank holiday and the capital itself was in celebratory mood, anticipating the break. As we got closer to Little Venice the outside terraces of the many canalside pubs and restaurants along the way were packed with office workers on long lunch breaks, braving the chill for the first decently bright day there'd been since winter. There were more walkers out than we'd seen for a long time too, and opposite Kensal Green cemetery, where the engineer Isambard Kingdom Brunel lies among hundreds of other Victorian worthies, we even saw a family perched uncomfortably on a blanket on the towpath eating a picnic in their overcoats.

They weren't the only ones taking advantage of the good weather. There were coots with white markings on their beaks like the nose guards on Norman helmets, busily nesting all over the place; and on a dislodged coping stone somewhere near North Acton we spotted a terrapin twice the size of a dinner plate which had dragged itself from the water to sunbathe. It had no doubt been an impulse buy at a pet shop during the Mutant Ninja Turtle craze of the mid 1980s when you could pick one up for a couple of quid and keep it in a tank until it threatened to eat you out of house and home, and finally threatened to eat you too.

We passed bus garages and roadworks and new blocks of flats; we passed artistic graffiti, street graffiti and just plain ugly graffiti. At one stage we passed under the Westway, arching over the canal on its way to the Euston Road. We were in a

queue of eight or nine boats now, most of them modern like
Justice, but a couple of them traditional narrowboats – great
70-foot chunks of industrial history built of riveted steel with
capacious, tarpaulin-covered holds at the front which in the
past would have accommodated forty tons and more of coal.
One boat in the convoy was having a hard time of it. It was
a relatively small craft driven by a painfully thin bloke in his
twenties, but it had broken down and he was being towed the
last bit of the route. This wasn't unusual: breakdowns happen
on the canals as they do on the roads, although there aren't as
many of them, and when they occur other boaters are generally
more likely to help you out than your average motorist is.

What was unusual about this breakdown was that the boat
seemed to be getting too much help. It was being shunted
around the flotilla like rolling stock in a goods yard. When
we first noticed it, it was being pulled by the first boat in the
convoy, but for some reason the one following soon took
over. The next time we noticed it was being towed by the boat
behind that. The way it was going, it would have been our turn
next. Perhaps this was the idea. Perhaps it was some festival
game I didn't know about. Perhaps you won a prize if you were
pulling it when you went under Ha'penny Bridge.

At length we passed the former council estates and the
moored residential boats along Delamere Terrace where Virgin
boss Richard Branson once had a houseboat, a pioneer of canals
himself. Soon afterwards we cruised under the attractive blue
cast-iron bridge which brings you into Browning's Pool, the
heart of Little Venice itself.

It's like entering a different world. Even if you didn't know its
reputation as one of London's most exclusive neighbourhoods,
it wouldn't take long for the penny to drop. The elegant houses
facing the water here are three, four and five-storey stuccoed

mansions with twenty rooms and more, a lot of them with their own built-in gyms and swimming pools in the basement which you can sometimes just about make out from the pavement if you're nosey enough. The poet Robert Browning, who gave his name to the pool, lived only a stone's throw away and for a long time it was generally thought that he'd coined the name Little Venice. In fact it was another poet, Lord Byron, who was responsible, though the term didn't really catch on until the estate agents got hold of it in the 1930s and marketed it to within an inch of its life. No doubt it appealed to their sense of hyperbole, for Little Venice isn't like Venice at all. Technically, it's where the Paddington Arm of the Grand Union Canal meets the Regents Canal main line: not even a Tiny Venice really, or a Minuscule Venice for that matter, just a wide waterways junction with a small island in the middle so boats won't hit each other.

Mind you, it's a charming spot; surprisingly tranquil and spacious for somewhere only a couple of miles from Trafalgar Square. There's a floating cafe, a puppet theatre on a barge and some good pubs. It's also the boarding place for the waterbuses which run a regular year-round service through Regents Park to Camden Lock a short distance away. Even the Paddington Arm, which for a long time was silted up and thick with rubbish, has undergone a renaissance. Only a few years ago it was as unattractive a stretch of canal as you'd find anywhere in a city; now it's been dredged and redeveloped with cafes and bars and sports clubs, and along its length are offices which are the headquarters of some of the biggest companies in the country like Monsoon, Marks and Spencer and Orange. Everyone wants a piece of the action with canals nowadays. To call them flavour of the month doesn't even begin to describe it.

The Canalway Cavalcade festival is a relatively recent invention. There'd been local fetes in the area since the 1950s, but these had been mainly small community affairs held on the streets rather than the water. However, in the 1960s, the basin was appropriated for the popular Boat Afloat show, a ten-day event which was held annually until 1974 when the last one was opened by the comedian Arthur Lowe of *Dad's Army* fame. By then it had become far too big and commercial and it was attracting criticism from local residents for the number of speedboats hurtling around the basin disturbing the peace and quiet of the area. They'd paid a lot of money for their peace and quiet and they didn't take kindly to seeing it destroyed by gangs of Hooray Henrys in blazers and captains' caps with pretensions to the briny deep.

Canalway Cavalcade is of a different order altogether and much more in keeping with the sedate tenor of the inland waterways. The first one was held in 1983 after the Inland Waterways Association organised a Waterways Fortnight to publicise the message that the canal system could be a tremendous national asset, given a decent level of government investment. The IWA is the pre-eminent organisation for those interested in Britain's rivers and canals, and the response of its London members was to mount a festival to celebrate the opening of the city's towpaths – a goal which had been achieved that year after long negotiation and planning.

The first festival to celebrate this new 'canalway' was small enough to be contained in the basin itself. The highlight was the arrival of two boats, one from the east and the other from the west, carrying the mayors of all the boroughs through which the canal passed. Since then Cavalcade has grown exponentially and today it attracts boats from all over the country, as well as many thousands of visitors who arrive by foot and tube, both locals and tourists. It's still organised entirely by volunteers, though. And it's still got that sense of a neighbourhood festival about it, the feel of village London. Kids paint their faces and eat candy floss, jazz and Caribbean steel bands play around the water's edge, and the beer tent does a raging trade all day, as do the food vans and the many towpath stalls which sell everything from second-hand books to joss sticks, painted canalware to garden herbs.

The transformation from quiet London backwater to busy festival site happens astonishingly quickly, a testimony to those who do the immense amount of work necessary to effect the change. One minute the basin's empty and peaceful, with just one or two Canada geese drifting around the island like stage props to emphasise the serenity of the scene. The next, as if at the sound of some celestial starting gun, it's packed with boats and the towpath's milling with people bustling about like extras in a movie. In no time at all the whole thing's set up: the boats are in their allotted places, the flags and bunting are flying, and the stalls are in place. No matter how often you witness it, the process seems somehow miraculous.

The event lasts the three days of the bank holiday weekend, and at first the crowds trickle in so slowly that you wonder if it was worth all the effort. By Saturday afternoon you know it was. By then the place is heaving, and it gets worse on the Sunday when a short, hundred-yard walk up the towpath can take half an hour or more because of the crowds blocking the narrow throughway shopping, promenading, or just taking in the atmosphere.

The basin is the focus of Cavalcade and throughout the weekend there's a programme of events happening in and around it, including a boat handling competition which is more of a highlight for the boaters at the festival than many of them care to admit. This is because they can have a drink and a few laughs at the expense of those suckers crazy or conceited enough to want to show off their skills in front of what must surely be the most critical audience of narrowboat experts you could hope to gather together in one place.

I, of course, had entered.

Why I had entered, and how this entry had come about, I am not altogether certain – although it was certainly not with Em's blessing. She set herself against the idea from the outset, declaring that if I was determined to make a fool of myself publicly I could do it on my own because she was going to go down into the cabin with the cat and have nothing to do with it. But there are ways the organisers have of signing you up to the event. They have long experience of it. It happened with me in the bar the night we arrived when I'd just started to relax and enjoy the atmosphere. Someone sidled up to me and engaged me in what appeared to be innocuous conversation. Whoever it was – and I forget now – had seen me on the cut somewhere when I was in a bit of tricky situation. Apparently I'd managed to extricate myself from it with exemplary skill. I might have been turning a tight corner or manoeuvring myself through a busy junction, I forget. But apparently whatever I'd done, I'd done extremely well. Or so I was told. Come on! Anyone would feel flattered at a compliment like that. You'd feel flattered.

I was bought a drink. There was more chat, not about boat handling this time, probably not even about canals. I certainly didn't agree to anything, let alone put my name on any sort of form. Which was why, when the lists were posted later, it was such a shock to find myself as an official entrant to the competition, scheduled to start in the arena the following morning at 10.30 a.m. I did not like that word 'arena'. It made me feel uncomfortable, very uncomfortable indeed.

And I was right to feel that way. Queuing up at the Paddington Arm to come in for my turn was a nerve-racking experience. And with Em and Kit below, it was a very lonely one. It was a gusty day and the conditions were playing havoc with the competition. From time to time I caught sight of my friend Martin who was competing ahead of me and who was still trying to complete his set manoeuvres a quarter of an hour after he should have finished them. Nothing seemed to be going right for him. His boat was being buffeted about uncontrollably from one side of the basin to the other. The crowds watching him were ominously silent. Not even a ripple of applause for his efforts.

At last he left the basin and I was shepherded in to take his place, a new sacrificial victim. I was already anxious, but this was as nothing to how I felt when I became aware of the number of people watching me. They were watching from the decks of the moored boats, and from the roofs of the boats, and from the towpath, and from the terrace of the road above which looks down over the towpath. I could see why they called it an arena now. In fact, arena doesn't quite capture the spirit of the place. Full of people like this, it's like the Emirates Stadium. By now I'd gone so jelly-legged I had to lean against the steering hatch to support myself. This, no doubt, added to my general appearance of insouciance, so alienating that small section of the crowd who didn't already hate me for being such a flash git as to have entered the competition in the first place.

But then, something totally unexpected happened. For some reason the gods smiled on me and the wind stopped dead. I did my first turn and reverse faultlessly. There was a faint round of applause from the crowd and I became aware of a commentator who'd been jabbering away in the background through a PA system telling people who I was. He was now saying something about how well I was performing. This acted as an incentive, spurring me on. Before I was aware of it I'd drawn the boat up against a pontoon moored against the island, and shaken the hands of a first judge as I was required to do by the rules of the competition. Back on board again, I swung *Justice* around the island and reversed down the Regent's Canal in the direction of the nearby Islington Tunnel where a second judge under the bridge was watching me like a hawk. There was another ripple of applause at my impeccable control.

There now only remained the final manoeuvre, the climax of the competition. This was the 360-degree turn in the very centre of the basin: a pirouette made no easier by the line of festival boats moored bow-outwards along the towpath on one side, restricting the available water space to the opposite bank where a couple of residential barges sat with their living room windows at a height which seemed, somewhat troublesomely, the same as my bow. But hey, what did I care? I was cooking on gas now; I felt turbocharged. For the first time I allowed myself to believe I could actually win this competition.

I brought the boat into the centre of the basin, accelerating as much as I dared so that I'd have enough power to sweep around in the confined space. At the last moment I pushed my tiller hard to the left so that the boat tipped and *Justice*'s bow arched to the right.

Unfortunately at this exact moment the wind blew up again. It blew up with a vengeance, like a military trumpeter saving his breath for a last piercing note on a morning reveille. It blew up directly behind me and I went hurtling towards the window of the barge opposite. I wrenched the gear control into reverse and revved up the engine as hard as I could. Clouds of smoke rose from the exhaust chimney and the propeller thrashed around in the water behind me, creating so much turbulence it flooded the stern deck. It didn't stop me, though. My momentum still carried me relentlessly towards the window, closer and closer. So close that I could make out the pattern on the upholstery inside and the photographs on the mantle shelf. So close I could see every contorted line in the faces of the owners watching from inside as it dawned on them what was happening.

But at the last moment, just as I was about to collide, *Justice* came to an uncertain standstill. Almost immediately she began to move backwards. At first it happened gently, barely perceptibly; but then, free of any forward momentum, the full power of the engine kicked in and she went into reverse, skating backwards across the basin. This was exactly the moment at which a waterbus emerged from under the bridge in the tunnel direction, and precisely the instant when a small cruiser appeared on the other side from Delamare Terrace. They both saw me at the same time and began to reverse as I accelerated forward once again in a last-ditch attempt to bring *Justice* under control.

For a moment it was inevitable I'd hit one of them, if not both. I panicked. The cruiser panicked. Even the driver of the waterbus panicked. Somehow in the midst of all this panic I managed to straighten up and weave between them, so that as I finished the course it looked as if I'd known what I was doing all along.

Of course no one was fooled. Well, no one who knew anything about steering a narrowboat, anyhow. As I left the basin for the short cruise to where I could turn and return to my mooring, I picked up a group of friends at a prearranged spot, one of whom had brought friends of his own. He lifted his eyebrows and looked towards the sky which really said it all.

By now Em had emerged from the cabin. She took over on the tiller while I downed a much-needed drink and acted as host. My frayed nerves made me garrulous. I talked too loudly, laughed a little too much at my own jokes. An hour or so later the friends of my friend left the boat thanking me effusively for my hospitality. They were French. They'd obviously enjoyed the trip. At one point they appeared close to kissing me with gratitude.

'Nice people,' I said to my friend after they'd gone. 'Where did you meet them?'

'Meet them?'

'The French couple. How do you know them?'

'I don't know them,' my friend said. 'I thought they were people you knew. You seemed to shepherd them off the towpath when you picked me up…'

Well, what can I say? What can anyone say?

No doubt at this very moment there's a young French couple in Marseilles or Auxerre or wherever, regaling their friends over drinks with the story of how hospitable are the English, how warm and welcoming and so unlike what everyone thinks them to be. *'C'est vrai,'* I can hear them say. *'Nous avons visité Londres* and at a fete in the Little Venice we were invited onto *un bateau* and given food and good wine and… Mind you, *ces Anglais*, they do not know how to steer their thin boats…'

And no, just in case you were wondering, I didn't win the competition.

SEVEN

Up the Grand Union to Black Jack's Lock

A man who's competed in the boat-handling competition at Cavalcade and walked away, if not with the winner's crown, then at least with his dignity intact, shouldn't need to apologise to anyone. Even so, I found myself apologising. What else could I do? I'd been caught red-handed eavesdropping in the festival bar on the final evening. Evidently I hadn't been doing it very subtly either. The bloke on the adjacent table eventually lost patience and invited me to join his group. 'You might as well,' he said. 'We all feel we know you now anyhow.'

To say I was embarrassed doesn't begin to express it. On the cut you live by a code of privacy, which probably originates in the old days of cargo-carrying when people brought up families on boats and were frequently forced to breast up side-by-side, sharing the intimacies of life for weeks on end as they waited around for work or the weather. In those days there was an unwritten set of rules about the things you did and didn't do on the canal – rules designed to protect what little bit of precious space you could carve out for yourself. There were rules about the way you crossed other people's boats to the bank, for instance; rules to do with whether you wanted to socialise or not.

It's more or less the same today, although the rules have changed. Nowadays, you don't breast up to other boats at all if you can help it. In fact, you don't even moor close to them; and if you have to, you'll keep as much distance between you as you can, like blokes do in urinals. After you've moored, you might wander over to a nearby boat to exchange pleasantries, but you won't stay long for fear of trespassing on their territory. That's why boarding other people's boats uninvited is so frowned upon. Or looking through their windows. People take a dim view of you listening into their conversations too – which is why I felt so bad being caught out in the bar like that.

But I was intrigued, that was my excuse. They'd been chatting about this crazy race round Birmingham's canal network – the BCN Challenge as it's known. And they'd had a few drinks; they were hardly whispering to each other. At first I couldn't believe what I was hearing. I'd been scheduled to take part in the event seven or eight years before but I'd had to cry off. After that, sadly, it was abandoned so I never got the chance again. Now, unbeknown to me, it seemed they'd resuscitated the idea and it was on again. I was genuinely excited by the prospect of competing; it was absolutely my sort of thing. Other people might get the hots for foreign travel, for trips to the exotic East, the Caribbean or to faraway South Pacific islands. Me though, what gets my juices pumping is a wet weekend in the West Midlands and the prospect of navigating up to Smethwick on the Old Line.

The following day, after I'd managed to extract as much information as I could about the competition from the people in the bar, I rang my mate Bob to see if he and his wife Rosemary were up for the trip. I needed help, you see; they were a key part of my strategy. I eventually got around to mentioning it to Em too. I'd wanted to catch her in the right frame of mind, and I thought at first I'd succeeded because when I raised the topic she didn't break down in derisory laughter or begin lecturing me on my mental health. In fact, she appeared to be intrigued by it. As was Kit. The two of them sat on chairs on either side of the cabin table looking at me, their heads cocked with curiosity at similar but opposite angles, like a mirror image of each other.

Except, of course, that one of them was a cat and the other wasn't.

'A race, you say?' said the one who wasn't.

'Well, a sort of race. It's more like an endurance event, really. We have to cruise for twenty-four hours. Through the night,' I added brightly.

'Ah, an endurance event. Through the night. I see. Just around Birmingham?'

'Well, anywhere in the BCN – the Birmingham Canal Navigations. But effectively that's anywhere between Wolverhampton and the M6, which gives us more than a hundred miles of waterways to play with. We get points for the distance we travel and for going up disused arms and around old loops.'

'Olds loops, eh? And Rosemary's agreed to this?'

'Yep.'

'Amazing,' she said. 'Quite astonishing.' Then she paused, looked at me quizzically and asked, 'Is she ill?'

'What?'

'Rosemary? Is she ill?'

'That's an odd question. Why do you ask?'

'Because I'm wondering why she might have agreed to this crazy idea.'

'Crazy idea?'

'Well, what would you call it? You want me to endure a weekend without sleep on an aquatic trek around the backwaters of Birmingham. You want us to use the boat to dredge the disused factory outlets of Dudley. I mean, it's hardly a family holiday at Center Parcs, is it?'

Mercifully, Kit at least seemed keener on the idea. You could see it in her eyes which had widened to large black marbles so they weren't like cats' eyes at all. She looked first at me and then Em. Perhaps she could sense the tension between us which she misinterpreted as excitement. Or maybe it was the thought of Birmingham which was getting her so pumped up. Maybe in her feline way she imagined Birmingham as one great boatyard like Banbury, only bigger. And filled with scurrying creatures of every delectable variety – a sort of Kenyan game park in the West Midlands.

Cavalcade marked the end of Em's holiday and she wanted to prepare for her return to work the following day, so we put the topic of Birmingham aside for the moment, consigning it to that bulging folder in the filing cabinet of our relationship headed, 'Things to Be Talked About Later But Only with the Greatest Caution'.

That night we left the boat in Browning's Pool and went back home on the tube. It was Kit's first trip on public transport and we'd both been worried how she'd react to the noise and the crowds. In the event neither of those things concerned her as much as the girl on the Bakerloo Line who persisted in trying to stroke her by sticking her fingers through the bars of the cat basket. She was only about eight or nine years old, a sweet little thing in a pink satin tutu coming back from ballet class with her mum.

'What's the pretty pussy-wussy's name?' she kept asking repeatedly, if somewhat nauseatingly, prodding her at the same time. 'What do you call the little pussy-wussy?'

Kit made a lunge at her with her claws. 'Fucking Attila the Hun,' I could almost hear her saying. 'Now piss off.'

Honestly, I didn't know where to look.

Before going back to the boat the next day I telephoned the BCN Challenge organisers and booked myself in. If Em wouldn't do it, she could stay at home as far as I was concerned. The date conveniently fitted into my schedule – even though I'd long since given up the pretence that I had a schedule. The truth about this cruise was I was actually going nowhere. I was just meandering about, travelling as and where the mood took me. I suppose at that stage, I had it in my mind to go north again to Rickmansworth, back up the Grand Union, where there was another festival in a couple of weeks' time which I'd heard good things about. Now, with Birmingham booked, Rickmansworth seemed to be an even better destination, positioned as it was conveniently on the route.

The weather was still fine and sunny, but back at Little Venice, Browning's Pool had emptied completely. When I arrived it was to discover that everyone else had moved off and I was now the only boat there. Well, almost the only boat. One of the waterbuses was rounding the island with a full complement of passengers. I heard it before I saw it. At first I thought, ridiculously, that the skipper was swearing at me. It must have been something to do with the resonance of his engine, the way it was echoing over the water – anyone could have made the same mistake.

But then I realised he really was swearing at me. Swearing quite animatedly, too. Like a gaggle of schoolgirls showing off to each other walking home from school.

I wasn't expecting it – although part of me wasn't surprised. London drivers are London drivers after all, whether they're in cars or on boats. The last time I was at Cavalcade one of these same waterbuses carved me up at a bridge and we collided badly enough to get some of the women passengers screaming as we hit. I wondered for a moment whether it was the same boat. Whether the steerer had been harbouring a grudge and seen his chance of getting even.

But surely not? Surely there had to be a more immediate reason for his behaviour?

What this reason was soon became apparent. It seems I was on his pick-up spot which had been suspended for the duration of Cavalcade. Now, with Cavalcade over, he wanted it back pronto. Actually he wanted it back yesterday, although this was his second preference. His first was not to have had to give it up at all, bloody festival boats just being a pain in the arse as far as he was concerned.

I walked over to explain that I'd be moving as soon as I could – but this didn't placate him. On the contrary, it seemed to wind him up even more, precipitating another string of profanities. They were good profanities, mind you. Genuinely resourceful, some of them. Indeed, one or two displayed such creative imagination I thought he was wasted in his current job. The cavalry tradition dying out in today's modern army, and the demand for troopers not being what it once was, he should have been a cabbie. Or a market porter. Or at the very least a journalist in the Malcolm Tucker mould.

Meanwhile, those passengers on the boat, and the one or two queuing to board, watched the altercation unfolding with growing curiosity. Some of them were Londoners and realised that intercourse like this, and the frequent vulgar references to it, were part of the rich texture of city life, a commonplace of the sort you can experience in the capital on most street corners most days. Some, however, were Americans, and they probably thought this sort of thing was part of the authentic Canal Experience, a show put on especially for them. A sort of celebration of how your average Cockney waterman loves nothing better than engaging in cheerful banter to make his dull day a little brighter; cor blimey, luvaduck, pearly kings and queens, and whelks and jellied eels.

I moored that night at Cowley Bridge just outside of Uxbridge. I hadn't intended to moor there, but getting off the boat I stepped back on the towpath without thinking and I felt my ankle twist under me awkwardly. As soon as it happened I could have kicked myself. Well, I could have kicked myself if I hadn't just done my ankle in. This was an old, niggling injury I'd sustained a few years back on a cruise across the Pennines. I should have known it was a weakness and been more careful. What was clear was that I was going no further that day. I hobbled up to the pub in search of an analgesic and fortunately the one I found came in such an attractively packaged pint pot I decided to have another, and one or two more after that.

Sadly, the next morning it wasn't just my ankle which was aching but my head too. I limped on past Denham, where Em and I had moored on our way down to London. But my mind wasn't on canalling. Neither was my ankle, which seemed to have developed a mind of its own. When I instructed it to do something, more often than not it would just lie there like a blob at the end of my leg, trembling uselessly and refusing to move. Worse, it seemed to have developed some pig-headed notion of leaving me. Or at least that's what it felt like. It seemed to be constantly pushing against my sock, as if trying to burst through the fabric like the creature in *Alien* breaking out of John Hurt's chest.

The reason became immediately apparent when I took a closer look at it. It was so swollen it was less like an ankle than one of those blood-red balloons they give out to kids at parties. Also, it was beginning to hurt like hell. The only way I could think to stop it was more analgesic, though I wasn't certain my liver could take the strain of the medication in the quantities of the previous night. On balance, I decided traditional medicine might offer better solutions, so I moored above Black Jack's Lock and secured *Justice* for what I knew would be a longer-than-average stay. At home, the doctor thought a rheumatologist might have more of an idea what to do with me, and the rheumatologist thought a physiotherapist might be able to help.

Meanwhile the Rickmansworth Festival came and went without me, better this year than ever before or so I heard later.

After two weeks of massage and exercises I eventually extricated myself from the clutches of the comely young dominatrix at Lewisham Hospital who'd been treating me. It was obviously only a fill-in job for her, anyhow. Her real ambition, no doubt, lay in becoming a torturer for a fascist dictatorship somewhere. She was, however, surprisingly concerned to see me go. In the period I'd been her patient she'd made me feel so much like a piece of meat I was convinced it was only a matter of time before she served me up on her treatment table on a dinner plate with two veg. Yet now, as the end of the treatment grew closer, she became all touchy-feely with me.

This new, kinder her was unsettling. It made me nervous.

'You're not fully fit yet; you know that, don't you?' she said

'But I have to go to work.'

'Well, at least you're only going to be sitting at a computer. That's right, isn't it? You're not going to be moving around much, are you?'

'Barely at all,' I said. 'Except for your exercises,' I added hastily. 'I'll do those religiously, I promise.'

Back at Black Jack's Lock it was as warm and sunny as when I'd left. Warmer in fact, and much sunnier: another exquisite spring day, so delightful that even despite my ankle, which was still sore even after (or maybe because of) all the treatment, it made my spirits soar just to be a part of it. Everything was just 'perfick', fried gold.

Except for the peacocks, that is. Peacocks – you know? Big, blowsy birds, like turkeys on diet pills. Showy, effeminate creatures with Gwyneth Paltrow necks and lustrous breasts the colour of a bolt of blue silk. And those enormous tail feathers, of course. Back plumes as they're properly called – like bouquets of old-fashioned lollipops.

There was a flock of them over the other side of the canal. An ostentation they're sometimes called. A muster. A pride.

No doubt at other times of the year peacocks are discreet, unobtrusive birds strutting about basking in the admiration of less decorative species. But take it from me, in early spring when they start mating they are a completely different proposition. There must have been a dozen or more of them at Black Jack's and the cocks were getting frisky. The trouble with peacocks is that when they get frisky you're best not to make any plans that might include sleep.

They do this crazy dance, you see. Shimmer their butts and rattle their quills as if they're doing a mambo. Then they let out this bloodcurdling cry to attract females. It's a sort of three-tone scream, like an old police siren or a cat with its tail trapped in the door. They do it through the day which is bad enough; but they do it at night too, and at night the cry of a peacock desperate to have its dirty way with anything in feathers is terrifying to hear. It sounds like an axe murderer hacking his victims to pieces. It sounds like the torture chamber in some Elizabethan dungeon.

Take it from me, when they're all fired up like this you wouldn't want to be a Native American in full traditional headdress.

Not that the females – the peahens – are much quieter themselves this time of the year. Once they've had their chicks they develop an infuriatingly plaintive cry of their own if they ever lose one. It can go on for hours and hours like a burglar alarm that no one will turn off. It is so heart-rending that eventually you'd do anything to make it stop, including cuddling up to her in the nest yourself just to make her feel better.

The cat, of course, loved it. A cat is not fooled by peacocks. A cat knows instinctively that despite all their finery peacocks are just birds, and although they may be louder and bigger than your average bird, they still come under the general heading of 'prey'.

Kit couldn't wait to get at them. She paced up and down the boat. She peered out of the portholes. She clawed at the front door. I didn't dare let her out. I had visions of her dragging one back, her mouth bulging with sapphire-coloured feathers which she'd be spitting out all over the place. It'd be weeks before I could get rid of them. They'd be turning up in my bed or in my Bolognese, a sad rebuke to my inability to control even a cat.

No, if it hadn't been for the peacocks, the mooring at Black Jack's Lock would have been ideal. Well, ideal apart from the dog, that is. The dog came from another boat, although I never worked out which one. It was a long-haired mongrel: a sort of overgrown terrier which was so unprepossessing you wouldn't have given him a second glance... except for the fact that he was missing a back leg, which is not a thing you see often in a dog. You couldn't help feeling sorry for him, and that was the problem. This was a dog that had traded on only having three legs from a very early age. He'd been spoiled because of it and was used to getting his own way.

I hadn't been on the boat five minutes before he started scratching at the door bringing me presents of sticks which he dropped on the deck. When I threw them off, he brought them back again. It was a great game for him; he could have played it for hours. I found it amusing enough for a while too, but the entertainment value of a stick is limited. Throwing one around for a three-legged dog doesn't turn it into a PlayStation.

But the damned thing wouldn't go away. When I walked up the towpath he followed me; when I went inside the boat he waited for me. I tried ignoring him and started cooking dinner but he sat peering at me through the porthole over the sink, a stick hanging from one side of his mouth and a drool of saliva from the other. This gave him a mournful look. It also ruined my appetite. I couldn't work out why he was so infatuated with me. Maybe he'd seen me limping around with my ankle and marked me down as a kindred spirit.

I'm too soft-hearted for my own good, that's my problem. Eventually I went outside again, with the intention of playing with him a bit longer. I ended up playing for nearly an hour, throwing sticks, again and again incessantly. It was boring for me and it must have been boring for the dog too. In time he disappeared and I thought I'd seen the last of him, except that a few minutes later he came back. Gone now was the stick. In its place was half an oak tree which he'd found somewhere. He dropped it at my feet provocatively.

'You wanted to play with me,' he seemed to be saying. 'Now play...'

Really, this was the last straw; I'd had enough. I'd had enough of dogs with disabilities taking liberties with me, and the peacocks which had started wailing again like banshees. I'd had enough of the damned cat too. She'd been following every move I'd made with the dog, part of her jealous at the attention I was paying it, part of her hoping to catch me unaware so she could give me the slip and go peacock hunting.

I cast off and headed north, pleased to be on the move again, but most of all pleased to be shot of Black Jack's. I was deliriously happy, so much so that I forgot all about my ankle.

At the next lock I jumped off the boat without thinking about it.

The next day it was as bad as it ever had been.

EIGHT

From Hemel Hempstead to the Tring Summit

It was agonisingly slow going. And very painful. Thirteen miles and twenty-two locks to Hemel Hempstead. Big locks at that. And every last one of them against me, not a single boat travelling in the opposite direction to make it easier. Even so, it was the sort of cruise I wouldn't have thought twice about twenty years ago. It wouldn't have worried me particularly even now if I'd been in working order. But I wasn't in working order. The ankle wasn't working at all. It had ballooned up again and I could hardly put any weight on it.

Late in the afternoon at Nash Mills Lock, a mile or two short of the town centre, it gave out on me completely and I had no option but to stop, slumping across the roof until the pain had subsided. I felt lightheaded, spaced out. I'd broken into a clammy sweat and felt shivery. It was crazy to push myself like this, I knew. This was just today's target. Tomorrow, if I was to have any chance of reaching Birmingham in time for the Challenge, I'd have to do the same distance again. And the same the day after that.

It was sunny again, and hot, more like summer than spring. Around the lock a couple of blackbirds serenaded each other, celebrating their confidence in the future. A woman with a pushchair passed, talking on a mobile phone, so engrossed in her conversation she was barely aware of me. But to be fair, I was barely aware of myself either. Sometimes, travelling single-handed on a canal, you can get like this. You push yourself beyond your limits and it drives you into yourself. When you're in this state of mind, travelling becomes more of an endurance test than a pleasure, and the outside world pales into insignificance as a result. What becomes important is whatever personal goal you're chasing and that blinds you to your surroundings.

I realised that for most of the day I'd barely been aware of anything outside of myself, except to register when I was approaching another lock. The last thing I could remember with any clarity was that morning passing through Croxley Green, where in 1830 John Dickinson had established one of his mechanised paper mills. Dickinson made the small village internationally famous, producing brands of notepaper like Basildon Bond for an age when writing meant a real engagement with the physical world through pen and ink, rather than just messing about with bits and bytes and binaries as we do now. The factory used to dominate the canal around Common Moor Lock but it was pulled down in 2002 to make way for a modern housing estate.

I slapped on an ice-pack and sat on the deck enjoying the weather, although it was hardly the most salubrious of surroundings in which to sunbathe. Nash Mills Lock was the site of another of Dickinson's paper mills dating from

1811, but this too had come to the end of its life and was being demolished. Parts of its walls had already been ripped out, exposing the blue-painted steel girders on which the building hung. Opposite, an open barge filled with refuse, and listing at an alarming angle, had been dragged to block off an arm which branched off the main line. For generations this had been used to deliver the coal from the Midlands which powered the factory machinery. All of that had been ripped out long ago, probably sold to China or India. Wires and a maze of twisted pipes trailing from the broken brickwork were the only clue that it had ever been there. The place was eerie, quiet and melancholic as factories always are when their workers have finally departed and they are abandoned. You couldn't contemplate it without feeling that something was wrong, that some part of the natural order had been disrupted.

Factories are tedious and mind-numbing places, as anyone who's ever worked in one can tell you. But at the same time they're places of fellowship and camaraderie, places of energy and enterprise, passion and ambition; and when they've gone they leave a black hole in the communities they served which is beyond politics and economics. To see a factory in this state – especially one which once produced such celebrated products – was chastening. But it was much worse in the 1970s and 80s when great swathes of industrial land were being cleared all over the country. In those days, when canals weren't so fashionable, and when they weren't the playgrounds for the well-off which they've become, a trip anywhere would inevitably bring you face to face with the discarded, dog-eared remnants of Britain's proud past.

Sometimes it brought you too close to it.

Once, cruising through the Black Country with my brother along a canal which itself was virtually derelict, we were confronted by a workman who bolted up the towpath in a panic as soon as he saw us, waving his arms about in a demented fashion like someone who'd just dug up a wasps' nest.

'Hold on! Stop there! Wait! There's going to be an…'

Judging by the enormous bang that followed, and the dust storm which billowed down the canal, and the bricks which came showering down around us, mercifully missing our heads (but not by much), I guess the word he was searching for was 'explosion'.

I was disturbed from these musings by my Blackberry. It was Bob monitoring my progress north. Bob now had a vested interest in tracking me since he was pumped up for the BCN Challenge and wasn't intending to miss it as a result of any cock-up on my side which might lead to me failing to get to the start-line on time. And he'd got no time for any ankle talk either; his tone was distinctly unsympathetic.

Even so, I wasn't expecting what happened next. That night, just after I'd let Kit out, I heard a knocking at the bow doors as if she was trying to get back in again. I knew I must be mistaken. Kit was a smart cat, but she wasn't that smart, not smart enough to knock on a door, anyhow. Besides, knocking wouldn't be her way. She was more of a meow and scratch cat. More of a wait-for-the-opportunity-and-dart-in-before-anyone-sees-her cat.

I prised back the front curtains, peering into the gloom. I didn't need to peer far. I saw a pair of bare knees directly ahead of me, illuminated by the light from the cabin. They appeared to be hovering there unconnected to any other body part, like those enormous plastic breasts you see hanging in joke shops. It was Bob; I knew immediately it was him. Bob is the only person I know who displays his knees with such indelicacy. He wears shorts all the time; and by this I don't mean he just wears them in the spring or high summer when the weather's warm. Perish the thought. This is not a fashion statement he's making, it's a political declaration. It is a V-sign to the world, the existentialist scream of an individual railing against a dull and uniform universe. And the colder it gets, the louder that scream becomes.

He wears shorts in the thick of winter when the canal is iced over and the snow's blowing horizontally. He wears them when the temperature is so cold people have to thaw out their words to hear each other talk. He wears them when they can't talk at all because their larynxes are frozen to their necks and their voice boxes have turned into fridges.

'What are you doing here?' I asked.

'And a big friendly welcome to you too,' he replied. 'I thought you needed some help.'

'You're not wrong,' I said, 'You'd better come on board…'

The next morning Bob got up so early it was still night. By 6 a.m. daylight had barely broken but we were already on the move, me alone on the boat, steering silently through the dawn mist; him on the bike specially kept for such occasions, his knees pumping hard as he cycled ahead preparing locks. Travelling this way – 'wheeling', as it's called – you move much faster since there's no time lost dropping off crew at locks and picking them up again afterwards. But it means that when there are only two of you, you barely see each other all day. I was aware of Bob being around at locks because the gates would be open for me when I arrived and they would close mysteriously behind me after I'd entered. Paddles would rise too, and water would flood into the chamber lifting me up to higher levels of the canal. But when I got there, he'd long gone, my only sight of him a sun-kissed pair of bare legs rounding a distant bend.

At Berkhamsted we caught up with each other for long enough to have breakfast, which we ate outside on the deck. Already it was turning into another wonderful May morning, even warmer than the previous day. Good weather late in autumn is called an Indian summer. But what's it called when you get an equally unseasonable early spell of sunshine like this? Global warming probably, but we won't get into that debate.

The canal through Berko – which is what canal people call Berkhamsted – is beautifully maintained, a real credit to the town. It passes some fine pubs and skirts the remains of the castle which was once the home of Edward, the Black Prince, and where both the archbishop-turned-saint Thomas à Beckett and the poet Geoffrey Chaucer were once constables. There's a lot of history like this in Berkhamsted which, as a result, has a rather high opinion of itself. So high, in fact, that it has sometimes been known to refer to itself as the 'real' capital of England – a view which, as a Londoner, albeit by adoption, I regard very dubiously.

Indeed, I'd like to remind Berkhamsters – or Berks as they should be called – that this hubris of theirs springs from the fact that after the Battle of Hastings in 1066, William the Conqueror accepted the surrender of the English in the town. However, I'd also like to remind them that although the local quislings offered to crown him there and then, William shared none of their illusions about the status of the place and insisted that something as important as a coronation was only going to take place in London.

London, do you hear? The real real capital of England.

So my advice if you meet anyone from Berko coming on strong about the town – reminding you of all the kings who spent time there and all the novelists, comedians and presidents like Graham Greene, John Cleese and Charles de

Gaulle who lived or were born there – is to whisper the name Esther Rantzen in their ear. She lived in the place too once, but somehow you never hear them crowing about her.

For anyone interested in canals, the real attraction hereabouts is Ashridge House, 2 or 3 miles north of the town. For centuries this was the ancestral home of the Dukes of Bridgewater, and it was the third duke, Francis Egerton, who is generally credited with being the father of Britain's inland waterways – though behind his achievements lies a sad and tragic tale of unrequited love, the irony of which has never been fully appreciated. For who was it that said that from the most trifling of human affairs untold consequences spring?

Probably me, actually. But it's true all the same.

It was certainly the case with Francis, who succeeded to the dukedom at twelve years old and who, as a young man, fell for the society beauty Elizabeth Gunning – the Dowager Duchess of Hamilton. Elizabeth was a sort of eighteenth-century it-girl, a bit of a goer in an age when the aristocracy went at it like rabbits on amphetamines. And in the same way that the paparazzi immortalise the rich and famous of today, so Elizabeth's bedroom eyes and fulsome cleavage were celebrated by every fashionable artist of the time, from Joshua Reynolds down.

Francis and Elizabeth got engaged, but it never worked out and they broke up within the year.

Part of the reason for this was the scandal associated with Elizabeth's sister, Maria, Countess of Coventry who was prone to having slanging matches with her husband's mistresses in Hyde Park, behaviour which Elizabeth refused to condemn. But this was just an indication of Francis and Elizabeth's incompatibility; they were different people with completely different outlooks on the world. You only have to look at them both to see it; you only have to know a little about them. She was drop-dead gorgeous, a head-turner; he was a bit of a dog, even as a young man. A relief of him made around the time depicts him as a proud, haughty man with a prominent nose, a thick bottom lip and early bags developing under his eyes.

Emotionally they were very dissimilar too. Elizabeth was a woman of passion and spontaneity who married her first husband on the night she met him, allowing herself to be spirited away from a Valentine's party and wed clandestinely using a ring from a bed curtain. From a bed curtain, can you believe that? What a delicious detail of history.

You can't for the world imagine Francis Egerton acting so impulsively. He was a diligent and dutiful man, the sort that changes the world and is the duller for it. The failed engagement must have dented his confidence. Afterwards he gave up women completely and retired to his country estate at Worsley, just outside Manchester, where he dedicated his life to getting coal out of his pits and into factories by this new-fangled concept of using canals as they did in France. He'd seen it done when he'd been on his Grand Tour and logged that the method could be useful to him. That was the sort of man he was – the sort who knew a potential earner when he was looking at it. In time it made him one of the richest people in Britain, perhaps the very richest after the king.

The fact that in acquiring his fortune he developed a whole new system of transportation, and radicalised industrial production, and precipitated the Industrial Revolution... well, all that was just a by-product, really. A displacement activity in the absence of a personal life. One of those untold consequences that result from trifling human affairs.

After his experience with Elizabeth, Egerton died unmarried and childless. I like to think that he probably regretted this later when he sat in Ashridge wondering what to do with the rest of his life. Eventually he set about rebuilding the house, but isn't life a bitch? No sooner had he demolished the place than he died, leaving those who inherited his fortune with a pile of rubble as his legacy. Mind you, he left them a pile of cash too, so I don't suppose they complained.

After breakfast Bob and I pushed on to Marsworth, where it was a toss-up whether the enormous reservoir there was filled more with birds or more with twitchers watching birds. They all seemed to have cameras with immense lenses the size of rocket launchers; and they were all were huddled in conspiratorial groups, whispering to each other as if they were involved in a dastardly plot of some sort. Perhaps they were planning to take out one of the many flocks of Canada geese which seem to be overrunning indigenous bird life in these parts. Or maybe I judge them too harshly. Maybe they were just exchanging recipes for duck à l'orange.

I could have done with a rocket launcher myself that day. It had turned very hot, and with the weekend approaching there were more boats out and about than I'd seen in a long time. Without wishing to be gratuitously rude, some of the handling techniques of their skippers struck me as being a little rusty after the winter and I wouldn't have minded blowing some of them out of the water. They were like Sunday drivers, only worse, because at least Sunday drivers know how to steer. At least they don't forget which side of the road to drive on. Some of the boats travelling that day seemed unable to recall the basic stuff and zigzagged across the canal from one side to the other leaving mayhem in their wake.

Marsworth reservoir is one of four grouped closely together, known collectively as the Tring reservoirs. They were built to supply water to the canal summit as it cuts through the

Chiltern Hills, although paradoxically the canal's not the best place from which to see them. Infuriatingly, at this point in its journey north it drops into a slight dip in the land and so from a boat you only catch tantalising glimpses of these man-made lakes, and you get no real sense of the scale of the whole complex which is a stunning piece of engineering as well as being a beautiful and remarkable haven for wildlife.

Not that Bob noticed the wildlife. The rate he was going he scarcely noticed the reservoirs. He'd fixed his teeth into a grimace and was still setting the pace on the bike, chasing the all-comer's record for the Most Canal Miles Travelled in One Day in the Service of Helping a Knackered Mate. It was exhausting watching him. Eventually even the bike found it exhausting and gave up the ghost with a broken chain. This at least meant Bob had to walk, although this scarcely impeded his pace, his bare legs pumping away like a couple of punks pogo-ing at a Pistols' gig.

At the two Ivinghoe Locks which take the canal past the small commuter village of Cheddington we encountered another boat travelling in the opposite direction: an old 70-foot working boat with a small back cabin and an open hold. It had arrived at the locks before us, its skipper one of that new breed of boater who is attracted to traditional canal boats in increasing numbers. He wore an impeccably clean set of overalls which looked as if they'd been ironed. And there was nothing he didn't know about canals and boats.

'You're opening that paddle a bit sharp,' he said to Bob. 'You should always open paddles gently.'

Since Bob had already opened more than a hundred paddles that day, not to mention the hundreds of thousands he'd opened in the past, many of them before Mr Know-All had had his bum slapped by the midwife, this didn't go down altogether well.

Bob harrumphed and shook his head incredulously and then squinted up his eyes in an attempt to look angry and offended at the same time. Sadly, it didn't work. He finished up looking like someone standing in a multi-storey who's forgotten where he's parked the car.

It was as much as I could do to keep a straight face.

Then Mr Know-All turned his attention to me: 'You're running that engine a bit rich, I can smell it from here,' he said.

I was speechless. Part of me wanted to engage him in conversation, to find out what on earth he was talking about; the other part of me wanted to punch him on the nose so that he wouldn't smell anything again for a day or two, let alone my engine which, of course, was completely odourless and a fresh as a mountain breeze. But then I saw Bob, the bastard, his shoulders shaking, spluttering to hold back his laughter.

'We should stop soon,' I said testily, 'it's getting late.'

NINE

Sweltering back up the Grand Union

B ob left me to go back home from the station at Fenny Stratford, an unremarkable suburb of Bletchley which is itself now a suburb of Milton Keynes.

The last time we'd been here together we'd been going to a football match at the MK Dons' stadium nearby and somehow, by that inexplicable telepathy that determines where visiting supporters herd in those few precious drinking hours before kick-off, we'd washed up in the pub bordering the lock. There must have been a hundred of us, maybe more. We were raucous and high-spirited, and so unlike anything you might associate with a typical canal scene that we might just as well have been creatures from a different planet.

A few boaters passed us while we were there, delayed by this one lock in a long, otherwise lockless stretch. You could see from their faces how disconcerted they were. Coming across us like this after cruising through the tranquil countryside, it was as if they'd been abruptly projected back into the present when they thought they'd escaped all that for an older, more sedate world.

But it was the same for many of the crowd going to the football. The same, but different. I watched them wandering out of the back of the pub, pints in hand, astonished at suddenly discovering themselves face to face with something that as far as they were concerned was a relic of a bygone age. Some who'd done boat trips as kids went glassy-eyed with sentimentality; but most of the others who knew little or nothing about the waterways were astonished to find a fragment of canal just lying there, hidden away. It was like coming across a dinosaur in a wildlife park.

What made the scene incongruous was that these were Leicester supporters, and Leicester's own ground overlooks the cut. In fact, the whole of Leicestershire is threaded with canals and rivers. So these weren't people unfamiliar with the concept of the waterways as such, just unfamiliar with the idea that all the bits of them which you come across link up into a countrywide network 3,000 miles long.

There were lots of questions for Bob and me who were known to be enthusiasts – but they weren't all easy to answer. But then Fenny Stratford lock isn't an easy lock to explain. For a start there's a swing bridge right across the middle of it which makes it tricky to get through because you have to open it before you even think about taking your boat in. It's difficult to account for that. I mean, why put a bridge over a lock? Surely it could have been positioned more conveniently?

The lock itself is just as intriguing. It only drops about a foot and doesn't seem to have any purpose to it, so that for a long time even canal experts used to think it was a surveying error. There were a lot of surveying errors in the early days of canal building, but you'd expect that, wouldn't you? The engineers were developing a new technology: they were inventing it as they went along.

When the canal was first conceived there was no lock planned for the 14.5 miles between Stoke Hammond in the south, near Leighton Buzzard, and Cosgrove in the north. But for various geological reasons this long pound proved difficult to keep watertight, and so in 1802, as a temporary measure, they built the lock at Fenny Stratford. This allowed them to drop the water level below the point at which it was leaking. It solved the problem straight off, but the drawback was that it held up boats, and twice in subsequent years the canal company considered removing the obstacle by properly repairing the canal. Both times they concluded the costs outweighed the benefits and that it just wasn't worth it.

Which means that the 'temporary' fix that is Fenny Stratford Lock has been in place for more than 200 years.

Not bad for a botch, eh?

It was Friday and later that day Em turned up for the weekend, exhausted from her battle to get out of London. We sat outside on the deck sipping ice-cold lagers straight from the fridge, our glasses cloudy with condensation. It was a beautiful evening, balmy and still; and though it wasn't far from the town, it somehow didn't seem that way. The swallows were back from Africa and after their long journey they seemed intoxicated with England, joyous to be home. We watched them skimming across the surface of the water around the boat, dipping their wings one way and then the other, so close to us sometimes that you'd think they were bound to collide.

Em, it seemed, was on a mercy mission to save me from myself. Or at least to save me from that bit of myself which was my ankle. That was her story anyway. The fact that the forecasters were predicting a scorching spell with record-breaking temperatures may have had something to do with her desire to get out of London too – although it would have been uncharitable to pursue that one with her.

Kit lay splayed at our feet, enjoying the way she could agitate passing dogs just by her presence. She wouldn't so much as twitch a whisker, but 50 yards before they got to the boat they seemed to detect her as if by some innate radar, and they'd start tugging on their leads, barking and making a performance of trying to get to her. What might have happened if one of them had succeeded, I don't know. I've no idea what Kit would have done either. She wouldn't have run, that's for sure. She was not a happy cat that May. The temperatures mystified her. She was a long-haired cat, a fur ball, and she was too young to have experienced a world this hot. It made her short-tempered and irascible. I guess a spat with a dog might have got it out of her system.

In the absence of that diversion she devised certain strategies to keep herself cool. She would go outside in the evening as soon as it got dark and hang over the edge of the boat roof where it projects above the deck, lying there like a dishcloth on a clothes line until she dropped off to sleep and lost control of her centre of gravity. They say cats always land on their feet when they fall. No they don't. Not if they're draped from a boat roof, anyhow. Not if they're dreaming their delicious cat dreams when they drop. When they do that, they're like bagpipes with legs. And they hit the ground with the same sort of sound.

Sometimes in the countryside, especially moored close to woods which were her favourite, she'd make for the undergrowth and blanket herself in the damp remnants of the autumn leaf-fall where if you went looking for her you might sometimes discern a half-buried pink nose twitching in the gloom.

Eventually I began to worry whether she was drinking enough. She'd been fed biscuits at the cat refuge, and we'd kept her on the same diet although we'd substituted the monstrously large half bricks they'd given her with something more in keeping with the scale of the kitten she still was. Even so, a diet of dry biscuits – any biscuits – means that a cat must have constant access to fresh water. I was like a first-time mum just out of the maternity ward fussing about making sure she got it. I'd fill up a bowl for her first thing in the morning, and top it up three or four times a day, maybe more, worried that the movement of the boat might lead it to it spilling, or that it might evaporate, or that she needed more than I was providing…

It became an obsession for me, this water thing. I'd find myself checking her bowl a couple of dozen times a day at completely inappropriate moments. I found myself doing it when I should have been thinking about steering the boat, or manoeuvring through locks. I found myself doing it in the middle of the night when I was disturbed by a dream or by my ageing bladder.

Imagine then how I felt, then, the next day when we stopped for lunch near the charmingly-named village of Grafton Regis (population approximately ninety-six), a mile or so from the canal. As soon as the engine went silent, Kit hopped off the boat. Normally I'd have discouraged her from doing this during the day, except that the forecasters had been proved right and it had turned out as hot as they said it would. The cabin had become stifling; I thought she needed fresh air.

But it immediately became clear it wasn't air she was after. She stood briefly on the towpath taking stock of where she was. Then, almost before I was aware of it, she leapt to the water's edge in a single purposeful bound. Her head dropped and for an instant she looked as if she was going to drink.

I shouted at her.

Whether this startled her into action, or whether it had been her intention all along, she suddenly launched herself into the canal. I could barely believe it. It was no accident, I'm sure. She didn't fall in, she didn't slide in. She didn't lose her footing and stumble. On the contrary, it was a very controlled immersion. She took a step forward to where the bank had eroded into the water to form a beach. Then, lowering herself in until she was half submerged, she pushed herself off, paddling in a graceful loop back to her starting point without any of the clumsy splashing I'd have imagined from dogs I've seen swimming.

Afterwards she shook herself down and went off rooting in the hedge as if swimming was the most natural thing in the world for a cat.

It was Em's turn to cook that day. I found her doing things with eggs in the galley. At first she didn't believe me, but then I showed her the tell-tale wet patches where Kit had emerged from the water. Finally Kit herself came back into the cabin, licking herself down, incriminatingly damp.

That settled it.

We seemed to have a cat that liked not just snow, but water too.

Interesting place, Grafton Regis. A prettyish Northamptonshire village. A fine church, some attractive stone buildings. A better-than-average gastropub called the White Hart serving real ale from hand-carved hand-pumps. During the nineteenth century one of the cottages not far from the pub was the home of a family called the Smiths who had an oil painting on an oak panel of a young, delicately featured man. It was dated 1588 and had probably been painted as a birthday tribute, for the man's age, twenty-four, was emblazoned in the top left corner. The painting found its way to County Durham where it hung for many years in the bar of the Bridgewater Arms in Winston-on-Tees and where, at the turn of the twentieth century, the belief grew that it was a portrait of the young William Shakespeare.

The main reason for this was that in 1588 Shakespeare was indeed twenty-four years old. If the painting's not him, he's an exact contemporary of the real subject.

But there's something more about the Grafton Portrait, as it's come to be known, that makes people believe it must be Shakespeare. For a start it looks like Shakespeare. Or at least it looks like that picture of him on the front of the plays we had to read at school. That was based on the 1622 engraving by Martin Droeshout which Shakespeare's contemporary Ben Jonson thought was such a good likeness. The young man in the portrait, whoever it is, has more hair, but he's got Shakespeare's trademark domed forehead. More than that, he's got a face that's evocative of Shakespeare – or at least what people imagine Shakespeare to be. Particularly his grey eyes. Sensitive, penetrating eyes, playwright's eyes, eyes that can look into your soul. He's got an appraising, critical look too. He's staring out of the portrait, pursing his lips beneath his thin moustache: not so much us looking at him, but him looking at us. Weighing us up, assessing us.

Despite all this, most experts nowadays believe the Grafton Portrait isn't Shakespeare. They say the silk doublet the young man is wearing is too opulent for someone as poor as Shakespeare was at that period when he had a young family and was just about to join a troupe of travelling actors. The exception is Peter Ackroyd, who's written a biography of Shakespeare and knows a thing or two about him. He believes the portrait is the poet, and for what it's worth I'm with him on this.

For heaven's sake, Shakespeare was an actor; he could have borrowed the doublet from the costume trunk. Or he could have scrounged it from somewhere else. And even if he didn't, the portrait's a painting, isn't it? It's not real. The artist could have embellished the clothing to make his subject seem more lavish, like I do sometimes with characters I write about here.

Besides, I want the portrait to be Shakespeare. I want it to be him because I love the idea of Shakespeare spending years presiding over a taproom in the Bridgewater Arms while the garrulous and the raucous, the vulgar and the boorish, the loud-mouthed and the bibulous of County Durham disported themselves around him.

And do you know what? I think he'd have liked that idea himself too.

That evening we moored at Stoke Bruerne again as we had on our trip down to London. This time, though, we tied up at the foot of the flight of locks that takes the canal through the village. The travelling canal theatre group Mikron were performing on the lawn opposite the pub and we joined a small crowd sitting on the grass to enjoy a boisterous and sometimes moving performance of a play about the history of the River Thames. As the sun went down it turned chilly though, and the damp made a beeline for my bum, in the way that as a kid my mum always said would happen if I didn't sit on something warm. Eventually we went back to the boat, only to find Kit waiting for us on the deck, impatient to get back into the cabin and bad-tempered with us because we'd forgotten to leave the side porthole open so she could get in. After making a big fuss all day because it was too hot, it was now, apparently, too cold for her.

Too cold for her, can you believe that? With all that fur. What was cat fur for if not to keep cats warm on nippy spring evenings? It wasn't sodding decoration, was it? I was beginning to wonder whether we'd spoilt the creature. Whether now she was our pet, or whether we were hers.

The following day was even hotter. I think the only time we were comfortable was going through the long 3,000-yard Blisworth Tunnel, when it was like cruising in a fridge. Afterwards though – after we emerged from it on the other side – the sun seemed even more relentless than it had been, the heat even more draining than before. Around us the countryside was lush: the trees thickening with fresh leaf-growth and the towpath already festooned with cow parsley. But it didn't seem authentic, it didn't feel real. The vivid colours were too flamboyant and intense for England. That luminous blue sky, those flaming yellow rape fields, that relentless green as far as the eye could see. It was as if during the morning we'd crossed into some other-dimensional lacuna.

And it was all so quiet and still. Understandable, perhaps, that the crews of boats might have found the heat unbearable and moored up to doze away the afternoon. But birds? They seemed to have roosted early too, and disappeared, the hedgerows and the trees lifeless as a result. Even the livestock in the fields were motionless. Sheep clustered like marble statues under the shade of trees. Cows splayed out on the ground, so laggard they could barely summon up the energy to chew the cud.

We kept going at a steady pace, although by the time we'd travelled the 14 miles or so past Nether Heyford and Weeden, and climbed the seven cussed locks in the Buckby flight, each of them as heavy and stiff as old church doors, we were on our knees with exhaustion. So wiped out we couldn't even be tempted by the crowd sitting sipping ice-cold lager on the canalside terrace of the New Inn. All we wanted to do now was to rest, but the trouble was there was nowhere to stop. The bank was under repair and fenced off from the water, so that the first opportunity we got was a couple of miles further on at the approach to Braunston Tunnel where the canal burrows into a cutting.

Normally the dampness of the atmosphere here and the gloom of the overhanging trees make this an unappealing place to spend the night; but that day it couldn't have been better, an ideal respite from the sun.

For the fact is, much as we all say we love the sunshine, it's not our English way to feel comfortable in temperatures like this. We may think it is and seek out places in the Mediterranean or further afield where the heat is so fierce it makes us melt. But this is not because we like the heat as such. It is because heat is the price we have to pay to be in a place where the rain's not constantly running down our necks. Generally, as northern Europeans, we can't stand these sorts of temperatures. We have a day or two stretched on a beach until we get lobstered, and then we spend the rest of our holiday slapping on calamine lotion, dreaming of our softer English climate that caresses us like a lover, not cooks us like a steak.

The next day – the heat more tolerable now, thank God – we cruised past Braunston and back onto the Oxford Canal, heading north this time, away from Banbury and towards Coventry.

At Rugby the canal passes over a steep embankment where two reservoirs nestle below. There's a flight of steps down to them, and a path to a viaduct under the canal which leads to the railway station. It was there I dropped Em for her trip back home.

'I'll see you in a week or so,' I said. 'After Birmingham.'

'After Birmingham?' she replied, a note of rebuke in her voice.

'Well, you said you weren't coming up for the Challenge...'

'I said no such thing. I said it was a crazy idea. And it is a crazy idea. But it's fun to do crazy things sometimes. Besides, it'd be enjoyable to spend time with Bob and Rosemary...'

I let it ride, kissed her goodbye. 'Well if you are coming, I'll keep my fingers crossed the weather keeps fine.'

Her response came just a little too rapidly. It betrayed the reason for her change of mind. 'Oh, I wouldn't worry about that, it's going to be another lovely weekend, sweltering again.'

'You checked?'

'No, no, I didn't check. I just... well, I happened to hear. On the radio,' she explained sheepishly.

That night I squeezed into a tight spot in a line of boats moored along the bank near Brinklow. Next to me was a young, well-to-do couple with a child having a drink on the deck. Their boat, I could see immediately, had been built by one of the more fashionable builders. It had imitation rivets and a long Nordic bow that rose into the air superciliously, as if turning its nose up at me. Gleaming brass-polished portholes adorned its sides and it had a paint finish you could have used for shaving. Remarkably, it hadn't got a scratch on it, not even along its hull, which led me to believe it must have been on its maiden cruise.

I cast my eye over it appraisingly, though as I did I became aware that the crew of the other boat, the child included, were doing the same to *Justice*. And it was clear they didn't like what they saw. You can understand it, I suppose. There they were relaxing outside on one of the best evenings of the year so far, and then this battered old tramp steamer of a boat turns up, dirty, scratched and bruised, with its skipper looking like a dosser who'd just turned out from the Sally Army.

'Hi,' I said to them as I was tying up. 'It's a grand evening.'

They gave me a forced smile but didn't engage me in conversation. When I looked again they'd gone inside.

TEN
Walsall

I am in Walsall, but Walsall is very confusing. It is not like I imagined Walsall to be. But then I live in London and I would react this way, wouldn't I? It's because I think London's the centre of the universe. All Londoners do. We think London's the only city in the country worth living in, and this makes us patronising about other places, particularly those in the North or the Midlands. We think they're all dumps, all cobbled streets and towering Satanic mills. It's called metrocentricity, this arrogance of ours. That's just a polite way of saying we're prejudiced.

Walsall confounds expectations. I stand on the deck of the boat in the recently re-opened canal basin listening to the frothing cappuccino machine in the coffee shop under the new art gallery where a David Hockney exhibition has just opened. People are sitting out at pavement tables chatting, or eating at the adjacent waterside bar which is doing lively business serving breakfasts in the warm spring sunshine. Around the corner is a prosperous pedestrian street which leads to the centre where there's a bustling market.

No, this is nothing close to what I imagined Walsall would be like. Walsall's in the West Midlands, isn't it? The Black Country? Traditionally its main industry has been leather manufacturing, which is supposed to stink to high heaven. For better or worse, I can't smell anything resembling leather manufacturing – or, for that matter, any other manufacturing. Neither is this bit of the Black Country particularly black. It's more a sort of warm terracotta as a result of the sun on the rich-toned brickwork from which so many of the buildings in the town are constructed. Today the sky is a faultless azure too, flecked by just an occasional indistinct cloud. A Californian sky like one Hockney himself would recognise from his painting *A Bigger Splash*. I am here with Bob who has been travelling with me for a few days now. His wife Rosemary joined us yesterday and Em has just arrived by train from London. Now we have all assembled, we are waiting to get going on the BCN Challenge which we can start anywhere on the Birmingham system, but which Bob has elected we should begin from here. He's navigator for the trip and he's seen the chance for some quick points by setting out from the place where the race is scheduled to end. He figures we'll be the only ones doing this and so we'll have the canal to ourselves.

This seemed like a good idea when he first proposed it. Now I'm not so certain. Surely, if there were easy points to be picked up, every boat in the competition would be here, wouldn't they? As it is, the basin's deserted; we're the only boat in the place. What's more, I suspect I know why. I think it's because all the other competitors realise that getting to Walsall by water is a pig. Doing it once in a weekend is quite enough for most people, thank you very much.

We'd had to learn this lesson from hard experience.

Bob and I had met up a few days before at the small Warwickshire town of Atherstone, only a gentle cruise from the outskirts of Birmingham. It was late May now. Heading towards the city along the Coventry Canal, the hedgerows were thick with the froth of hawthorn blossom; and the adjoining fields, once spoil heaps, quarries or pits, were like the undulating hills of Devon, incandescent with glowing buttercups. We stopped that first night at Curdworth, which the canal guides describe as set in the shadow of motorways and close to the sewage works. It's also near a road freight terminal – all of which makes it a place not greatly recommended for a long stay. However, it is useful as an overnight stop for narrowboats on their way to Birmingham, the last safe suburban mooring before the badlands of the inner city. Unfortunately, when we got there, every spot between the town bridge and a short 57-yard tunnel – the only space in Curdworth where you can moor – was taken up by a local boat club out on an early-season cruise. So jam-packed was it that craft were even breasting up together. We had no option but to stop further along where it's so shallow we could barely get close enough to the towpath to get off.

Manchester United were playing Barcelona that evening in a televised Champions League match, and once we'd let Kit out for a few gentle hours terrorising local wildlife, we found a pub which was showing the game. It was chock-a-block and raucous with it. You stepped inside the door to be regaled by a solid wall of perspiring humanity, the dominant scent of which was Eau de Male, a heady little number composed of stale sweat with top notes of fag smoke and stale lager. Getting a drink in the place was a nightmare; knowing where to take it afterwards was even worse. There were no seats in the main part of the bar, which was dominated by two or three TVs, but around the perimeter of the room were a series of small booths. Some of them were filled with expatriate Man U hardliners wearing red club colours and more tattoos than you'd find at the Edinburgh Festival. They eyed us up and down suspiciously with a look that seemed to warn us not to even think about sitting near them. Others were occupied by factions of indigenous Aston Villa supporters in claret and sky blue, or by their closest rivals from Birmingham City in royal blue. There was even a group of Baggies from West Bromwich in blue and white stripes. The supporters from the different clubs were all glowering at each other provocatively, though their loyalties in this match were far from clear – even to themselves.

Some, regardless of their team allegiances, were rooting for The Reds. After all, Man U was an English club playing Johnny Foreigner. It was upholding values of civilization and culture in an anarchic world, showing the way of progress and advancement. Not that there was general consensus on this; far from it. Half the pub was shouting for Barcelona. As far as they were concerned the Catalans may have been greasy dagos reeking of garlic and cheap wine, but what they weren't was Manchester United, and Manchester United is the most hated team in the country among English football supporters.

Believe me, trying to get a seat in this place wasn't so much a matter of taking the weight off your feet as declaring a tribal affinity. You needed more diplomacy than the United Nations. Goals presented the most difficult dilemma. United lost 2–0. How do you react as a disinterested non-partisan when half the pub's feeling suicidal about the score and the other half's cheering hysterically?

By the time we got back to the boat the two of us were traumatised by the experience, and it was as much as we could do to drop into bed exhausted.

The following morning the trip to Walsall took its first turn for the worse. I'd got used to Bob, his shorts and the spectacle of his knees, but today, as if to provoke the fashionistas, he appeared from his cabin with the addition of a flat cap on his head. This was made of a fetchingly loud design of tweed which I assume he'd put on to protect himself from the sun, which was fierce even at this early hour. He obviously thought it was a becoming item of apparel. Actually, I did too. I thought with his shorts it was becoming ridiculous. However, since I was all too aware of my status as a dependent invalid, I kept my own counsel. Besides, the dress sense of my crew, such as it was, soon became an irrelevance as the journey went on.

After a couple of miles we stopped to fill up with water at one of the service points provided along the canal for the purpose. It's the sort of routine task you do every couple of days on a boat, but this time it wasn't so easy. The level of the canal had been down all morning, but now we became aware of how bad it was, so shallow that we couldn't get anywhere near the bank. In fact, there was so little water in the canal we could barely float in the middle of it. The edges had become mud-banks, studded with old bricks and rusty bikes; the canal a black, slimy stream through the middle. Thankfully, a British Waterways man appeared as if from nowhere, clearly alerted to the situation. He looked concerned and started prodding around with a stick, mumbling about seepage and leaks and outflows. The upshot of all this was that as soon as he was able to manage it, he came on board and we took him up to Salford Junction while he used *Justice* as an inspection launch, examining every culvert and drain on the way.

Salford Junction is where the Birmingham and Fazeley Canal bends a sharp south towards the centre of the city, and where it meets the Grand Union coming in from the same direction. If you do any driving, you'll have been here many times, except you'll have been passing high above it on one of the many motorways or slip roads which compose the Gravelly Hill Interchange – Spaghetti Junction as it's more commonly known.

You probably think that as unpleasant motoring experiences go this is about as bad as it gets; but let me tell you, driving over Spaghetti Junction is nothing compared to the experience of travelling under it on the fetid, graffiti-covered canal below. Concrete jungle doesn't even begin to describe it. There are 559 columns dotted around here, supporting roads on five different levels. Some of them are nearly 80 feet high. As you cruise underneath it's like being in a forest of petrified tree trunks or the set of a movie of some Brothers Grimm fairy tale directed by Tim Burton.

The noise is unnerving, though it's not what you'd expect. It's not like traffic noise – or at least not the sort of deafening sound you'd hear if you were standing at the side of a motorway. This is a far-off rumbling resonance, echoing far above your head. From underneath, the roads seem to groan in agony as the traffic passes over them; the supporting columns seem to strain under the pressure.

It's dark, dirty and damp too, even on a hot day like this. And yet it's surprisingly arid as well, cut by sharp, dusty winds and prone to sudden flurries of air blowing up from out of nowhere like small tornadoes. The steeply sloping areas under the roads never see daylight, and they're so contaminated by the toxins from the traffic that nothing grows. The whole place is a hostile wasteland, abandoned to drunks, drug addicts and feral kids; and if you think my imagination's running away with me and that I'm inventing menace that doesn't exist, think again. At one point, you come across a simple red granite memorial like a gravestone on the towpath, a reality check if ever you needed one. It's a monument to Detective Constable Michael Swindells of the West Midland Police who was stabbed to death here in 2004 by a man he was trying to arrest.

This is one mean area, make no mistake. You don't want to hang around for long.

But then you get to the bottom of the thirteen Perry Bar locks on the Tame Valley Canal, a matter of a few hundred yards further on. There, a little beyond the junction, the tenor of the canal alters suddenly in a way which is entirely unexpected. Under Spaghetti Junction you were in the middle of an uncompromising cityscape, harsh and relentless. Now, a couple of locks up, you could be in deepest rural Cheshire, say, or Shropshire. The flight winds up the hill under a thick canopy of trees which insulates it from its surroundings.

Bob went on ahead and we slipped into a locking routine. Occasionally we passed kids on bikes who were using the towpath as a cut-through; once or twice we came across anglers who were taking advantage of the good weather for an hour or two's quiet fishing. Mostly, though, the canal was ours, with not another boat or person on it. We stopped for lunch, which we ate outside on the deck in the sunshine, and as morning turned to afternoon the city seemed to dissolve in a heat haze, only the occasional far-off sound of a train or a dog barking in the distance reminding us it was there.

At the top of the flight is Rushall Junction, where the M5 joins the M6 amid a welter of confusing approach roads. It was rush hour when we arrived but there wasn't much in the way of rushing going on. From the canal your whole vista is of motorways at different levels crossing and merging from all directions. That day every one of them was at a complete standstill. We watched the drivers sitting impatiently in their immobile cars and trucks, drumming their fingers and picking their noses while we overtook the lot of them at an imperious 4 mph. It was as much as I could do to avoid smirking. Or maybe I did smirk and wasn't aware that I was doing it. One of the drivers gave me a V-sign anyhow. That might explain why.

Soon we arrived at another junction where the Walsall Canal branches north.

No sooner had we turned into it than *Justice* slowed to a sluggish crawl, though her engine beat remained constant. This is the definitive sign of a fouled propeller, and there was nothing for it but to go down to the weed hatch to clear whatever was holding us up. The weed hatch is a box that sits over the propeller, high enough to be above the water line but placed so you can get your arm through and access the shaft and blades.

From inside, the Walsall Canal looked cleaner than you might imagine. OK, it was the colour of stale urine, but at least it wasn't muddy; at least you could see the bottom. Mind you, you didn't want to look at the bottom for long. It was like a rubbish tip, strewn with every object you could imagine lying among the reeds and lily roots. Obviously people in this part of town didn't believe in dustbins. I believed in dustbins. From where I was stretched, my arm immersed up to my shoulder, I could see at least three of them half-buried in the canal bed.

What had fouled us was a flowered living-room curtain which I unwound carefully, bringing it dripping to the surface undamaged. I threw it onto the towpath, which was a bit of a shame really because no sooner had we got the engine started again than the prop fouled once more. It was a curtain exactly the same as the other one. If I hadn't have thrown the first one away I'd have had the pair.

We proceeded for another hundred yards or so before the engine stopped again. This time Bob volunteered for weed hatch duty. He brought up a table lamp with the flex attached. Ten minutes later it was my turn and I pulled up a rug. He followed this up by extracting us from an easy chair, but I trumped him soon afterwards by freeing us from the cushion of a settee.

Believe me, if we'd have saved all this stuff, we could have furnished a three-bedroom house.

Eventually the going got a bit easier – but not that much easier. I don't know whether the Walsall Canal was just shallow, or whether it was actually a deep canal which was being used for landfill. Perhaps the council was just tipping there hoping that no-one would notice. Or maybe it was their idea of art. An underwater installation? Something to do with the new gallery possibly?

At least it was a beautiful day; shirt-sleeves weather. And at least people were friendly, though as the light waned and evening fell, we began to attract the unwelcome attention of lippy 11-year-olds, most of them girls and most of them dressed in skirts so short and make-up so thick you'd have thought they were out for a night's clubbing. Whether the interest shown to us was due to the rarity of boats on the canal or to Bob's sartorial style, I couldn't say. With his shorts, his knees and his flat cap he looked enough of a sight to start with; but spattered with mud from his excursions down the weed hatch, he presented a real spectacle. Mind you, I didn't look any better myself. The pair of us, both in need of losing a stone or two around the midriff, were like a couple of happy hippos who'd been rooting around at the watering hole. And yet despite the rubbish, despite the kids and despite the stream of featureless business parks and vandalised council estates we passed, the Walsall Canal – indeed the whole of the BCN – was wondrous.

There was an astonishing concentration of flowers along its length: foxgloves, banks of oxeye daisies, bursts of sunshine-bright gorse, and blue lupins all over the place. The water lilies were in full bloom too, both yellow and white, carpeting the canal from one side to the other in places.

These lilies got thicker as we approached Walsall, and they began to cause problems that were worse than the rubbish. The propeller couldn't cut through their thick, pliable roots and they wound themselves around the blades like rope, leaving the engine screaming with the effort of just turning over. Bob and I were like a couple of jack-in-the-boxes going up and down the weed hatch. Eventually, just to entertain ourselves, we began to time our excursions, like athletes performing against the clock. An early best time of 6 minutes 23 seconds, dropped to 5.49 and then to 4.18. Finally Bob broke the 4-minute barrier and try as I might, I couldn't get close to it.

Not that it mattered much at that stage anyhow. We weren't far from Walsall, and the closer we got, the sparser the lilies became. It was just as well they did. We'd been on the go since early morning. All this bouncing up and down attending to the propeller had exhausted us. Besides, it was getting dark. We were beginning to dream of a shower and that first pint of the night. It was only about 3 miles to our destination, an hour's run – two hours at most, given how slowly we'd been travelling all day.

Then we went under Spinks Bridge.

You will probably find Spinks Bridge engraved on my heart when I die, as Mary Tudor said Calais was engraved on hers.

Justice suddenly rose in the air, lurched to the right and then stopped dead in her tracks. No amount of engine power would move her, no amount of pushing or pulling on ropes or heaving on the barge pole. A cursory examination was enough to establish that she'd lodged on something under the water, probably a lump of concrete from the adjacent site which had once been a factory, but which was now being levelled. One thing was obvious: she wasn't going anywhere like this. The only thing we could do was to reverse her off and try a different tack. With the engine revving at full power, and with Bob pulling from the towpath and me levering from the arch of the bridge, she finally began to move backwards so we could release her from the ledge on which she'd stuck.

By now it was dark and we were both sweating freely from our exertions. The evening was balmy, which was the good news since you really wouldn't want to be stuck like this in the rain. The bad news was that this meant there were more people around than you'd expect, given the late hour. We were beginning to attract unsolicited attention again – and this time not just from prepubescent girls. Trapped as we were, unable to move, we couldn't help but feel vulnerable and intimidated by the situation, threatened by everyone who passed. This was because most of those who did pass looked either drunk or stoned, or were in loud, aggressive groups where you couldn't but feel that the slightest wrong word on your part could turn an already unpleasant situation nasty. At one point a young couple appeared, staggering up the towpath, both of them out of their heads on something or another. They were pushing a young child, sound asleep in a battered pushchair. They were affable, if a bit loud.

'Want a hand, mate?' the man asked, his voice slurred and indistinct.

I threw him a rope. 'Thanks a lot. Grab this. We're going to need all the help we can get to deal with this one.'

I reversed *Justice* a little further from the bridge and drove it under the arch at full power, scouring the coping stones on one side in order to avoid the same obstruction that had stopped me before. For a moment or two it looked as if this strategy might succeed and that I'd get under, but then *Justice* juddered to a halt again, no more than halfway through.

The three of us yanked and wrenched and jerked at the ropes mindlessly for about twenty minutes. At first Bob and I were concerned the guy helping us might fall in; he lurched around dangerously on the edge of the canal, scarcely able to stand upright. Soon, though, perspiration began to run down his face and the effects of whatever it was he was on wore off. None of us had got any real idea of what we were doing; we were crossing our fingers, hoping that something would happen.

Then, as much by luck as design, it did. We started to swing the bow of the boat from one side of the canal to the other, the bloke pulling on the rope from the towpath side, Bob pulling from the site of the demolished factory. The effect was to 'walk' the boat over the obstruction, half centimetre by half centimetre, much as you might walk a heavy crate across a room on its corners.

It was arduous going, exhausting, but in an hour we were free. Afterwards, the stranger who had helped us, and the woman and child who were with him, stumbled off into the night, waving away our thanks as if rescuing boats was the sort of task they were called upon to perform every night. An hour later we pulled off the main line of the canal down the arm which leads to Walsall Basin. It was pitch black except for the boat headlight perforating the gloom, and the shimmering lights of the waterside bar at the end where we could the hear the remote, muted sounds of music rising to the sky.

They're another world sometimes, the canals. It's part of their charm, though it's not always charming.

ELEVEN
A Weekend in Brum

I t's 9.30 a.m., and in Walsall the BCN Challenge starts to
a fanfare of indifference. No starting gun, no cheering
crowds, no jostling for early position. In fact, nothing and no
one except for a crusty old fisherman sitting in the sunshine
watching his float from one of the mooring piers in the basin.
But then, this is not a race in any real sense of the word.
There are rules, yes, but most of them only the organisers
properly understand, and the rest are left to the honesty of
the competitors who could, if they wanted, start ahead of time
without anyone being the wiser.

Basically it's a twenty-four-hour endurance contest, though
participants have to take a mandatory six-hour stop at some
point during the event, which extends it to thirty hours.
The idea is to keep going. You earn points for the miles you
travel and the locks you pass. The more difficult the canal
and the harder the locks, the more points you earn. Someone
somewhere works all this out afterwards. It takes an age to do

and generally by the time the winning boat's announced the crew has forgotten it ever competed in the event.

Em finally succeeds in marshalling us to our positions. We are all to take turns locking and steering. She has decided to start off on the tiller, though this, it soon transpires, is a bad mistake. We are all feeling a little fragile from our late meal the previous night which, judging from the empty bottles we woke to find rattling around on the deck, got a bit out of hand. Clearly Em is feeling more fragile than the rest of us. She immediately crashes the boat against some outcrop on the bank – at which point she hands the tiller to me with the sort of alacrity that suggests she was hoping no one had noticed she'd been steering in the first place.

This is a mistake. My mobile phone has just rung and I am taking a call from my friend Claire who I haven't spoken to for ages. My mind is in the wrong place and so is the tiller. I immediately crash as well. Eventually Bob takes over from me, and as we turn from the Walsall Arm back onto the main canal, he is so overwhelmed with all this crashing going on around him that he decides to join in the party and crashes too.

This really isn't going too well. We've only come a couple of hundred yards. At this rate we'll have trashed the boat by lunchtime.

Finally, we sort ourselves out and begin to climb the eight Walsall Locks which take us 65 feet up to the Wyrley and Essington Canal – or the 'Curly Wurly' as it's affectionately known. It's one of the oldest canals on the BCN, so-called because it's a contour canal: that is, one that winds around torturously following the lie of the land – a system of construction which meant the original contractors didn't have to build expensive locks.

We stop at the top to take on water adjacent to the old Boatman's Rest mission hall. This is a simple but elegant redbrick building which at first sight seems very un-ecclesiastical in its design, until you notice a row of six Gothic windows tucked away at first floor level, presumably put there so as not to frighten the clientele by looking too religious. There were originally five of these halls built by the church authorities around Birmingham to minister to the needs of working boatmen; and although this sort of patronising attitude to the poor is out of fashion today, in its time it provided a key service to men who needed to get a wash somewhere, or have a letter written for them or just sit and relax away from the pub. Only two of the mission halls survive today. This one in Walsall, built in 1890 at a cost of £350, used to be a canal museum until the bean counters got to it a year or two back. Now it stands proud but unloved, abandoned to its fate, and just waiting for vandals to put a match to it, something that will surely happen unless someone finds a use for it soon.

It cheeses me off. I'm sure if a building of such historical interest was located in a more salubrious area – in some posh Northamptonshire village, say, or a Staffordshire market town – someone would have found a role for it, if only as a charity shop. But out here in the nether regions of Walsall, away from the town centre, it's difficult to know what you can do with it. We're like the Italians in this respect, we English. We have too much heritage for our own good and as a result we don't always value it as much as we should. We finish up preserving those bits like stately homes and aristocratic gardens that make us feel warm and cuddly about ourselves, but buildings which speak of ordinary lives and the struggles of working people barely get a look in.

Thankfully the canals themselves, which are a living tribute to the people who built them and earned their living on them, have survived that post-war low of the late 1940s when they were seen as ugly remnants of bygone industrialism, vulnerable to politicians who were too blind to see a role for them. But the battle's not yet won. The canals are administered by British Waterways, who still operate under the constraints of the 1968 Transport Act, which classifies canals under three headings: commercial waterways, cruising waterways and the remainder. Among the latter are the Walsall and the Wyrely and Essington canals.

British Waterways is under no legal constraint to keep these 'remaindered' waterways open, and the fact that it does is a credit to them and the army of volunteers who turn out in their spare time every weekend to clear the rubbish they attract. So unless I'm willing to go out and join them I should keep my mouth shut and stop belly-aching about the state they're in.

At least they're here to complain about, and for that I should be grateful.

Actually none of us is complaining about the Wyrely and Essington Canal. In fact, it's a terrific waterway and we can't speak highly enough of it. Some of us remember not so long ago when cruising it in a boat as deep as *Justice* would have been about as feasible as taking off at Heathrow. This weekend, though, the water is clear and bottomless and we are slipping through it as if we were on some sylvan river meandering through the shires.

Of course, the weather has something to do with the way we are feeling. It is not yet midday but already the temperature is in the high eighties and rising. Em and Rosemary are splayed out on the roof sunbathing; Bob and I are on the stern deck steering. Suddenly I am aware that him wearing shorts doesn't look as much the attention seeking device it normally does. On the contrary, I'm the one who looks out of place since everyone walking along the towpath seems to be wearing shorts too – or if not shorts then summery frocks, which will no doubt be Bob's next thing once he realises the rest of the world's caught up with the lead he's set and he has to think of something new.

We are the centre of attention on the Wyrley and Essington today. So few boats travel along it that everyone we encounter stops to watch us go by. We pass families out strolling in the sunshine; we pass kids playing on their bikes and lovers on trysts. We pass the elderly with grandkids glued to their hands; we pass young mothers clinging to all-terrain, three-wheel pushchairs with tyres so thick they could traverse mountain ranges. We pass the whole of Birmingham, it seems, the whole of the world.

The only things we don't pass, however, are other boats. Neither do there seem to be any following us. In fact, the canal is so empty that we are beginning to think perhaps we've got the date wrong and the BCN Challenge isn't this weekend at all. We suddenly become very self-conscious about the boat, which we've decorated in gaudy bunting as the organisers requested. Perhaps the reason we are attracting all this attention isn't because there are so few boats on the canal, but because the only one that is looks like a floating primary school classroom.

Eventually, thank God, we do meet another boat competing in the event; and though it may be our imagination, its crew look every bit as relieved to see us as we are to see them. They look about as sheepish as we do too, but that's probably because their decorations are even tackier than ours. We wave at them. They wave back at us. This provokes another bout of waving on our side which leads to more waving from them so that eventually we are all waving dementedly at each other. In my opinion there is too much waving taking place between these boats for it to be healthy. Finally, we pass each other and the canal once again becomes ours alone.

The Curly Wurly is a remarkably rural waterway for one that is entirely contained within an urban area. It snakes through a sort of municipal countryside, the urban edgelands; and though you're always aware of the presence of houses in the distance, they never seem to impinge even when, as occasionally happens, they trespass close enough for the odd garden to tiptoe timidly to the water's edge. For the most part, though, as it winds its way around a series of anonymous West Midlands' suburbs, the Curly Wurly passes alongside scrubby fields, characterised by a great many shaggy-shanked shire horses which seem to be tethered everywhere.

We make slow but undemanding progress through the hot day. A boat can't travel faster than the water will allow it and for a large part of our journey we are pottering along in tickover, *Justice*'s massive engine sounding like a sewing machine. At Catshill Junction at Brownhills we swing south on what is called the Daws Branch and the depth increases, which allows us to speed up slightly. An hour or so later we reach a flight of nine locks on the Rushall Canal. Astonishingly – despite the better part of a day's travelling – we are only about 3 miles from our starting point in Walsall. Grateful for the chance to stretch our legs after such a long, lockless stretch, we work our way down in sunshine that seems to be fiercer in this late afternoon than at any time during the day.

I take the opportunity to check on the cat, and for an instant I find myself panicking as I fail to find her in any of her usual places. For a mad moment I even start to think she might have jumped off the boat somewhere along the way; though this, I have to admit, seems unlikely, given that to do it she'd have had to claw her way over Em and Rosemary who for the last few hours have been sitting with their feet up on the front deck, having been forced off the roof earlier in search of shade. She finally comes to light in the main bedroom where Em and I sleep and where she knows she's not supposed to be.

Lying pitted into the eiderdown, she stretches herself luxuriously when she sees me, shameless that she's been caught red-handed like this. But that's cats for you, isn't it? We don't discipline them; we suggest they make lifestyle changes. They'll comply if they feel like it, and nothing we can do will alter that, so we might as well get used to the idea.

I ignore her wilfulness and give up. At least here I know where she is.

Back on deck I discover we are back at Rushall Junction, where the Rushall Canal meets the Tame Valley Canal, and where not so very long ago Bob and I were slipping past the rush hour motorway traffic on our way to Walsall. All the talk is about where we might take our enforced six-hour break, which has already reduced to five because of odd stops we've already made. Originally the strategy was to spend the night around here, but we've made better time than we anticipated, and what's left of the evening promises to be so agreeable that it would be a shame not to make as much of it as we could. Besides, since reaching the junction and turning towards central Birmingham we are meeting other competitors coming up the Perry Barr flight of locks which we are descending. This means they are all set in our favour and it would be a travesty not to take advantage of what is, to adapt a sailing term, about as near as you'll get to a following wind on a canal.

However, after ten hours on the go already, we're all starting to get tired and hungry; we are beginning to get short and impatient with each other too. Eventually we decide that we ought to have a proper meal and so we put on a joint of boiling bacon which we are planning for dinner. Five minutes later, it comes off again. Bob is on the tiller, and he misjudges his line and goes crashing into a gate. The bacon slides off the stove, hits the floor in an explosion of boiling water and goes slithering towards the door as if it's suddenly become a pig again and is making a dash for freedom. We retrieve it off the carpet and dust it down. It is evening now, and soon it will be that strange period of the day when the light fails and the shadows on the cut become ghostly and unreal. It is no time to get precious over details of hygiene.

I take over steering, and with the remaining locks in our favour and everyone now out on the towpath working me through, we are down the flight before we know it. Now we're back in the hellhole under Spaghetti Junction – though this isn't the same grim and threatening place Bob and I had experienced so recently. A vibrant sunset has burst into flame behind us and an extraordinary transformation has taken place. The grey concrete columns supporting the motorways are now burnished pillars of gold, and the space beneath the motorways is like the inside of some vast Byzantine church. Even the dull and dusty towpath has undergone a mystical transubstantiation. Washed with this light, it is as if it's been draped with gilded gossamer, as if a precious and insubstantial mist has blown across it.

We make a sharp turn towards Aston Locks and the National Indoor Arena; we've revised our plans and have now decided to stop in that area. The contrast is startling. Suddenly, out of the sunshine, it is night and very dark. Ahead of us the canal is as black as an oil slick, cutting through a chasm of industrial buildings which rise like grotesque castles at either side, their chimneys lonely turrets reaching for the sky. I see Bob disappearing into the gloom, visible now only by the reflection of a yellow fluorescent jacket which he has dug out from his cabin and slipped on without me noticing. He pushes on ahead preparing locks for us, and I soon lose sight of him completely, so that it is only the ghostly figures of Em and Rosemary on the towpath which reassure me that I am not entirely alone in this strange, unfamiliar world I've somehow stumbled into.

Past the eight locks at Aston, just beyond Digbeth Junction, we begin the ascent of the nine Farmers Bridge locks. This relentless climb of eighty-odd feet will take us into the very heart of the city, past the British Telecom tower which is Birmingham's tallest building and one of its most famous landmarks. The locks come thick and fast now, and the surrounding buildings bear down on the towpath, with roads crossing overhead every few yards on low, tunnel-like bridges with scarcely any headroom, so that the canal resembles one of those chambers in that nightmare we've all had when the walls and ceiling are relentlessly closing in, threatening to crush you.

From the canal the urban night is eerie. Between the locks it is blank, empty silence; but passing under bridges the tumult of the city insists that it be heard: cars and rumbling buses and the late-night sound of revellers turning out from the pubs amplify and merge into a clamorous cacophony which hangs in the air. Yet no sooner have you passed underneath than it suddenly dissipates, the canal becoming soundless once more as if the noise was just a figment of your imagination.

It's a different world down here at night, a strange surreal netherworld completely divorced from any you're familiar with. Odd high-spirited youngsters occasionally venture from above to use the towpath as a short cut, or a urinal, and from time to time you hear their low voices or their unnerving shrieks echoing over the water. But they are outsiders, interlopers as you are, trespassers into a domain which at this hour is the preserve of the loveless fumbling towards each other under bridges, or dossers desperate for a warm place to sleep or alcoholics sharing companionship over a can of strong lager and a fire made of rubbish pulled from the water; every one of them, each last pathetic soul, part of this city's dark throbbing heart.

At one stage, beneath the floodlit Telecom tower – that garish and outdated symbol of the twentieth century – I navigate the boat into a cavernous space like a section of an underground car park which the architects have forgotten. It's lit from the window of an adjacent night club where drinkers lounge lazily at the bar, watching me as I pass. They see me but appear disengaged, as if they are looking at images that aren't real, like events on a TV screen. I emerge into a new development of executive flats connected to the towpath by a pedestrian bridge, reminiscent in a much smaller way of the Millennium Bridge over the River Tyne at Gateshead.

A young couple is waiting there for me. It seems *Justice* wasn't as invisible to the clientele in the bar as I had thought. They had seen the boat and decided to join me. Now they walk up the towpath with me, chatting amiably, keeping me company. Or maybe – am I imagining this? – they are uneasy in these surroundings. Maybe they're latching onto me for reassurance?

At the top lock Rosemary closes the gate behind me, then walks along the towpath a short distance to Cambrian Wharf where Bob and Em are waiting to help me moor. We eat the bacon which has long since gone cold; we drink too much wine too quickly. It is strange to be here at the very nucleus of this city at this time, sharing it with all the clubbers, the insomniacs and the nighthawks; peculiar to be eating at this improbable hour, trying to be sociable when we're all so dog-tired we can barely summon up a word to say to each other. Even so, we all feel a sense of exhilaration and wonder at the novelty of being part of this Saturday night city and seeing it from this unique perspective. We all feel somehow stirred by our predicament.

Cambrian Wharf is floodlit, blanketed with security lights, and this too adds to the bizarreness of our situation; for it's the early hours now, and yet it is as light as day. We go to bed and what is left of the night passes – that is to say, a few hours of it does, though it seems I've only just closed my eyes before Bob is starting the engine once more and we are skidding around various short loops and arms lined by derelict factories, with him hopping up and down excitedly because we've passed the back of some station or old tram depot that he recognises from those top-shelf transport magazines he reads.

All these detours are an attempt on his part to pick up easy competition points, but as I look at him straining at the tiller to turn a succession of tight bends, it doesn't look too easy to me. I sit on the deck still in my dreams, nursing a bowl of cereal and watching the city as it stirs around me. Em and Rosemary are still in bed. Or maybe they're not. Maybe they're up and about. I don't notice them, anyhow. Mind you, I'm so gaga from sleep deprivation that I wouldn't notice them if they were sitting on my lap juggling pineapples.

We pass through Winson Green, Soho and Sandwell, suburbs that slip by as quickly as they slip off the tongue. We go through three locks at Smethwick and through another three at Spon Lane, and then suddenly it is the morning – not the early morning mind, the morning we'd woken to, but the real morning, the clocks finally at a respectable hour and Birmingham at last awake on what is a gloriously sunny Sunday, a day promising to be as hot as yesterday had been. The towpath is alive with dog-walkers and joggers and guys who've just popped out to buy a paper, and others who've just come out for a walk, or a quiet fag or just to enjoy the sunshine. Meanwhile the laggers from the night before, from parties, clubs and stag nights, drag themselves back home lackadaisically, nursing their hangovers and desperate to get their heads down for an hour or two's kip.

There are other boats involved in the competition around too, we notice for the first time. Coming down the flight of eight locks at Ryders Green we pass one stranded in a pound by something wrapped around its propeller, and I lend the skipper a Stanley knife to hack off whatever it is that's causing him such trouble. He promises to return it when we next see each other at the finish line in Walsall, but in the event we encounter each other much sooner than that; for almost immediately after we leave him *Justice* jams solid under a bridge, blocking the canal completely. Even with two crews on the job we can't move her and it is only when a passer-by lends a hand that we start to make progress. Even so, it is an exhausting business; the temperatures are sweltering.

The man helping introduces himself as Si which I take to be some derivative of Simon. He is with his dog Rambo, an enormous Chow which he assures us is as gentle as a lamb, though I find this difficult to believe. If it was as gentle as a lamb, I can't help wondering why he didn't name it after a lamb and call it Larry. In China, Chows are known as puffy-lion dogs. In my opinion you don't buy a puffy-lion dog and name it after a psychopathic ex-Vietnam veteran for no reason.

Si seems harmless enough, though. He's in his late fifties, maybe a bit older, and in between heaving on ropes, he chats about his boyhood. He was brought up in the area and was always messing around the water, summer and winter alike. One year he fell through the ice and had to be pulled out by a boatman who thought he was mad for being out in that sort of weather when he could have been at home in front of a fire.

'But I love this canal,' he says in a Brum accent so thick you could have spread it on bread. 'I couldn't keep away from it then, I can't keep away from it now.'

Eventually we get the boat moving and get underway again, though I am left stranded on the towpath by all the manoeuvring; and Em on the tiller isn't so stupid as to ground us again by coming in too close to the bank to pick me up.

'You'll have to catch us up somewhere it's deeper,' she shouts as she disappears around the next bend.

Si takes me under his wing and shepherds me to a nearby car park.

'I know somewhere nearby you can meet up with them,' he says, directing me into the front passenger seat of his car. This is thoughtful of him and I am very grateful for his kindness. Even so, I'm not entirely comfortable with the prospect of sitting in the place he suggests. Judging by the dog hairs on it, it's obviously Rambo's seat and I guess he'll be disinclined to give it up to a stranger who's just appeared from out of nowhere. I am not wrong. Si puts him in the back of the car but he immediately leaps to the front onto my lap, catching me in the pit of my stomach and winding me in the process. He is enormous, the size and weight of a couple of sacks of potatoes. Si attempts to put him in the back again, but this time he worms his way to the front by wriggling over the gear lever. He's a half-hundredweight ball of muscle but he seems under the misapprehension that he's some thin and svelte creature whose movements will go unnoticed.

I am feeling very awkward at all the trouble I am causing 'Oh, don't worry about him,' I say eventually. 'We're not going far. Leave him. He's all right.'

But he is not all right. He is fractious and ill-tempered because of being shunted around so much, and he is growling quietly in the back of his throat. I cannot be certain that he will not transform into a snarling killer any moment now. I don't want to risk it and so I allow him to take liberties with me I don't even let Em take. I let him sniff my crotch, for instance – though, lest there be any misunderstanding, this is not something Em is inclined to do very often. Well, not at all, actually. Neither is she inclined to stick her tongue up my nose, though this is something else Rambo appears to take particular delight in.

Having established himself on my lap, he now tries to dislodge me from the seat completely by wriggling behind me and forcing me off. When that fails he attempts to displace me by brute force. He wedges the bottom of his spine against my hip and tries levering me off by pushing with his legs against the door. When that doesn't work he adopts a new approach and spends the rest of the journey with his paws on my shoulder attempting to drown me with his fetid saliva.

Si is oblivious to all this. He is lost in memories of his past, recounting to me how as a twelve-year-old he watched the coal boats come down the locks in the winter with their cabin stoves belching thick smoke behind them.

'Ah, the smell of that smoke,' he says, waxing lyrical. 'It's the smell of my childhood, the smell of my past...'

Unfortunately all this reminiscing is taking his mind off driving. I suspect that even at his best Si is no advanced motorist, but with his concentration gone he's lethal. His speed has crept up and now we are hurtling down narrow alleyways and through a maze of small lanes at a rate you would not think was conducive to quiet recollection of anything, let alone the events of your early life. He tears around corners, swings a left, then a right, a right again and then three lefts on the trot so that eventually I am hopelessly lost, with no idea of how I'd get back to the canal if I had to walk. I am completely fazed by all this. How was I to know he'd be such a lunatic behind the wheel? It crosses my mind that I am being abducted. Perhaps Si is an agent for one of these sweatshops I have read about in the papers. Perhaps he is going to sell me into slavery. Or maybe he is making off with me to feed to his dog. Is this why Rambo's dribbling over me so much? Is this why he's tasting me all the time?

Eventually he screeches to a halt in what appears to be a terraced cul-de-sac but which I see connects through a narrow alleyway between two houses to the canal beyond. As if by magic *Justice* is passing at exactly that moment.

'Where on earth have you been?' Em asks once I have got back on board.

'I'll tell you when we've got more time.'

'You look wet, for heaven's sake, whatever have you been doing? And what's that rancid smell…?'

'It's a long story,' I say.

We're now nearly back in Walsall again, pottering along in a queue at a speed determined by the leading boat which is barely moving as a result of the rubbish and the depth. We're third or fourth in line, behind the boat whose crew helped us out earlier under the bridge and which Em, out of courtesy, has allowed to overtake. However, we soon become aware that it's in trouble. Its engine seems inconsistent and unreliable; it's cutting out every few minutes and has to be constantly restarted. Before long its skipper pulls over and waves us through. We imagine his propeller must be fouled, for no one's exempt from trouble in this department today. The problem turns out to be more serious, however. The boat's engine is overheating in temperatures which are even higher than yesterday's, and the skipper's unwilling to go on for fear of causing permanent damage. Eventually, after some consultation, he asks if we'll tow him, and the queue behind us halts in its tracks while we rope up together, bow to stern; and it is like this that we eventually pull into Walsall basin a few hours later after a round-trip that's taken us 41 miles through sixty-two locks. It feels like we've done more. In fact, it feels like we've circumnavigated not just Birmingham but half the globe.

Kit emerges cautiously from the cabin as soon as she hears the engine stop. She peers around the door to see us celebrating, quaffing lager and taking pictures of ourselves and our fellow competitors as they limp home, filling the basin with boats. She goes back inside very soon. She has been to Walsall before; she recognises the place and it bores her now. She wants to be somewhere else.

I feel the same way. It's time to move on.

SUMMER

TWELVE

Towards the Shropshire Union

Forty years ago there was barely anyone using the canals apart from enthusiasts and a few hippies like me – Woodstock wannabes that hadn't quite managed to make it to the party. Then canals got discovered. How they got discovered I couldn't rightly say, even now. Maybe I had something to do with it. Perhaps it was something I said. The fact is I've always bigged up waterways. Every chance I've had I've stood on my soap-box preaching about how we could develop them for leisure use, how we could promote them for tourism, how we could use them as the basis for urban renewal…

Then one morning I woke up and everything I'd been banging on about had happened. It was a shock, I can tell you. I'm English, bred in the democratic tradition. I'm not used to anyone taking any notice of me. But what's that old Chinese proverb about being careful what you wish for? With all the boats crowding the canals nowadays, I sometimes wish I'd kept my mouth shut. Mind you, if I had kept my mouth shut there wouldn't be any canals left, the rate they were filling them in all those years ago. Looking back, I don't suppose I had much choice, really.

Today the waterways attract visitors from all over the globe. They're particularly popular with the Dutch and Scandinavians, who all speak English with the same accent, but whose country of origin you can distinguish a mile off since they insist on displaying huge national flags on the backs of their boats. Aussies and Kiwis do the same but their flags are barely distinguishable so it doesn't really help, except to further weaken the bond between the English-speaking peoples when you get them wrong and start to talk to someone from Auckland as if they're from Sydney.

A lot of people from the southern hemisphere live on canal boats in the summer. This is usually because they have roots in England and boats are a cheaper option than hotels if you want to keep in touch with the family. They're also a good deal more liberating than having to park yourself for months on end on some great aunt you don't really know anyhow. Besides, our summer is as close as it gets to cold in their part of the world, so by this means they avoid ever having to suffer a winter anywhere. This is a smart move on their part, and it partly explains why Kiwis and Aussies on the cut always look so smug. They tend to name their boats nationalistically too. One New Zealander has called his Tui after one of the country's loveliest songbirds. One Australian's christened his *Fair Dinkum*. He travels around in a Drizabone greatcoat and a bush hat, short only of a rim of hanging corks to be completely and authentically outback.

They're not strong on irony, these Australians.

It was June now and still flaming hot. Em and Bob and Rosemary left me in Walsall after the Challenge, and the next day I began the ascent of the eight Walsall locks again – this time without a crew. It was a pig of a job. So many boats had been using the flight over the Challenge weekend the locks were drained, and so to get through them I had to feed water from the summit. This is a process I won't even begin to explain, apart from saying that it involves you walking up to the top of the flight and back again, opening and closing every paddle on the way, just to go through a single lock.

By the time I'd finished I'd done the equivalent of a route march. And it felt like it. My legs ached, my knees ached, my thighs ached. Most of all, with the strain of having to do everything without a crew, my ankle had flared up again and I was limping once more. There wasn't a breath of wind in the air, and to add to my discomfort the heat was unbearable, like trying to do a workout in a sauna. It was as much as I could do to keep cool. I put on a T-shirt and dragged out an old pair of paint-stained Levis from the engine room which I ripped off at the knees. I found some sandals there too, and a battered old Panama hat, so that I finished up looking like something from the Mississippi Basin, needing only a corncob pipe to complete the image.

And I have the effrontery to mock Australians...

The Wyrley and Essington, going west towards Wolverhampton, is more urban and less well dredged than it is heading north-east along the route I'd travelled with the others on the first morning of the Challenge. I was reduced to a lazy crawl, travelling barely above tickover, winding my way along an empty waterway flanked by factories and endless suburbs. I stopped for the night at Sneyd Junction where an old British

Waterways maintenance yard has been commandeered for moorings, presided over by an amiable Welshman who was happy for me to stay until the morning, once he was reassured I was respectable and wasn't going to rob him during the night. The next day, the weather still as hot as ever and still showing no sign of breaking, I pressed on through an area of what the map said was disused collieries, part of which had been reclaimed as a country park. This was typical of this section of the canal where the industrial landscape is regularly broken by tracts of open, semi-derelict land which makes it constantly interesting.

At Wednesfield they were building a new bridge and I had to wait while they brought in a crane to lift the temporary steel platform they'd laid to get plant and machinery from one side of the canal to the other. At least the wait allowed me to clear my propeller, which at that stage was hanging heavy with rubbish which I'd been putting off clearing all morning. I suppose I was hoping it would just miraculously disappear. In fact, the miracle was that the propeller was still turning at all given all the crap that was clinging to it. I pulled out a first load of lily root entangled with industrial polythene and threw it onto the towpath. The second load seemed to be clothing, enough of it to stock a charity shop. After that, holding everything at the core of the bundle, was 10 or 12 feet of that brown industrial tape which can take the weight of a detached house.

Removing this was a more formidable task. I had to get a Stanley knife and hack through it. It took an eternity. Well, long enough for me to need a cup of tea halfway through the job. Long enough for me to get a blister doing it and long enough for the blokes messing about with the platform to get it moved. Mind you, it was clear they were unhappy having to interrupt their work for a boat – though surely even they must have realised that in blocking a canal it was a risk they took.

'We didn't expect a boat,' one of them said to me.

'Well, what a coincidence,' I said. 'I didn't expect a JCB parked over the canal either. Funny old world, innit?'

Soon after I'd got underway again I passed a bright new retail park, resplendent with a row of major chain stores; then a sparse red-brick estate only recently built, every house with two or three cars squeezed onto the hard-standing in front.

It was then that I first spotted them in the distance.

They were the more noticeable because until I'd come across the contractors I hadn't seen any sort of movement on the canal all day. No boats at all, and precious few people on the towpath either apart from odd fishermen I'd taken for herons. Or maybe, thinking about it now, it was herons I'd seen which I'd taken for fishermen. It's an easy mistake to make, believe me. They both sit on the towpath hunched over the canal for hours on end watching for fish. And they both have that sad stoop of the back too, as if they're carrying the woes of the world on their shoulders. Some fishermen even have beards like herons, which confuses things even further.

Anyway, these were neither heron nor fishermen. I couldn't make them out clearly at first, but they seemed to be a gang of workmen: about half a dozen of them, maybe more, all decked in fluorescent yellow jackets which stood out so much you could have used them as runway markers at Heathrow. They appeared to be standing around on a couple of boats, listening to a lecture being given by an older man. There was some slogan on the backs of their jackets but I was too far away to make it out.

My curiosity, however, was fully aroused. Even the boat itself seemed inquisitive about what was going on, and it seemed to speed up on the straight stretch of canal leading to them.

Eventually I was able to make out the words on the jackets. They read 'Community Payback'. At almost the same time they noticed *Justice*'s name. They were suddenly reduced to helpless laughter, so disabling that whatever canal-related activity they were scheduled to be doing that morning to atone for their crimes and misdemeanours would have surely had to be abandoned until I'd passed.

At Horseley Fields Junction, in Wolverhampton, the Wyrley and Essington joins the main line as it heads into the centre of Birmingham. As waterway beauty spots go, this is hardly the most picturesque. The Curly Wurly suddenly darts from under a low, graffiti-covered bridge like a cockroach scurrying from under a skirting board. There's a railway line adjacent, and opposite is a terrace of derelict factories where pigeons roost in the crumbling brickwork. Even so, it's a significant junction for anyone travelling in or out of Birmingham for it effectively marks the boundary of the city.

I knew I was approaching it, but I hadn't been expecting to arrive there as soon as I did and it caught me unawares. One moment I was lost in my thoughts, dreaming of the countryside and foaming pints of ale; the next, the canal suddenly narrowed and I was at a T-junction, straining on the tiller to get around a 90-degree bend. It was only then, as I stepped up the engine revs to give myself extra turning power, I noticed a boat coming towards me from the opposite direction. It was, I registered in that fraction of a second I had to register anything, a very beautifully painted boat. Very shiny and gleaming with brass. It was driven by a retired bank manager – or at least someone who looked like a retired bank manager. He was squat and overweight; wearing round piggy glasses and green Terylene trousers of the sort that would have been the height of fashion at the time Kennedy was assassinated. And he had a white captain's cap on. It was pulled so far down over his forehead to shade his eyes from the sun that it was clear he hadn't seen me any more than I'd seen him. He was probably lost in his own dreams too. Probably fantasising about Oeics or ISAs or how to screw more money from the Treasury for his pension. Or more likely just wondering how he could get through Birmingham as fast as possible without getting mugged.

We both went into reverse at the same time, powering our engines to their maximum. The junction, which only moments before had been torpid, almost stagnant, now became a churning spume of water as our propellers fought to hold us back. But it was no use, nothing could have stopped us. We crashed broadside with a sound that rent the silence of the afternoon and sent the pigeons fluttering into the air.

Honestly! Isn't life cussed? I hadn't seen another boat on the move since leaving Walsall two days before.

And the first one I meet, I hit.

Around the corner from Horseley Fields Junction are twenty-one locks known to boaters as the Wolverhampton 21, or 'the 21' for short. The flight starts around the corner from Wolverhampton railway station, and it drops downhill, becoming increasingly more rural until it touches the edge of a race course where it joins the Staffordshire and Worcester Canal which does as it says on the tin and links Stafford with the cathedral town of Worcester on the River Severn.

The 21 is an unusual flight, changing so much over its course that I can never decide whether I like it or not. My attitude seems to depend on which direction I'm travelling. Going towards Wolverhampton it always seems ugly and urban, but coming from the opposite direction it strikes me as remarkably pastoral, even pretty in parts. The water used to add to my sense of uncertainty about the flight, for it used to be unusually clear for a canal, something I've always put down to the geology of its construction. I have some notion that it's built on rock so that it never needed as much of the 'puddling', or mud, that seals the bottom of other canals to stop them leaking.

Whether this is true or whimsy on my part, what is indisputable is that there was a time when you could see the bottom of the canal in some pounds on the 21, the water as limpid as a Pennine stream. But seeing the bottom is OK in mountain streams when you're looking at a delightful rocky bottom, dappled with the green fronds of reeds through which speckled trout might dart. On the 21 it wasn't quite like this. In fact, on the 21 it wasn't like this at all. You could see the bottom all right and there were reeds. But there were also rusted bikes, Coke cans and oil-drums; sodden bundles of abandoned free papers, black plastic bags of discarded rubbish, Kentucky Fried chicken bones and half-eaten hamburgers. And there was other stuff too, stuff you don't even want to know about: dead stuff, and stuff eating dead stuff. One summer years ago Em and I made the unwise decision to have lunch on deck coming up the flight. We'd laid the table and brought out the food before either of us noticed what was on the canal bed underneath us. After that we didn't fancy eating.

At one of the locks Kit emerged from the boat and peered at me along the gunnels as if asking me when we were going to stop. This was a signal she wanted to get off and was part of the routine she'd developed for life afloat. She was doing it increasingly often as she became more sure-footed and more confident of the boat as her territory. Normally, though, going through locks where there was a risk of getting bumped about, she'd stay inside curled in her favourite spot under a low coffee table in the main cabin. Today, however, she seemed to have her mind on other things. She'd obviously had her fill of cruising and wanted to get off the boat. I'd never known her to be so assertive at this time of day or so restless; I couldn't understand it. Or at least I couldn't understand it until I'd put her back inside the boat and closed the door on her. Then I became aware myself of what she must have registered instinctively. A gentle whiff of a cooling breeze had blown up in the trees, cutting the sultry afternoon. It carried with it the delicious scent of the nearby countryside: the odours of fields warmed by the sun, and of the May blossoms in the hedges. There were notes of rich woodland, evocations of hot tarmac on dry, dusty lanes, and the hint of grasslands, so faint as to be barely a suggestion.

I headed north at the Staffs and Worcester Canal, and a hundred yards or so further up, as it veered east, I turned onto the Shropshire Union. Soon the suburbs were behind me and the village of Brewood (pronounced 'Brood') appeared from out of the greenery on the hill like a ship caught in the swell of the sea, the elegant spire of the Anglican church of St Mary the Virgin and St Chad a mast at its bow. I tied up as soon as I could and it was a toss-up whether Kit was fastest getting onto the bank or whether I beat her limping off to the bar of the adjoining Bridge Inn where I cleansed my throat of a week of Brummie slag.

I wasn't the only boater in the pub. The Bridge is popular with those travelling the canal and around me were a selection of the people you'd find in any waterside watering hole anywhere in the country. There were one or two hire-boat crews looking exhausted and ready for bed. Everyone tells them canal holidays are relaxing; no one ever mentions they can be physically gruelling too. There were a couple of retired liveaboards at a table on the last course of a lavish meal. They'd obviously sold their house for a life afloat and they were just as obviously getting rid of the proceeds before the kids got their hands on it. Oh yes... and there was this heavy bloke with a beer belly in a battered Panama hat and jeans ripped off at the knees, sitting at the bar downing beer as if there were no tomorrow. He had a florid, sunburned face, white hair and wild undisciplined eyebrows, as black as crows. He looked for all the world like an ageing Huckleberry Finn.

'Are you staying long?' the barman asked me, in a way that was probably just conversational but which I couldn't help investing with deeper significance. Maybe what he really wanted to know was when I was planning on leaving the pub. Perhaps he thought my solitary drinking habits, not to mention my sartorial style, might be putting off customers. Or perhaps he was just asking when I was planning to leave Brewood?

The fact is, I didn't have the first idea. Brewood's a nice enough village despite the social schizophrenia it must induce spelling your name one way and pronouncing it another. It has some nice shops and an amusing eighteenth-century turreted house with Turkish-type windows, said to have been built on the back of the winnings of a horse race. It's very affluent, well-kept and maybe a touch self-satisfied as a result. I reached this conclusion a few years back when I left a car there for a week while I was cruising, and Em went to pick it up only to find it penned in by vehicles on either side.

Any doubts she had that this had come about accidentally were resolved when she began to extricate herself from the situation and a deputation of residents gathered on the pavement, arms folded confrontationally. Not a single one of them made the slightest effort to help her by moving their cars. In fact, no one even said a word to her, presumably thinking that eventually she'd have to appeal to them to let her out. Unfortunately, they didn't bargain for someone like Em schooled on London streets, where space is at so much of a premium you learn very quickly how to park in places a foot shorter than your car. She made nothing of her task in Brewood; and after a few nifty turns of the steering wheel and some clever clutch control, she was away faster than it would have taken her to say, 'Up yours'. Even so, I won't forgive the village for its unkindness to her. It strikes me that any place which so misunderstands the concept of a 'public' highway might just as easily misinterpret other more basic freedoms we take for granted in the twenty-first century. Who's to say the burghers of Brewood won't impose a curfew on you if you're up too late, for instance? Or that they won't commit you to the local lock-up for the heinous crime of walking on the pavement when they want to walk there too?

I didn't know whether I wanted to stay in the village longer or not. Would you want to stay long in a place like that?

In the event, though, I didn't have a choice about the matter. I woke the next morning and Kit wasn't there. She'd disappeared. Gone on another of her walkabouts.

THIRTEEN
Storms up the Shroppie

Do cats think we're stupid? Do they think we're idiots? Don't they realise we can see through them like a window? I'd fallen for this one in Denham and before that in Banbury; there was no way I was going to be a sucker a third time round. OK, it was true that as we travelled through Birmingham Kit had been penned up in the boat longer than either of us would have wanted. But Birmingham wasn't exactly an earthly paradise for a cat. It was noisy and busy and there were too many other cats about. I was reluctant to let her out and when I did, she was reluctant to go. It was too much like home in London, that's what it was.

Of course, I could understand why she'd gone off. She'd gone off in a huff; she was bored. She'd gone off in search of fun and excitement and hedgerow creatures to eviscerate. There might have been an element of reprimand to her behaviour too, I grant you. She was probably cheesed off with me, thinking to herself that if I wasn't going to take her to the sort of places she wanted to go, then she'd go there anyhow and I could go hang myself. Well, she was wrong; I wasn't going to stand for it. She was just winding me up. She'd come back eventually, I knew that. Besides, I had other things on my mind, matters of more pressing concern. Foremost among them was that the dining table in the main cabin had collapsed. I bought the damned thing years ago from a junk shop in Gloucester and it was always collapsing. This time, though, it had collapsed with my dinner on it and I didn't trust it any more. A lapful of lamb pasanda with a side order of sag aloo can change a man's relationship with his dining table, take it from me.

So I left the cat to its own devices and I caught a bus back to some suburb of Birmingham where I bought a new table at IKEA. What a waste of time, though. Having to trek all the way back to Birmingham like that, I mean. Call me a dreamer for even thinking it, but why couldn't the table have collapsed while I'd been travelling through Birmingham? Why had it decided to give up the ghost somewhere a bus ride away? But that's the thing about tables, isn't it? They're so inconsiderate. It's a trait they share with the rest of the material world which sometimes seems as if it's out to get us at every opportunity.

Leaving the cat that day I ensured the side porthole was open so she could get in. I topped up her biscuits and even left a token of my undying love and affection in the form of a delectable sliver of the steak I was planning on having for dinner that night. I didn't want to settle any scores with her or punish her for the trouble she was causing me; it was just that I wasn't going to be forced into playing cat games as I had in Denham. I was determined not to humiliate myself again walking up and down the towpath shouting for her in some silly voice when she was a couple of feet away hiding from me behind a tree. Why should I be arsed? I knew if I ignored her she'd come back in her own good time anyhow and I'd find her under the coffee table again as usual.

Except that when I got back from IKEA she wasn't under the coffee table. Or anywhere else on the boat, either. The biscuits and the steak I'd left were untouched, so I knew she hadn't been on board. Even so, I resisted the temptation to panic. I'd panicked before and it hadn't won me any prizes unless you count the T-shirt with 'Sucker' printed all over it. No, this was a simple battle of wills and it was a battle I intended to win.

I unpacked the table from its flat pack and was delighted to discover that rather than there being fewer components than there should be – as usually seems to be the case with IKEA furniture – there were actually four more than I needed which would keep the fire going some autumn evening when it turned chilly. There were also two extra Allen keys to add to my collection of IKEA Allen keys which had now grown so large it would soon be worth selling for scrap. This at least was vaguely reassuring, as were the instructions which seemed useless in the way IKEA instructions always do.

I reckoned it would take me ten minutes to put everything together, but after half an hour I realised I had a problem: I couldn't get the fourth leg on properly, until it struck me that I'd put it in the position of the third leg, which was where the second leg should have been. Somehow – by some miracle – I had succeeded in getting the first one in place correctly, though how I'd managed to do that I haven't the first idea. If I'm honest, all the legs looked the same to me. But, of course, they weren't all the same. There was a tiny variation between each of them which I'd have known about if I'd read the instructions properly. But you don't read IKEA instructions properly, do you? Most times you don't read them at all. That's not what they're for, is it? They're for scribbling shopping lists on. They're for making paper planes. They're for folding up to jam under the legs of tables which are always wobbling because you didn't read the instructions before you assembled them.

The thing is, with their simplified diagrams IKEA instructions look as if they've been put together by a class of Swedish kindergarten kids who haven't learnt to write yet. They look so crude. Other people might need them, but not anyone who's handy with tools and knows his way around a DIY manual. It's only when you get in a mess you realise that they're more sophisticated than you gave them credit for.

It's then you understand why assembling IKEA furniture is so frustrating. It's frustrating because it makes you realise just how dumb you can be.

I found the whole process demoralising. The job took me far longer to finish than I'd anticipated, and afterwards – missing cat or not – I was fit for nothing except dropping into bed, too wiped out to worry about anything, let alone feckless felines. Besides, I was confident Kit would be back the next day; I'd have put money on it. I felt relaxed about the whole thing, calm and laid back… well, I felt that way until the next morning when I woke up and she still wasn't back. That's when I lost it completely and went haring up the towpath making a fool of myself screaming out her name like a madman.

She appeared almost immediately, sauntering nonchalantly out of a hedge as if she hadn't a care in the world. She hopped onto the boat and into the cabin where I found her nibbling biscuits.

I could have wept with frustration at her behaviour. It seemed designed to make my life a misery. I dropped into a chair and dug my fingers into my eyes. What was it with this cat that made her want to wind me up like this? Why did she seem to get so much pleasure out of tormenting me?

She saw the new table and leapt onto it. 'Nice table' I could almost hear her say in that grating Sarf Lunnonese she'd made her own. She explored it with her claws.

'Stop that,' I screamed at her. 'That is a brand new table. I don't want you destroying it before Em's even seen it.'

'Please yourself,' she seemed to say, arching her back and stretching. 'It's no good, anyhow. Cheap wood, you can tell. It's like butter…'

I set off the next morning as early as I could. I was travelling northwards now, heading for the salt town of Middlewich, where there's a boat and folk music festival which has been growing in popularity over the last few years so that it's now a feature of the waterways' summer calendar. The Shropshire Union Canal along which I was cruising is a late waterway, built in the early nineteenth century against the background of rail expansion. Whereas early canals meandered around the countryside, the only game in town as far as bulk transportation went, the Shroppie sliced through the countryside in a straight line, perched on high embankments or buried in deep cuttings. The idea of building it in this way was to try to speed up carrying times. The engineers who planned it were all-too-aware of the competition posed to narrowboats by those monstrous new steam locomotive thingies dashing about all over the place at unheard of speeds.

Their individual histories give canals their individual character and this is more evident travelling along the Shropshire Union than on any other waterway. The canal managed to hold off the competition from railways longer than most, but it was eventually bought out, and in time it was left to quietly decay. When I first started exploring the waterways, its characteristic cuttings were like jungles, shaded by trees and overhung with trailing creepers that swept across the top of your boat as you passed underneath. Travelling through them you could almost believe you were Humphrey Bogart in The African Queen. Today the canal is incomparably better maintained, but it still feels a bit the same. The cuttings aren't as wild as they once were, but they're still overgrown, damp and dark, and in places the towpath is reduced to an impassable quagmire.

The embankments on the Shroppie have their own particular appeal too. When they were built they must have been dreadful to look at, great mud scars on the landscape, standing out like some awful icon of the industrial age. Boatmen got the best of them then, for they are high and command spectacular views of the countryside. It's all different nowadays. Today, looking at them from any distance you'd be hard pressed to notice they were there. They've grown over and they seem a natural part of the topography, whatever natural means in this context. But the downside is that the views have gone. Trees have grown so high that in places they arch over the canal forming a canopy so impenetrable that from a boat you can't see beyond them and hardly know you're on an embankment at all. Even so, if you're alert, every now and again you can still catch a glimpse of an enfolding panorama through the foliage, the fields stretching away to the horizon for mile upon mile in a patchwork so quintessentially English it takes your breath away.

It's odd to be hovering above the ground like this on a narrowboat; it makes you feel somehow separated from the landscape of which you're usually such an integral part. You're high up, and feel somehow higher than you are, part of the sky rather than the land. In the wrong conditions that can make you feel strangely vulnerable.

I was crossing an embankment when a summer storm suddenly broke around me and being up there I felt like I was in the very eye of it. There was an abrupt, unannounced crash of thunder and rain started falling so heavily I couldn't see to steer and was forced to bring the boat to a halt alongside the towpath where I stopped to take shelter without even bothering to tie up.

Inside the cabin, the sound of it hammering on the roof was deafening, like being inside a kettle drum. More spectacular, though, was the way it hit the canal: a million comets, trailing tails behind them, exploding onto the water. The canal bubbled like soda water in a glass, frothing up until it seemed to create another surface 2 or 3 inches above the existing one. At the same time the sky darkened and lightning began searing the sky, which is never a comforting prospect in a metal boat. I stood at one of the portholes watching everything unfold around me. Kit, who by rights should have been terrified by the whole business and cowering under the coffee table, seemed indifferent to the commotion. She stood on the step at the door, as transfixed as I was by the display.

Then, just as suddenly, it all stopped. The thunder. The lightning. Even the rain. I went out onto the deck which was already bathed in sunshine so hot that within moments thin wreaths of smoke-like steam were curling off the boat roof as if it had been hit by one of those bolts of lightning and was smouldering, ready to burst into flame.

I went back to the tiller and cruised on, passing Shelmore Wood and then Norbury Junction where the now abandoned Newport Branch once joined the main line, connecting with the town of Ironbridge and the famous china-producing factory at Coalport. In no time I was tying up outside The Anchor at Bridge 42 where I planned to spend the night.

The Anchor is one of those archetypal canalside pubs which have barely changed in centuries. It's in the tradition of old public houses and that's what it looks like: as if someone's put up a sign and just started selling beer from their living room. It's set back from the canal behind a lawn, and the two downstairs rooms on either side of its front door are small, no-nonsense bars with wooden floors and rude settles around the walls. In the past it was a regular overnight stop for horse-drawn boats which used the stables it had at the back, and it's still as popular with craft travelling the waterways today. My plan was to have a pint or two there before going back to *Justice* for dinner, but it was such a splendid evening I decided first to walk up the hill to the church at nearby High Offley, from where you can just about make out The Wrekin in the south rising above the luxuriant flatness of the surrounding countryside. The Wrekin's more than 1,300 feet high, a landmark visible for miles about. According to local folklore it was created from a shovelful of soil which a giant with a grudge against the place was planning to drop on Shrewsbury.

Some shovelful of soil. Some grudge.

The hedgerows were thick with honeysuckle, campions and the most intensely perfumed dog roses I have ever come across. It was a flawless evening: the sky scoured by the recent rainstorm was clean and sharp, the air warm but fresh. As I'd been leaving the boat I'd grabbed my camera as an afterthought and I was pleased I had it with me, for later on I felt so euphorically happy I had a compelling need to record my happiness. Pausing at the gate to a field on one of the lanes I passed, I took a photograph of myself on the self-timer. God was in his heaven that day, all was well with the world. The picture shows me framed by the hedgerow and radiant in my contentment, my eyes smiling, flashing with what the French in that phrase we've stolen from them call joie de vivre – the joy of just being alive. I look bronzed by my trip, caught in a moment of near ecstasy.

But nothing can be as ideal as that, can it? Or at least not on this earth.

On the way back I passed a cottage on the bend of a lane where I noticed an unusual sign pinned to the gate. It was handwritten, roughly scrawled, though it was professionally laminated as if the person who'd done it wanted it to last. It was evidently aimed at cars using the driveway and at first glance it seemed to be a helpful warning about some nails which had been accidentally dropped there. There were two or three similar signs on the same topic, though as I read them it gradually dawned on me that they hadn't been put up in any spirit of charity. On the contrary, they'd been put up as a threat. NO TURNING! one of them said. These nails can penetrate a car tyre. Another, more menacing one, read: If you are going to turn here, leave us your address so we can do the same at your house. A third hammered the point home: don't forget if you've turned here, let us have our nails back.

The tone of unpleasantness was unmistakable. And it was shocking in this impeccable pastoral setting on an evening so beautiful. It was like an ink stain on a delicate watercolour, a crack in a cut-glass vase. It was like those signs I'd seen on the posh houses in Denham on my way north from London; like something you might find on a run-down city council estate, or in the backwoods and backwaters of the southern USA. But this was in the heart of rural England, as lovely a place as you could imagine in your dreams.

It troubled me. What on earth compels people to announce their malevolence so publicly like this, I wondered. Were the people living there genuinely inconvenienced by a constant stream of traffic using their driveway? I couldn't see it. The lane they lived on barely carried any traffic at all. I'd hardly encountered a car in either direction during my walk.

Perhaps they were just naturally acrimonious people; or maybe, which was my hunch, they were just people who needed to get out more and engage with the real world instead of locking themselves away in this enticing prison where they'd nothing better to do than nurse festering grievances.

Ultimately, who knows why they were acting as they were? Maybe they didn't even know themselves. This was Shropshire, after all. A place where giants wander abroad bearing giant-sized grudges.

FOURTEEN
Market Drayton to Audlem

I was sitting in a pub in Market Drayton chatting to a bloke I'd met when the conversation turned to contemporary manners and the fact that people today didn't seem to trust each other in the way they once did.

'Everyone's so protective of their privacy nowadays,' he said. 'It's even getting to be like it on the canals now. In the old days people at least used to talk to each other; there was a sense of community on the cut. These days a lot of the newcomers are just stuck up. They wouldn't give you the time of day if your life depended on it.'

I could see what he was getting at: there are people on the canals like this. But there are people everywhere like this; why should it be any surprise to find them on the canals too? Of course, canals aren't the same as they used to be but show me anything that is the same as it used to be. Apart from Bruce Forsyth, that is. Oh, and the *Daily Express*'s obsession with the death of Diana. And I suppose England's poor performances in World Cups and…

OK, so scrub that idea.

Even so, the fact is there are more people enjoying the canals nowadays than ever; and though there's no denying that this has changed the social relationships between boaters, canals are still one of the friendliest environments you'll find in the contemporary world.

I'd just found myself talking to a grumpy old man, that's all it was. I should have known when he started talking about 'the old days'. Whenever I hear anyone talking about 'the old days' I reach for my gun. I know about 'the old days', you see. I lived through them.

I took a swallow of beer. 'You're on a boat, I take it?' I said.

'I've been on boats all my life,' he replied. 'I was born on the canals and I used to work on them until I was laid off. My father was a boatman too, and his father before him. The whole family's been on the cut as far back as anyone can remember.'

My first response to this was to think how kindly the years had treated him. Commercial narrowboat carrying effectively finished in this country after The Big Freeze of 1963, when boats were iced in for months on end and couldn't move. For him to have been a working boatman at that time must have meant that he was at the very least sixty years old. Yet he looked much younger, not a day over fifty.

I'd have probably made some flattering remark about it, but I got no opportunity. Before I could say anything he launched into another homily about his ancestry. Not only was his father a working boatman, he told me, but his mother was from a boat family too, and her people had been on the cut for generations as well. It seemed all his brothers and sisters were on the boats, all his aunts and uncles, all his cousins and second cousins twice and thrice removed. That was the way of it in the old days, he said, when boat people were on the margins of society, water gypsies who married each other and kept themselves to themselves.

It struck me that maybe he was telling me all this to establish his own canal credentials because he had me down as one of those stuck-up boaters he was talking about, too protective of their privacy for their own good. And maybe he was right; who knows? I sometimes do feel stand-offish about other people on the cut, especially people in boats that I know cost as much as my house, the 'newbies' who've only been on the canals ten minutes and think they own them. Maybe the way I feel is rooted in my past. Maybe like the old boat people I once believed that by being on the cut I'd somehow got away from the world. Maybe the influx of new people over the last few years has unsettled me because I feel other people are trespassing on my territory.

I must have said something to him along these lines, though I can't remember exactly what it was. All I know is that it came out wrongly. I was trying to be self-critical; he thought I was criticising him. I became aware that he'd taken offence. He glowered at me suspiciously.

'I love the canals,' he said as if I'd somehow suggested that he didn't. 'They are my spiritual home,' he announced earnestly, his eyes widening with a fervour that made him look messianic.

He suddenly barked out a question. 'Have you ever been on the Kennet and Avon canal?' Without waiting for me to answer he started to tell me at great length about a journey he'd made to Bristol in the 1980s. This bothered me. My memory isn't as good as it used to be, but I had some notion the K&A was closed at the time he was talking about. I had an idea it had only reopened in 1990 after being derelict for years. I couldn't understand how he could have cruised it at the time he was saying.

There was no chance to pursue the matter with him, though. Having told me about his expedition to Bristol thirty years ago, he now began recounting stories of trips he'd made as a working boatman in the 1950s. And then – bouncing around randomly, moving from year to year and place to place – about an expedition he'd made in 2000 along the Thames to Greenwich when he'd cruised past the Dome the day Tony Blair and the Queen had celebrated the millennium New Year there.

These tales were interesting enough, but there was something about them that didn't quite gel with me. The accounts followed too familiar a pattern: they were formulaic like Wikipedia is formulaic: packed with facts but short of telling detail and personal anecdote. They reminded me of bad lectures I'd attended at university, except that at least the tutors then were making an attempt to communicate with me. He didn't seem to be even trying to reach out beyond himself. Most of the time he seemed to be involved in a tortuous soliloquy, the primary aim of which was to ensure anything he said didn't develop into a dialogue. If I picked up on any detail of anything he said or asked a question about it, he changed the subject immediately and started on another tack.

'Where are you moored?' I asked when I did, finally, manage to make my voice heard.

He looked at me dubiously. 'I'm on the seventy-foot Woolwich near the bridge…'

'I didn't notice a seventy-foot boat near the bridge.'

'The other side of the bridge,' he corrected himself. 'The opposite side to you.'

This struck me as the oddest thing he'd said yet. How could he have known which boat I was on to know where I had moored? Had he seen me on it? Had he been watching me without me knowing? The idea was spooky. But I was beginning to think there was something spooky about him: something I couldn't quite put my finger on. This boat of his, for instance. Did it even exist?

I never did get the chance to find out. Perhaps seeing the scepticism in my eyes, my determination to get the bottom of who he was, made him feel exposed. Or maybe he'd been toying with me and he'd got bored. Either way, he got up abruptly and mumbled about having to go for a pee; and though I waited for him longer than I should, he never came back. It was left to a young guy at the bar to explain why.

'He's always doing it. He's a bit soft in the head,' he told me. 'A bit of a romancer, if truth were told. He means no harm; he does it to everyone who'll talk to him. He finds out what interests them and then winds them up about it.'

'Are you sure?' I protested. 'It's just that he seemed to know a fair bit about waterways. He was very convincing...'

'Oh, he is convincing. And he knows a lot of stuff too about a lot of different things. I was in here having a drink a month or two back when a bloke comes in from Chester way and before I knew it they were at it thirteen to the dozen arguing about French literature.'

'French literature? Did he know much about French literature?'

The young guy shrugged his shoulders. 'I'm blessed if I know,' he said. 'They were talking in French most of the time.'

Robert Clive, the man credited with securing India as part of the British Empire, came from Market Drayton. The Clives were from old Shropshire stock and could trace their antecedents back to the time of Henry II. Robert was the oldest boy in a family of thirteen and as a youngster he honed the skills he'd need to loot Bengal by running a protection racket vandalising the houses of local merchants.

Derek 'Poddy' Podmore was another Market Drayton man. His party trick was swallowing frogs for a bet in local pubs, a pastime which eventually brought him into conflict with the RSPCA and led to a much-publicised court case in which the law in its majesty ruled that swallowing live frogs didn't actually count as causing them undue suffering. Mind you, what did Poddy know about undue suffering? He once nailed himself to a tree in Stafford by his ear in protest at a fine he'd tried to pay with a wheelbarrow of half-pence pieces.

It's odd like this, Market Drayton; and it's not just the people who live there and turn out not to be what you first think they are. The place itself is like that too. You visit thinking it's a prosperous and gracious Georgian town – which to some extent it is, since most of the town was destroyed by a fire in the seventeenth century and not much survives from before then. But you don't have to be there long before you realise that it's actually run down and poor too, and at a bit of a loss to know what to do with itself except make sausages, which is its main industry.

It's been the same for as long as I can remember, and I can remember back a long way because I've been visiting Market Drayton on and off for nearly forty years, every time I've come up this way on a boat. It's the sort of place I continue to visit more in hope than expectation. I always think places like this have got so much potential; though I just know they'll never get close to realising it. They're like English strawberries in that respect, towns like Market Drayton. You keep going back for more out of some spurious belief that next time they'll be better. Only they never are.

The place certainly seemed as if it were going through a bad patch that day. Even in the sunshine it looked a bit tired and unloved. After finishing my drink I walked into the centre to do some shopping and discovered that The Corbet Arms, a once-prosperous old coaching inn where I'd spent a happy evening a few years back, was now closed, boarded up and overgrown with Virginia creeper. So was the cycle shop I've used a number of times in the past and where I was planning on getting the bike repaired which Bob had broken coming up the Grand Union. The shop next to it was closed down too, as were half a dozen others dotted around town, including a sandwich bar where I once bought a chicken baguette as good as any I've ever had at twice the price from posh London delis.

The market itself, after which the town is named, has been around for 750 years and just about struggles on, though the range and sad state of the vegetables on sale that day wasn't improved by the few gaudy balloons some of the traders had put on their stalls in an attempt to cheer things up. Call me old-fashioned, but if I have to have bright red objects hanging from a greengrocer's stall I'd prefer beetroot any day. At least you can eat beetroot, which is more than you can say for cheap Chinese balloons that always seem to deflate inside the hour to a wizened bag the texture of Keith Richard's face.

The trouble with Market Drayton is that it doesn't know what it's for any longer. A lot of traditional English market towns have the same problem. They grew during an age when walking was the only way to get around. People shopped in the towns they lived in because they had no option, so places prospered or not on the back of their own local economy. Today, with the motor car, that's all changed. The reason shops are closing down in Market Drayton is simple enough: it's because people who live in Market Drayton are shopping somewhere else. There are a couple of supermarkets in the town, but that hasn't helped; in fact, it's probably made matters worse.

Supermarkets sell everything and you don't need many other shops when you've two of them in a place this size.

Small towns get sucked into a cycle of decline: people don't use them and then they begin to look so run-down that nobody wants to.

I cast off as soon as I got back to the boat and left Market Drayton behind me. Apart from the storm I'd experienced on the embankment, the weather was holding up surprisingly well for an English summer – though you never like to admit as much since it's tantamount to inviting the rain gods to dump on you continuously for the next forty days and forty nights.

It was another terrific evening, the late June sunshine already beginning to etch long shadows across the fields. I cruised through the remote countryside without seeing another boat until I arrived at the top of the flight of five locks at Adderley where one was moored for the night. As I was passing I heard the voice of a man in the bowels of the bilges, obviously up to his neck in oil and water repairing his engine.

'All I said was pass me the washing up liquid,' he was saying.

'And all I said was that I hadn't got any,' a female voice responded.

'Don't take that tone of voice with me,' he snapped.

You hear a lot of fragments of conversation like this on boats, some of them intimacies, some embryonic arguments. Part of it's because narrowboats are small places and couples who don't get on with each other in five-bedroom houses aren't likely to get on any better in the sort of space where one of them breathing can sometimes seem like an unforgiveable provocation to the other. Much of it, though, is because you're so often isolated on a boat, moored up miles from anywhere and not really expecting anyone else to be around to overhear you. Especially in the summer when us canal folk tend to throw open our doors and windows and spill out onto the towpath as if it's our own personal patio.

'I will not have that creature in the house any longer,' I once heard a woman screaming from a boat in Berkshire.

'But she's my sister, you can't treat her like that.'

'Lionel, she's not your sister, she's a dog for heaven's sake...'

Another time on the Trent outside Nottingham I heard another woman in the middle of a conversation with her husband which I think was about yogurt of all things.

Then she went silent.

'Andrew, you're not asleep, are you...? Don't you dare go to sleep on me. If you go to sleep again while I'm talking to you I'll kick you, I swear it. Andrew! Wake up! ANDREW!'

I moored that night in Audlem which is another of these picturesque canal villages you seem to come across on the waterways so frequently that eventually you begin to get a bit blasé about them: 'Oh another picture postcard hamlet, it must be a Wednesday then' – that sort of thing. Audlem, though, is particularly attractive; you'd have to be blind not to see it. It lies at the foot of a flight of fourteen locks spread out over a mile or so and fringed on both sides by trees and lush fields where indolent cows graze. The lock surrounds here are so meticulously mown you could be forgiven for thinking you'd strayed onto someone's lawn. I always feel self-conscious using them, as if someone's going to start bellowing at me to keep off the grass. Walking on a surface this perfect seems a heresy; digging your heels in it to pull on a rope, a sacrilege.

Audlem village itself nestles in a shallow wooded cutting flanked on one side by a redbrick Georgian-looking mill, which for many years has been a canal shop; and on the other by the Shroppie Fly pub, outside which stands an old-fashioned crane with a pulley wheel tucked in its crossbeam. This structure has become as iconic an image of the British waterways as narrowboats themselves, photographed a thousand times and used in hundreds of guides, books and brochures. It's not original, though, any more than the Shroppie Fly is an original pub. The pub used to be the wharf warehouse; and though there was once a crane outside, the one that's there now is from a railway coal yard and was erected in the early 1970s. And while we're on the subject, The Mill's not Georgian either: it was built in 1916 during World War One.

Not that I'm knocking Audlem. What's not to like about the place? It's friendly and easy-going, and if it's a little too twee for some tastes, it's nevertheless still tasteful. Even so, it has to be admitted that there is an element of theatre to the place – and I'm talking the Globe here, not the National. The bar of the Shroppie Fly, for instance, is done out like the front of a boat with lots of brass and copper on the wall, and recesses covered with shelves full of books bought by the yard. It's not everyone's cup of tea, and to be honest these last few years whenever I've been in the village I've gravitated towards the other canalside pub in Audlem, unimaginatively called The Bridge after the bridge that takes the main road over the cut to the village. This used to be an altogether more industrial drinking hole, though recently even this has developed ideas above its station and now boasts an adjoining restaurant.

I was in The Bridge in 2006 the day the England football team broke its habit of losing to Germany in the World Cup and lost instead to Portugal after a penalty shoot-out. Afterwards – unusual I know, but true all the same – most of those in the bar threw themselves into the canal in despair. The water was so thick with writhing bodies it was like a Saturday afternoon at the municipal swimming baths. One bloke decided to go further than the rest and leapt off the bridge. Everyone was drunk, but he must have been particularly drunk. He missed, landed on the towpath and broke his wrist, all in one smooth action.

That night I went for a swift one and happened to mention to someone at the bar the last time I'd been there, and the knuckle-dragger who I thought was lucky not to break his neck let alone his wrist.

'Er… that was me,' he said.

'Good to meet you again,' I said. 'I'd stay longer but I've, er, left a chicken in the oven. I'd best be pottering along…'

FIFTEEN
Hack Green

The heat was getting me down. It was relentless. Day after day of it, scorching the surrounding grasslands to a crisp; burning the countryside brown and making it all but impossible to keep lager at a decent temperature once it was out of the fridge.

OK, I know I shouldn't have been such a wuss. After all, it was only a warm spell in June which is one of the summer months and therefore supposed to be warm. But hey, I'm English: I'm not used to temperatures like these for more than a couple of days on the trot. In my book when it gets this hot it counts as a heatwave, and I can't handle heatwaves. I decided to rest up and take it easy for a few days until it cooled off.

The cat – long-haired, remember; unsuited for these sorts of temperatures – lay splayed out on the deck like the limp hairball she turned into whenever it got into the seventies. I was no better. I lost interest in moving. I lost interest in eating. I even lost interest in breathing. I'd reverted to the Huck Finn outfit and was lying flat out in the coolest place in the cabin with the fan on full power, seeing how well I could balance Beck's bottles on my belly while I was drinking from them. I got quite good at it. At least, I was good at it as long as I didn't drop off to sleep. It was just hard not to drop off to sleep in that heat. I often woke up reeking like a brewery, looking as if I'd wet myself.

'It's about time you pulled yourself together,' said Em when she rang at lunchtime. 'You're losing it. You always get like this when you've been on your own too long. Get outside into the fresh air, for heaven's sake. Go for a walk.'

'I can't walk,' I said. 'I'm injured. My ankle still hurts when I move.'

'I'm surprised you're aware of it,' she said. 'Tell me, when exactly was the last time you did move?'

Her reproaches stung me into action and later that afternoon I forced myself to take her advice and get some exercise. The sky was cloudless; the atmosphere still and sultry, heavy with that silence of summer when not even a breeze rustles the trees. I set off at a fair limp down a footpath to the village church of St James which is set on a mound in the middle of Audlem and dominates the place. Built of sandstone, it's more the size of an abbey than a church. On a dull day it's a grey, foreboding building; but when the sky is clear it catches the sun and turns a miraculous flushed pink, the sort of colour a four-year-old girl would choose for the icing on her birthday cake.

I hadn't walked far, no more than a hundred yards or so, when I became aware of a light footfall behind me, a soft rustling in the grass. I swung round thinking someone was creeping up on me, which was partly true, only it wasn't someone but something. It was Kit. She rolled onto her back and began writhing around like an open hosepipe with water gushing through it. When I walked on, she jumped to her feet and began following me, stalking me in the undergrowth and then running past me to hide herself again. She'd never done this before and I was at a loss to know how to react. The question now was should I take her back and lock her in the boat despite the risk of her suffocating in the heat, or should I let her do her own thing and try to pretend that she wasn't anything to do with me?

In truth, I was a little self-conscious being followed by a fluffy cat with a tail like a feather duster. It was like taking a cuddly toy for a walk. Other blokes you met out walking had dogs – the bigger the better it sometimes seemed. Great slavering brutes with jowls dripping saliva; monstrous creatures the size of horses with teeth as sharp as razor-wire. Even if they had little dogs, they had little ones with attitude: pint-sized yappy ones which could fillet a rat in seconds; or lanky, leggy ones that could sprint around a field at the speed of a Porsche, terrorising rabbits until they begged to be put out of their misery.

A cat didn't really cut it. A cat was a bit girlie for a bloke like me, especially one with the sort of belly I had. On balance I thought it was best to take Kit back to the boat. It was only a matter of time before someone started to impugn my manhood.

The problem was she wouldn't let me get close enough to pick her up. She followed me, sometimes at my heels, and as soon as I stopped, she'd stop too, which she obviously thought was clever. But as soon as I bent down towards her or made any sort of move in her direction, she backed off. She probably thought this was clever, too. This toing and froing between us went on for a long time, too long. Eventually I lost patience with whatever game it was she was playing and I gave up on her. If she was going to mess me about like this she could do as she damn well liked. She could follow me to hell and back for all I cared. She could even follow me to the pub if she felt like it. If she was that clever she could buy me a pint.

Of course, once she realised she'd won the game, she didn't want to follow me at all and went her own way with her tail up and a curl to her lip which was as close to a snigger as I've ever seen in a cat and made me want to throw something at her.

Em rang again once I got back to the boat. I wasn't expecting another call from her, though the timing of this one was good. Any earlier and she'd have caught me in The Bridge; any later and I'd have been playing belly bottles again. As it was I could brag about the fact that I'd just come back from a walk. This was useful in demonstrating that I took what she said seriously.

But on this occasion she showed no interest in what I'd been doing. Instead she kept going on about Crewe. For some reason she seemed to have developed an unhealthy infatuation with Crewe. 'You're near Crewe, aren't you?' she asked.

'Crewe? I guess so. Crewe's near Nantwich, isn't it?'

'Not far,' she said. 'Could you get a local taxi to pick me up there?'

'Pick you up? Where from?'

'From Crewe. From the station. I'll be leaving the office in ten minutes. I'll let you know when I'm arriving.'

'Arriving where?'

'At Crewe, for heaven's sake. At the station.' I could hear her take a deep breath. 'Steve, are you being obtuse or am I just not making myself clear? I'm coming up to visit you. I am leaving London as soon as I can get away. I'm coming to spend a few days on the boat with you…'

Apparently, as I was to learn later, she had a meeting in Crewe on the Monday and since it was now Thursday she'd decided on the spur of the moment to take the following day off and make a weekend of it. Not that at that stage I really cared why she was coming up; the fact that she was coming up at all was enough for me. The news left me in a state of blind panic. If I'm being frank, I'd rather let standards slip the previous week or so and everything was in mess. I was in a mess; the boat was in a mess; even Kit was in a mess. She was covered in burrs and teasels from her rustic wanderings, and she had unspeakable things hanging from her bum end. I was totally unprepared for a visit.

Added to which, I'd got no food in. Or at least no food worth talking about. Certainly nothing in the rocket and shaved parmesan vein which was Em's preferred summer diet, and a long way from the cold baked beans with mustard and Worcester sauce which had been my staple these last few days.

Realising she was on her way at such short notice was like waking the day of an exam to discover the alarm hadn't gone off.

I dashed to the shops before they closed, throwing things into a basket with the same sort of desperation they show on those cooking shows where contestants have to come up with a menu off the top of their heads. Then I started to clean up and I cleaned solidly for the next four hours. I cleaned the boat. I cleaned myself. I even cleaned the cat and got scratched for my trouble, since I groomed her so infrequently she thought this was some new game like the one we'd been playing walking to the church.

In the process of all this – by the sort of multitasking us blokes aren't supposed to be able to do – I managed additionally to produce a tomato salad with basil, and a portion of lightly-poached tarragon chicken in cream sauce. Indeed, I'd only just finished finally checking my seasonings when I heard Em walking up the towpath and felt her step onto the boat.

The table was laid. The wine was opened. The candle was lit.

'Wow! I hope you haven't gone to all this trouble on my account,' she said, as she took everything in. At the same time, she kicked off her boots in a way that left most of the mud clinging to them on my newly vacuumed carpet.

'Just as easy to cook for two,' I said, fixing my face into a rictus grin and kissing her on the cheek. 'It's lovely just having you here.'

'And it's lovely to be here,' she said. 'Although – and I hope you don't mind me mentioning this – there does seem to be a strong smell of stale beer in the air. Or is that my imagination?'

We got away the following morning as early as we could, which wasn't very early at all since we'd both had a disturbed night, the cabin too hot and stuffy for either of us to sleep well. After we'd negotiated the remaining locks in the Audlem flight we cruised through the secluded countryside where after an hour or so we came across the tiny hamlet of Hack Green, a scattered settlement of farms next to a couple of locks. It was there Em drew my attention to a sign in the hedgerow. There are a lot of these sorts of signs in hedgerows near canals nowadays. They're usually discreet little notices advertising nearby pubs, or local shops, or farm eggs at exorbitant prices. But this one was different. It was advertising a 'Secret Nuclear Bunker', although 'secret' in this context was stretching it a bit since the sign was the size of a road hoarding and big enough to have been seen from the next county. I discovered it was also marked on the waterways map, which somewhat mitigated its security classification too. There was even a star to highlight it just in case you weren't expecting to see a secret nuclear bunker marked on a map of the English canal system. I couldn't help thinking what other information might be contained in these unassuming books which I'd used for years to navigate. Perhaps if I looked at them more carefully they might tell me the whereabouts of emergency food stores, or control and command centres, or war operations rooms. Perhaps I just hadn't seen the information about these things because all I'd wanted to know, in my naive way, was how many locks were coming up and whether there was a post office in the nearest village.

We moored up and walked to the place through the blazing midday sun, the temperatures higher than ever and still rising. I don't know what I expected a secret nuclear bunker to look like. They're secret: I hadn't seen many. For all I knew they might look like Tesco superstores. Well, that would make sense, wouldn't it? Tesco superstores are springing up all over the place; there are thousands of them now, so many you hardly notice them. In fact you don't notice them at all unless you're looking for somewhere to shop. This has to be good for security. I'd bomb them all tomorrow, but that's just me – I've got a thing about supermarkets. Most people wouldn't give them a second glance, certainly not members of al-Qaeda who probably shop there too, if truth were told.

This nuclear bunker at Hack Green didn't look like a Tesco store: it looked like a barn built out of breeze blocks with a mobile phone mast stuck in the top and a sign out front telling you that it was a prohibited place under the terms of the Official Secrets Act. In fact, it looked just as you'd imagine a secret nuclear bunker would look if you'd ever thought about it.

It can't ever have been very secret, though. Even before the sign went up on the towpath advertising the place as museum of the Cold War, I can't believe that local people didn't know exactly what it was. For a start it's in the middle of nowhere with nothing but hedges and flat fields for miles around. Nothing except for the phone mast, that is. That stands out like a sore thumb even now, but it must have stood out more in the days before mobiles when there weren't communication masts all over the place. In fact, the whole complex must have been a local landmark, the sort of place you'd have mentioned if ever you'd been giving directions to a stranger. 'Straight on by the three rape fields, left at the big oak tree and then take a right past the secret nuclear bunker...'

It wasn't so funny, though, once we'd got behind the heavy-duty blast doors which once protected the place. Yes, there's a 'find-the-mouse' game designed to keep the kids quiet, and a faux NAFFI canteen for granny, built as a nod to World War Two when Hack Green was an RAF radar station. But this couldn't detract from the awfulness of what, in more recent times, the bunker had become; for in the event of a nuclear war Hack Green was one of a network of seventeen similar places built across the country to be regional seats of government, nerve centres for small groups of people it was hoped would survive to keep alive the very concept of civilisation itself.

Inside it's chilly, literally and metaphorically. It's that sort of chill which gets into your bones. The sort that makes you want to curl up and die. Underground there is a labyrinth of corridors. Threaded between air-filtration units, water storage facilities and a power generating plant is an endless succession of decontamination chambers, dormitories, operations rooms and the like. There's even a briefing room with a BBC studio attached, from which some harried official with a posh accent was presumably supposed to broadcast to a population which the authorities believed would not just be alive, but compliantly receptive to their messages.

The whole place is profoundly depressing. It's where government was supposed to operate, but there's no sense of power about it, no aura of magnificence in its empty, echoing halls. It's more like a town hall crammed into a few basement rooms. And like a town hall the place reeks of institutionalism. From its polished brown floor tiles to its white concrete ceilings it is as utilitarian as a buff envelope from the Inland Revenue. The desks are all standard local authority inventory, the phones functional 1970s-issue, the chairs basic green plastic and tubular steel.

At the centre of the complex – notionally if not actually – is the Information Room, a menacing black space built around an operations wall on which sits a diagrammatic map of the UK surrounded by illuminated grids and charts and clocks showing the time in Moscow, Washington and at NATO headquarters. It seems on too small a scale to be real, more like a set in a low-budget movie. Yet this was the sharp end of the Ballistic Missile Early Warning System that was designed to give us a four-minute alert before we were consigned to eternity.

As if to rub home the futility of even this modest ambition, there's a row of computers set into the desks here taking pride of place, like trophies of the new technological age. Everything would have depended on them, I suppose. Yet their screens are tiny, like miniatures of the real thing. And I guess not one has a fraction of the memory of a modern mobile phone.

Really! What did these muppets blindly leading us to the edge of the abyss expect would happen if the Soviets had bombed us? Did they honestly believe that their world inside the bunker would survive the holocaust? Did they genuinely have any confidence that there'd be a world outside worth governing? Were they even confident there'd be a world outside at all?

Talk about the blind leading the blind. Talk about the ship of fools...

We were relieved to leave the place and get back into the fresh air. Outside, despite the muggy heat, the countryside was wholesome and cleansing, brighter than usual. Even the birds seemed to be singing more loudly than they normally did at that time of day. Or maybe that's just the way it seemed. Maybe because we'd been somewhere with such a subtext of death we'd begun to see life like this in all its vibrant glory. I'd felt the same way years earlier leaving my father one sunny day after visiting him in hospital during his final illness. For all I loved him, I was relieved that it was him in that ward that day and not me.

We'd left the boat at a blissful mooring on a verdant stretch of towpath near the locks, the countryside laid out before us like a green grid punctuated by occasional trees clawing the cornflower sky. It was so wonderful we thought about calling it a day and staying there overnight; but when we talked about it neither of us really felt comfortable being there. We needed to put space between us and the bunker which threw a shadow over us longer than any the sun could ever produce.

SIXTEEN

From Nantwich to Church Minshull

We moored that night near to a boatyard on the top end of Nantwich embankment and the following morning I took the bike into town to get it repaired. I knew there was a bike shop in Nantwich, but after Market Drayton I couldn't be certain it would still be in business. Maybe Nantwich was also suffering from the recession; or perhaps cycling was just going out of fashion in these parts. On both scores I was reassured; the shop was open and it was remarkably busy. The guy running it wanted a tenner for the work. I did a quick calculation. He was going to fit a new chain and replace a few other parts too. As far as I could see, they would cost more than ten pounds on their own, let alone the price of his labour.

'That can't be right,' I said. 'You're doing yourself. Make it twenty quid at least.'

'No, too much. How about twelve?'

'For heaven's sake,' I urged him, 'take fifteen.'

'Thirteen,' he said. 'My final offer.'

Nantwich can be a bit like this, a bit skewed in the way it sees the world: bustling and contemporary on the one hand, but a bit old-fashioned at the same time. Modern values in a traditional setting, as John Prescott might have put it. It's the sort of place that's all cream teas and Bath buns in the daytime, but come the evening it's filled with drunken young women with skirts up to their armpits looking as if they want to procreate publicly. Architecturally, what first strikes you about the place as a visitor is that it's filled with half-timbered buildings, some of them so crooked they look as if they're about to collapse. They probably would if they weren't half-timbered. The town is built on salt reserves and half-timbering allows buildings to move as the ground beneath them shifts, which it can do when salt is being extracted.

One particular structure that intrigued us as we walked around taking in the sights was a splendid old black and white pile used now as a bookshop and cafe. It was leaning so badly it looked as if it wouldn't survive the afternoon, and we were surveying it from a safe distance on the pavement opposite when a bloke accosted us and struck up conversation. He was huge, like a building skip on legs; and covered from head to foot in tattoos. He had a beer belly so enormous it hung over the waistband of his shorts, giving the impression that he wasn't wearing any. More alarmingly, it made him look like he was bereft of his private parts which, while no doubt a relief to Em, left me disconcerted, pondering on the dreadful things drink can do to a man.

Actually, despite first appearances, he was a pleasant enough sort, even if he was inclined to go on a bit. Since Roman times Nantwich is a place which has made a living from that basic need we humans have to put something on our chips apart from just vinegar. I was interested enough when he was telling us about the salt industry and the hundreds of salt houses there used to be in the place. I began to flag a bit, though, when he got on to Nantwich's Civil War history and its unique position as the only town in Royalist Cheshire to declare for Parliament in 1642.

Normally I love this sort of stuff, but I love comedy too until I see a bad comedian. This bloke's delivery was dreadful. I didn't trust his facts too much either.

Which is why I perked up no end when, from out of nowhere – a little twinkle of starlight in an otherwise black void, as it were – he mentioned *Big Brother* which at that time was running on Channel 4 in the middle of its umpteenth series. Nantwich was buzzing with it since as well as the Nottingham single mother-of-two who was looking for 'direction' in her life, and the London window fitter whose ambition was to be a porn star, the town had its own contestant in the form of twenty-year-old topless model Sophie Read, the sheer scale of whose 30GG breasts were a match for our man's belly any day.

Sophie, however, resented being thought of as just another blonde bimbo. She wanted to be taken seriously and be president of England.

Mr Building Skip was inordinately proud of Nantwich's latest claim to fame, though personally I couldn't see what there was to crow about in having a contestant on the show – even if like Sophie they eventually go on to win it. Civically, surely, it must be like developing psoriasis: it's one of those vaguely unpleasant things which you can't help and can't really do much about, but which you don't want broadcasted too widely if you can help it.

Em left the next day after her lightning visit and the weather broke with a vengeance almost immediately afterwards, a massive storm blowing up with great thunderous clouds suddenly materialising overhead from out of nowhere, making the sky as dark as night. At first I was relieved: relieved to see the back of the heat-wave, and, if I'm honest, relieved to be alone again and allowed to regress to the squalor of my bachelor life afloat. But after a couple of hours sitting in the cabin watching the cat playing in the rain as it hammered down on the front deck, I'd had enough of it: I'd had enough of the rain and I'd had enough of being on my own, too.

I gradually became aware that I was in a bad mood which I could trace back to all the talk about *Big Brother* and Channel 4. Now don't get me wrong, I used to be a bit of a fan of *Big Brother* in the days of 'Nasty' Nick Bateman when it was all very dangerous and cutting edge. I used to do a lot of work for Channel 4 around that time and it was that sort of TV channel then – even if it did take itself a bit seriously at times. *Big Brother* changed things. Before, I used to go into C4 meetings trying to sell programme ideas and the suits would look at each other gravely and ask searching questions about whether my project touched the contemporary zeitgeist, or whether it had intellectual credibility, or 'weight' – a word they used to bandy about with much relish in those days.

Afterwards all they asked is whether it would get big audiences.

Beyond Nantwich the Shropshire Union passes Hurleston Junction where the Llangollen Canal branches westwards up four locks and into Wales. Rain or not, I decided I'd be better off on the move and I pushed on through the murky morning to where the canal divides, the main line continuing north to Chester while an arm veers off at 90 degrees towards Middlewich and the Trent and Mersey Canal to the east. This was the route I took. Em was coming up again the following weekend to meet me for the Middlewich festival, so with time to kill, and the forecasts predicting the weather was unlikely to improve for some time, I moored on the scenic embankment overlooking the village of Church Minshull in the valley of the River Weaver, where I planned to spend a few days.

The renowned waterways writer L. T. C. 'Tom' Rolt moored at virtually the same spot with his wife Angela in the autumn of 1939, after their honeymoon was interrupted by Hitler's invasion of Poland and the world war which resulted from it. It was not a happy period for them. They'd married in the face of poisonous opposition from her father who banished her from his sight afterwards in the manner of some mustachioed pantomime villain. Once war was declared they came here, close enough to Crewe for Tom to commute to a job as an engineer at Rolls Royce which, as a 'reserved' occupation, meant he wouldn't be called up in the forces. They must have figured that this way they could stay together and that Tom would at least be doing something he liked.

But it didn't turn out like this. He'd served his apprenticeship in factories but he hadn't worked in one for years, and the mindlessness of it left him so bored that in his autobiography he admits that even visiting the toilet came as a relief from the tedium.

The upside for him was living in Church Minshull which he saw as the exemplar of an English village, and he eulogised it with shameless nostalgia in his classic waterways book *Narrow Boat*. This was published after the war when six years of death and killing had put people out of sorts with the present and disposed to look back to what they wanted to believe was a better world. It's no exaggeration to say that *Narrow Boat*'s elegiac account of the canals at a time in their history when they seemed to be on their last legs was the single most influential factor leading to the modern waterways restoration movement.

But my, it can be mawkish at times.

In the book Rolt paints a picture of Church Minshull as if it was trapped in a time warp. It is a village where the blacksmith is at his anvil, his clinking hammer 'the music of the street'. Where the wheelwright reconditions old pony-traps, eschewing modern spray-guns to paint them in the old traditional way by hand. It's a place where the wooden water-wheels of the old mill keep turning as they have for centuries, and where at the end of the day menfolk repair to the local pub for a glass of beer after work while the women – 'housewives' all – 'foregather in the post office for a gossip, on the pretext of a stamp or half a pound of tea'.

I wonder what Tom would make of Church Minshull now? In truth, it was never the place he described, even when he was describing it. He was just using the village to air his personal regret at the passing of a world which, in reality, had ceased to exist generations before, the smithy and the wheelwright redundant occupations even then. All the same, as a keen observer of contemporary social history, Rolt was one of the first to identify the erosion of the English village as a centre of rural community, a trend which has accelerated since and which you can't help thinking would make him despair if he was alive today.

Nowadays you wouldn't find many women foregathering in post offices in English villages to gossip, for the simple reason that you'd have trouble finding a post office in an English village at all, so many of them having closed over the intervening decades. The one at Church Minshull is typical in this respect: it disappeared years ago. It's the same with village shops which are such an endangered species they ought to be put on a conservation list. Again, what happened in Church Minshull is characteristic of what's happened across the country. The shop there closed in the early 1980s, about the time Cheshire Council shut down the local school which had been running for 124 years and which had originally been built, not with public money, but money raised in donations from people who lived in Church Minshull itself.

The village pub, The Badger, clings on by its fingertips – though it's not a place you'll find me getting sentimental about. There was a period when every time you went there it seemed to have a new landlord, each promising to return it to its glory days. Regrettably, those days seemed to be the ones when Church Minshull was so self-sufficient it didn't need the passing trade of outsiders. At least that's how it seemed to me, because regardless of who was in charge whenever I ventured inside I was always made to feel like I shouldn't be there. One of the landlords once rounded on me because I was wearing muddy boots. Too right I was wearing muddy boots. That's because I'd just walked a couple of miles through muddy fields to give him my money in exchange for beer. That's what you do in pubs. And that's what you do in the countryside, too, since in the countryside you have to walk through mud to get anywhere. Because when you get down to basics, mud is what the countryside's made of, and muddy boots go with the territory. Literally.

On another occasion, I was served a pint so rancid you could have used it as paint-stripper. This was under another landlord who'd run the pub down so badly it was filled with the sort of weirdos you'd usually find in inner city spit-and-sawdust bars close to football grounds – God knows where they'd come from. When I complained about the beer, my host told me with the sort of charm you associate with Simon Cowell that I was nothing more than a freeloader who was out to cheat him.

'It's not at all cloudy,' he said. 'Look, clear as a bell...'

'I didn't say it was cloudy,' I replied, 'I said it was sour. Taste it if you don't believe me.'

So it was with no surprise, and certainly no regret, that I heard a few years back that The Badger had finally closed down for lack of trade. Imagine my amazement then, walking past it this time, to discover that it was undergoing a major renovation. From the street it looked much as it always had, but from the rear you could see that it had been gutted and stripped back to bare brickwork. The outbuildings at the side had been totally demolished too, and in place of what had once been the garden there was an enormous hole in the ground.

I slipped under a fence and was peering over the edge of this when I became aware of a bloke shouting at me from the other side. Despite the rain, he was stripped to the waist and was sporting a mortar hod on his shoulder in the fashion of some medieval weapon of war. He wanted to know what I thought I was (expletive deleted) doing and didn't I know I was on (expletive deleted) private ground. Since there were half a dozen signs scattered around the place with the word 'Private' prominently displayed on them, and a couple more with 'Keep Off' added to ram the message home, I really didn't have much of a leg to stand on; he was soon marching me off the site, making me probably the only person in the history of the world who's been thrown out of a pub before it's even been opened.

The indignity of the incident didn't do much for my mood which, I confess, hadn't improved any since the *Big Brother* conversation in Nantwich. Thankfully, though, the church of St Bartholomew next door was more welcoming. Despite the misleading date of 1702 highlighted in dark brick on its tower, the church was erected to replace an older wooden structure a few years later, about 1704/5. Recently it has required some TLC, necessitating substantial grants from English Heritage. The fortunate result of this is that where so many country churches are locked for security, this one has to be kept open for visitors at certain set periods; and since it has to be supervised when it is, the local ladies' sewing club have taken to using it at the same time, killing two birds with one stone.

They're a vivacious, garrulous bunch who obviously don't get many people dropping by and who are delighted to welcome the few that do. They sat me down with a cup of tea and a large slice of Victoria sponge and cross-examined me at great length and with much charm about where I lived, where I'd come from and where I was going on the canal. In return, once they'd identified me as the sort of person who was interested in local tittle-tattle (and they weren't wrong there), they gave me an insider's briefing on the pub which they told me was scheduled to be open by Christmas, although there'd been delays and postponements in the work and all manner of Machiavellian goings-on with the council at planning level. Apparently the big hole in the garden was to become a small development of executive housing, though permission for it was dependent on the pub being brought back into use. The council – no doubt canny to the ways of developers in this part of the world – had insisted that this was done before the houses were put up, at least ensuring that The Badger wouldn't finish up converted into flats like so many old village pubs around the country.

I hope it all works out. Pubs are such a key feature of small villages like this that when they're forced to close what's lost isn't just a place to drink but a social centre, a community focus, a central meeting point. Village pubs are part of our rural history, a tangible link with the past; and when they close we lose part of that bond which ties us to preceding generations. In villages like Church Minshull where so much of what made them what they are is lost already, the pub's as important as the church in encapsulating the core identity of a community: it's one of the lodestones by which we can all chart our relationship to the past.

After all, people are social creatures – they always have been. Pubs are traditionally where people have gone to mix and mingle and it's important in any community that there's a place like this – a place where everyone can gather and feel comfortable. It's a basic act of humanity which binds us in fellowship. The English pub is essential to England in this respect.

Why, then, am I so fearful of its survival? Possibly because the factors that will determine its future lie outside our control. Writing this book, I rang to check about The Badger – only to discover it was still being renovated. It was almost a year behind schedule and no one in Church Minshull was holding their breath for the grand opening.

Paradoxically, however, it was probably the best thing for me personally. The Badger being closed, I mean. I wasn't exactly Mr Happy at this stage in my journey and the way I was it would have been a penance to other customers to have me imposed on them. It was probably a good job the weather was so bad too. The way I was I'd have cast a shadow over a Mediterranean morning.

I walked back to the boat with the rain running down my neck, gradually beginning to realise after being manhandled by the thug with the trug that my bad mood had turned into a vile mood. The cat didn't make me feel much better, either. I found her on the deck, dripping wet and hunting midges. She was in her element, much preferring the rain to the sunshine.

When I went into the cabin she followed me inside for as long as it took to shake herself down and soak the place. Then she went out again, got herself wet once more and repeated the process. I eventually locked her out until I saw her little pink nose pressed pathetically against the glass. At which point, like a mug, I capitulated and against my better judgement I let her in. She, of course, immediately did her shaggy dog act again with renewed vigour.

She gave me that little twisted look of hers, the sort of half smile that isn't a smile at all. If I hadn't known better, I'd have thought she was winding me up. Except, she's only a cat, of course. Only a mindless animal.

Not helped by the continual rain, my disposition didn't improve any the next day or the day after that. It was no better even after I'd left Church Minshull behind and arrived at Middlewich, and even after Em had arrived from London for the festival. Mind you, she wasn't all sweetness and light either. There'd been problems at work and we spent a few miserable days moving from pub to pub, drinking too much and not talking to each other enough.

We met some friends, which was fun, and we missed a party we'd been invited to because we were confused about the time it started, which wasn't. There was nothing wrong with Middlewich and nothing wrong with the festival which has been running since 1980 and is one of the best folk festivals in the country. But the weather wasn't kind to it that year and we weren't kind to ourselves, and by the end if I'd have heard another version of 'The Black Velvet Band' I'd have run from the town screaming.

'It would be fun to go to Cropredy this year, wouldn't it?' Em said on the last afternoon before she went back to London.

'Maybe you could pop back there with the boat as part of your journey?'

We were sitting in the cabin waiting for the taxi she'd booked to take her to the station. Before us lay the detritus of a Sunday lunch, the dregs of a bottle of something or another in our glasses. I looked at her open-mouthed. What she meant by Cropredy in this context was the annual reunion of the folk/rock band Fairport Convention which takes place in Cropredy in Oxfordshire every year, one of those many music festivals which punctuate the English summer like the rain that so often characterises them.

Why on earth she wanted to go to a wet music festival after having just spent a weekend being miserable at one was difficult to grasp. But how she thought I could possibly get the boat down there in time was beyond me. The concept of 'popping' anywhere in a vehicle with a top speed of 4 mph is absurd, but popping back to Oxfordshire, a distance of some 125 miles away with God knows how many locks in between, was preposterous. She might as well have suggested popping over to the Hindu Kush for a short walk.

Besides, it was already the end of June. The Cropredy Festival takes place in the middle of August. We'd taken the boat there once before twenty-five years ago and though we arrived so late in the day the music had already started, we were nevertheless able to get a mooring near the festival site very easily. But as the popularity of canals has increased, so too has the popularity of Cropredy for music-lovers with canal boats. Nowadays to get a mooring anywhere near the festival you need to be there a couple of weeks before, if not more. To be in with any chance I'd have to hare down south at what for me would be a breakneck speed.

And this wasn't the end of it, for immediately afterwards I'd have to hare back north again to Stafford where I had a commitment to another canal festival which I wouldn't have been able to get out of even if I'd wanted.

'I'll think about it,' I said non-committally. 'It's... er... an interesting idea.' But she was having none of this prevarication.

'I think I'd enjoy it,' she said. 'Steve Winwood's headlining; you know I've always liked him. And it'd be useful for you, too. You're supposed to be doing this project visiting waterways festivals, aren't you? Well, Cropredy's a festival. And it's on the waterways, isn't it...?'

SEVENTEEN
Middlewich to Stone

The old boatmen used to be able to move around the canals sharpish. They had to. They were paid according to what they carried: piecework, it used to be called. Most of them would be doing local runs, travelling from a pit to a nearby power station, doing three or four trips a week, more if they could fit them in. Some boats used to do longer runs: they'd take coal down to London, for instance; or pick up lime juice from the ships berthed in the East End and take it up to Roses' near Hemel Hempstead.

But these were professionals, blokes operating in teams to a deadline with money at stake which is the best incentive you can have for working hard. I wasn't working at all; I was supposed to be enjoying myself. And I was travelling singlehanded with a cat on board which was likely to go AWOL at any moment. I didn't have any incentive to move fast at all, unless you count Em breathing down my neck because she'd got the hots to see Steve Winwood who she's fancied since she was at junior school and he was a fifteen-year-old playing with the Spencer Davies Group.

What it amounted to was that if I was going to get to Cropredy in time to get a decent mooring I had about sixty-odd solid hours of cruising and nearly a hundred locks to do over the next three or four weeks. It wasn't that this was an impossible task, far from it. But it wasn't desirable either. It wasn't the sort of thing you did on the canals which were all about pottering through the countryside at a sedate pace with no real imperative to get anywhere.

The next morning it was filthy with high winds and driving rain, but even so I started out early with the intention of getting a few miles under my belt by evening. But it didn't work out that way. Em and I had moored for the duration of the Middlewich Festival on the Shropshire Union, just short of its junction with the Trent and Mersey Canal, so my first job was to negotiate Wardle Lock which brings the two together. Strictly speaking Wardle Lock is on the Wardle Canal, Britain's shortest waterway at all of 154 feet long – less than the length of a couple of bowling alleys. But this quirky statistic masks a sharp bit of business practice, for at the time when the canals were run by separate private companies, all of them in competition with each other, this 'canal' (if you can grace it with that name) was built by the Trent and Mersey Company to control the intersection.

Navigationally it's a pig, mainly because of a hump-back bridge which spans the canal just after the lock, and which restricts your view in both directions. Turning onto the Trent and Mersey from the lock you've got a problem if you haven't got crew since there's no one to warn you if anything's approaching. You can crane your head around the bridge as much as you like, but however often you do there's always the threat of something appearing from out of nowhere in the minute or two it takes to get back to your boat and get it moving. So there's a point at which you just have to cross your fingers and go for it.

I'd been particularly alert to the hazard. Even so, what I feared might happen is precisely what did happen. No sooner had I got *Justice* underway than a small cruiser swung around the corner bearing down on me like a wasp to a jam jar. It's the sort of cussed thing that happens on canals: it's nobody's fault but it makes you think that if there is a God up there he's got an impish sense of humour. We both slammed our engines into reverse and after much thrashing around we managed to avoid colliding and no damage was done. Well, not at that stage anyhow. Later, though, as I went for the turn a second time, I stepped onto the bank to give *Justice* a push from her bow and I suddenly found myself splayed out on the ground. This occurred so quickly that for a moment or two I couldn't quite understand what had happened. I wasn't disposed to fall down on canals any more than I was disposed to fall in them. Trust me, it isn't part of the typical pattern of my cruising which experience has taught me is best conducted from an upright position.

I lay on the ground gradually becoming aware of my dodgy ankle, the war wound from my Pennine trip, which I'd tried to make myself forget about over the weeks since I'd injured it again in Uxbridge travelling up the Grand Union. At first it was so painful I felt nothing, but it soon began to throb with a searing intensity until I could have screamed with the agony of it.

'Are you OK?' It was the skipper of the cruiser. He helped me to my feet and I stood unsteadily for a moment or two clutching his arm while I tested my weight.

'I think I missed my footing,' I said.

'More likely you stepped in that hole,' he replied, pointing with his foot to one so well camouflaged with grass that even when you knew it was there you could hardly see it.

I realised straight off I wouldn't be doing much more cruising that day; yet at first I pressed on, hacking it as best I could, hoping the pain would go away. Finally I had an attack of common sense and realised I'd have to stop and rest up for the day, though resting didn't really help much. Nowhere near as much as a few stiff whiskies did. Even so, that night I slept fitfully, tossing and turning, unable to get comfortable. Kit seemed to realise I was discomforted. Normally as soon as it gets dark she goes out exploring the countryside, returning every now and again to eat and perhaps to reassure herself the boat is still where she left it. Sometimes I'd hear her come back through the porthole I leave open for her; sometimes I'd hear the scraping of her bowl on the floor of the main cabin as she rooted around for biscuits. That night, though, she didn't go out at all, and in the early hours, waking whimpering from a disturbed half-sleep, I found her sitting at the side of my bed licking my hand which had trailed out from under the eiderdown.

In the morning the ankle had come up like a balloon and I could barely support myself on it. There could be no debate about what I had to do now. I made a couple of calls and found a temporary mooring at a boatyard, and later that day – carrying Kit in her basket in one hand, and a small holdall of dirty washing in the other – I limped back to London as best I could.

On the way I called Em to let her know what was happening. 'You sound as if you're on a train,' she said.

'That's because I am on a train. I'm on my way home. Do you mind me coming back or would you rather be on your own?'

I heard her laugh uncomfortably. 'It wasn't a very cheerful weekend in Middlewich, was it?' she said. 'Maybe what's happened is a blessing in disguise. It's an ill wind, as they say. At least it means we'll be able to spend some time together. And it'll be a novelty for me to live with someone again. I was beginning to think I was single.'

So we kissed and made up, and for the next month I sat with my leg propped up on a cushion watching daytime TV and doing the physiotherapy exercises I should have done before but didn't. Day by day, under a strict regime of ice packs and hot compresses, the ankle slowly improved until one day I woke up and realised it was better. Well, maybe not better. Not completely better. Not 'I-could-run-a-marathon-now' better. But at least the pain had stopped. At least I could walk without limping.

That afternoon before Em got back from work I packed up a holdall and got the cat basket out of the cellar. As soon as she saw it Kit began scratching at it excitedly trying to get inside. Em was less pleased. She thought I was crazy even thinking about going back to the boat at this stage in my recovery. She thought I should abandon the festivals idea for the year. She thought I was making trouble for myself and that it was only a matter of time before I had another accident and came back home with my tail between my legs looking for sympathy.

'What I don't understand,' she said, 'is why on earth you're persisting with this ridiculous project of yours anyhow. I could understand you taking that trip a few years back down the Severn estuary to Bristol. That was all about you getting older, wasn't it? Feeling that your life was slipping away and wanting to do things while you could? And that journey across the Pennines the other year: that was about your mum dying, it was obvious. But I can't fathom why you're just wandering around the country aimlessly going from one waterways festival to another. I mean, it's not as if you even like waterways festivals, is it?'

This was a difficult question, not one I could easily answer. Yes, she was right in one sense – though to say I didn't like festivals, full stop, was too crude a way of putting it. I'm a gregarious person; I like the sociability of them. I like the opportunity of spending time with other people who share my esoteric, anorak interest in the waterways. But this process of coming together in some sort of common celebration confused me. It was too much like going to a church service for my liking. For me narrowboating has principally been a solitary pastime, a way of getting away from the world. Or rather a way of getting away from a part of the world: that fractious, tetchy, discordant part that is twenty-first century urban life. Canals provide the means to reconnect with a rural England; they are a conduit to simple, solitary pleasures. The contemplation of a quarrelsome flock of ducks as you throw them bread; or a storm as it gathers over the hills; or a far-off fox as it threads its way across the fields in the failing light of an autumn evening. Canals allow you to reflect on your existence. They allow you the space to deliberate on the world and your brief stay in it. Canals are a balm to a troubled mind, a solace to those in mental turmoil. They are a place, I suppose, to reconnect to your god, whatever he or she or it might be.

They reconnect me to my past too, to my childhood and the small Leicestershire village close to the River Soar where I was brought up and where I still feel rooted. Though why that should be, I can't understand. The village isn't the same village any more, not the village I once knew. That was destroyed years ago by an influx of commuters from the city and the creeping suburbanisation which went with it. Executive estates built on the sites of old factories. Posh shops appearing round the village green. Hanging baskets all over the place. But why do I still care? I haven't lived in the place for more than forty years. Why should it have this hold on me?

What puzzled me as I attended festivals was how differently so many newcomers felt about the canals. For them the attraction wasn't their solitude and seclusion, but the opportunity they offered for having a few drinks and a knees-up. Nothing wrong with that, of course. Even so, I couldn't help but find it sad. It was as if people had lost any community where they lived and sought it instead on the waterways among us old hands who've been boating for years. I sometimes speculate whether some of these people are actually committed to boating at all. I sometimes wonder if they might not be just as happy making friends with their neighbours.

I've noticed, I suppose, a certain middle-class uniformity falling over the waterways like a funeral pall over a coffin. Canal boats I remember from the past used to be idiosyncratic and unique – old lifeboats salvaged from God knows where, ancient cut-down wooden working boats patched with whatever would keep them afloat, or rowing skiffs of various sizes with a shed tacked on the top or a bit of canvas stretched over the front for shelter. Now boats are all much of a muchness, homogenous, each of them basically the same size, shape and design. And Em and I are as guilty as anyone. We once had a unique 30-foot home-made boat built out of a gas holder; now we've got a ubiquitous 60-foot traditional-style floating cottage.

The canals too, which were once unkempt – wild, shallow and remote – have now for the most part been restored, the towpaths cleared and the locks renovated so that there's no adventure left in them the way there once was, no sense of risk or discovery any more.

Em was right: why was I pressing on with this ludicrous project? Was it a painful process of forcing myself to come to terms with the present or was it a reluctant admission that canals, the last refuge of the 1960s hippy that I still essentially felt that I was, had been invaded and overwhelmed by outsiders. Or was it simply that I'd given up the fight and concluded that if I couldn't beat them I might as well join them?

'So what are you planning next?' Em asked. 'Will you go straight to Stafford now?'

'Of course not. I'm going to Cropredy; that's the plan, isn't it?'

For a moment she looked at me as if I was winding her up by cracking some tasteless joke. Then she exploded.

'Steve, you can't be serious, can you? If you'd set out for Cropredy four weeks ago you'd have been hard pressed to get there. But you don't have a hope of getting there now, not in two weeks, not in the state you're in. Besides, even if you did, you'd get there too late to get a decent mooring. This is madness, complete and utter madness. And what's more it's selfish. Who's to say that the next time you fall it won't be into some lock miles from anywhere or some weir where you'll drown before you know it? No, I'm not having it, worrying about you all the time. It isn't fair.'

And she walked off slamming the door behind her.

Of course, I could understand the point she was making, but like all arguments there are two ways of looking at it. I mean, it wasn't as if I was one of those blokes who went rock-climbing, or paragliding, or potholing, was it? I didn't spend my weekends bungee-jumping or off-piste snowboarding. There are risks with singlehanded boating, but it's not exactly a dangerous sport. You couldn't really see it figuring in the X Games, could you? Looked at this way, my decision to make a dash for Cropredy wasn't selfish: it was a sort of noble gesture which highlighted the domestic compromises I normally made.

Or something like that.

Besides, Cropredy was her idea in the first place; she was the one who wanted to go and see her precious Steve Winwood. If I'd got the idea lodged in my head so far that I was obsessed with it, well, that was her fault, wasn't it? It was hardly me being unfair.

Even so, if for no other reason than to maintain domestic harmony, I felt it prudent to accommodate her concerns at least part of the way. If she was worried about me boating alone, then I'd get some help. I rang my mate Dave who'd just got an early release for good behaviour after serving a forty-year stretch in the classroom. For the last couple of weeks he'd been kicking his heels, terrified he might run into one of his old Year 10s offering him a car wash at the supermarket. Dave was with me on my first canal holiday and has been around boats as long as I have.

'I was just about to call you,' he said straight away. 'Em rang me about going on the boat with you. Yes, I've got a few days free; I'd love to come. She said you were a bit reluctant to ask me, though I don't know why...'

So the next morning we drove north together and that night, the canal beginning to turn more industrial as it approached Stoke on Trent, we moored in the suburb of Hassel Green where we were so exhausted after the journey and the atrocious weather which had battered us through the afternoon we hadn't even got the energy to go for a drink in the local pub. This was a shame, since the local pub is said to be haunted. Mind you, we probably didn't miss much. So many pubs are said to be haunted nowadays that you feel cheated if you're not having a pint with a poltergeist somewhere in attendance. Still, it brings in the tourists, I suppose. And it's a ready-made excuse for when you drink too much and fall over. 'It was the ghost, I swear it was. Honestly, I felt something push me...'

Stoke stands astride the Trent and Mersey Canal like a man from Dyno-Rod looking for where the problem might be. At first the canal's a sewage pipe more than a mile and a half long passing through the Harecastle tunnel, 237 feet under the hill near Kidsgrove, one of the longest waterway tunnels in the country. After that, as it drops down past the station, it's more like an open drain, littered with cans of Tennants Extra and decorated with graffiti which the kids spray on the brickwork like dogs cocking their legs up against lamp posts. Finally, where they've built the new road, it turns into a concrete culvert: brutal and blockish, as if someone had bulldozed a channel through the middle of a 1960s council estate.

Dave and I have had problems with Stoke in the past. Once when we were passing through one of the outlying estates the local hooligans started catapulting half bricks at us using an enormous length of elastic they'd found somewhere. If one had hit us it would have taken our heads off. The police, to give them credit, were at the scene very fast. Even so, it's not much of a recommendation for a city, is it? Come to Stoke; when someone tries to kill you the police will be there quickly.

We had a sandwich before we went into the tunnel. It's not wide enough for boats to pass each other so you have to take turns, one direction at a time. This sometimes means waiting. We had to wait so long we were beginning to think the tunnel had collapsed, which I always worry it will do one day, so unstable does it seem, so narrow and constricted where the black, wet brickwork of the roof has bowed and buckled under the weight of the earth above. Eventually we got the go-ahead from the British Waterways' man who works in a cabin at the tunnel mouth controlling everything. That's when I discovered that *Justice*'s headlight wasn't working. This is par for the course for me going through the Harecastle; something always goes wrong. The last time I went through I forgot to turn on the headlight which, admittedly, wouldn't be much of a problem on a normal boat, but which on *Justice* meant I had to clamber up the slippery gunnels in the pitch black to turn it on. This latest problem with the headlight meant we had to miss our turn and hang around even longer while I fiddled with the electrics. Since I know nothing about electrics this didn't help much. Why I thought it would help isn't clear. Perhaps I was thinking of what they say about chimpanzees, that if you give them a typewriter and enough time they'll write *Hamlet*. Perhaps I was thinking if I just fiddled for long enough I'd be bound to find the right wire. If that was it, I was mistaken. An hour later I was still fiddling around, randomly pulling at odd bits of cabling. Eventually I gave up and rigged up an internal lamp from the cabin on an extension lead. Of course the minute we were inside the tunnel the headlight came back on of its own accord. Dave thought it was as a result of what I'd done and that I was damn clever.

I thought, as I have done so often before, on the canals and away from them, that life's a bad joke – though obviously there's someone up there who thinks it's funny.

Stoke came, Stoke went. The next day we were in Stone, one letter and 10 miles or so further south. I'm supposed to like Stone – everyone else does. There is a quaint boatyard like something off the set of a costume drama; there is a superb lockside pub called The Star Inn which is said to date from the fourteenth century; and there is an elegant canalside brewery building, one of two which used to grace the town until they were bought out and closed down by Bass (the basstards) during that period before Small is Beautiful when it was Big is Best.

Stone was always a boat town, even before the canal when its location on the River Trent made it important. After the canal was built in the 1770s it became more important yet, and for a time the canal company was based in the place. Recently – a bit like Braunston further south – it has reinvented itself for the new canal age. They build new boats in Stone now; they repair old ones. There's a hire-boat company there too, and in summer everyone seems to be on a boat – and presumably buying bits and bobs for them as well, because there's an enormous chandlery too.

In many ways Stone is a model canal town, though I've had a downer on it from years ago when I moored there one autumn. In those days when there were no mooring restrictions, and not enough craft cruising on the cut for it to make any difference, I left a boat with a cruiser deck there for a couple of weeks, but I got ill and finished up having to abandon it for a month. It rains a lot in Stone. I reckon it rained continuously the whole month I left the boat there.

A cruiser deck is open, and though it's advisable to cover it with a tarpaulin it can still leak if the wind gets under it. It leaked in Stone that time and when I came back the bilges were filled with so much water that the boat was close to sinking. She was just 3 or 4 inches off going down, maybe less. When I first saw her I almost had a seizure. She was listing at such an angle she looked as if she was about to tip over at any moment. I'd just come up from London on a train and I'd taken a taxi from Stoke, arriving in the early hours. It was raining that night too, I remember, hammering down horizontally. I told the taxi driver to hang around for a bit. I told him that I might need him to take me to a hotel if I couldn't sort this one out. I told him I might need pulling out of the cut as well if it went pear-shaped and I couldn't salvage her.

Yet there was no one in this celebrated canal town who'd bothered to do anything to prevent her getting into this state in the first place. Not one boat enthusiast of the many who must have passed during the time I was away who had thought – for the sake of charity if not pity – to empty her of few gallons of water with a bucket. No one cared. I couldn't understand it; I still can't. If you love canals, you love canal boats – any sort of canal boat, however run-down or shabby, however ill-kempt or apparently unloved.

Because all of us on canals know that there isn't such a thing as an unloved boat. There is only a boat waiting for someone to love it.

If I was walking anywhere – in the middle of the deepest countryside, say, in the middle of the night even – even if I was wearing my best suit because I'd just come from a wedding – even if I was drunk, because you do get drunk at weddings, don't you? – even if it was raining too, and I was up to my knees in mud – if I saw a boat close to sinking, any boat, I'd try to do something about it.

But they don't in Stone, apparently. Or they didn't twenty years ago. And this has coloured my view of the place ever since.

EIGHTEEN

Down the Trent and Mersey and onto the Coventry Canal

The bad weather had become a national news story. Part of the reason was that in its long-range forecast the Met Office had been injudicious enough to predict a 'barbecue summer' which, to be fair to them, it had been so far – give or take the odd bad spell, which you have to expect in England this time of the year. Now, though, the schools were out and it was holiday time. No one notices the weather when they're at work; now they couldn't help but notice it. It rained every day. It rained relentlessly. It rained incessantly. And not just fine, English rain either, the light, sappy type that caresses your face so softly it's like being sprayed by an atomiser. This was the hairy-arsed version, great muscular outbursts of the stuff pummelling you from the air like a power shower.

On the canals it cannoned onto the top of steel boats like artillery shells, exploding on impact. Sometimes the sky would darken and there would be ominous grumblings of thunder; then it would turn to hail which fractured into shrapnel as it landed. The fields had become a claggy no-man's-land of mud. In places the towpaths were running streams. No one was out boating; no one was out walking; no one was out at all if they could help it, even the hire boaters who you couldn't help feeling sorry for. This was their holiday, after all. Their once-a-year chance to enjoy the canals.

We were the exception. However bad it got, however heavily it came down, we just kept pushing on regardless. For my part, pride made me determined to get to Cropredy for the festival or die in the process, and that meant making as much use of Dave as I decently could in the few days he was with me. I don't think he knew what had hit him. At least I could keep dry steering the boat – and steering the boat was the only thing I could do with my dodgy ankle. I tucked myself into the traditional steerer's position on the step just inside the stern deck and closed the doors of the back cabin behind me. This insured I was sheltered from the waist down. The upper half of me I covered with a sou'wester and a waxed poncho of the sort used by sheep farmers in New Zealand, where I bought it. With all this I was completely protected, heated too from the warmth of the engine rising around me.

Poor Dave had it much harder. He was out in the elements preparing the locks: a sacrificial piece of blotting paper on two legs. Away from the shelter of the boat it was impossible for him to keep the rain off, however many clothes he was wearing. He'd brought a coat of his own and I lent him another to go over it, and a cape to go over that. But whatever he put on was neither here nor there; the rain somehow managed to percolate inside. It was a shame we couldn't have put it in bottles. With all the layers it had filtered through, it would have been purer than Volvic.

We pressed on down the shallow Trent valley, the river (a stone's throw to the west) narrow and meandering, little more than a stream at this stage – a shadow of what it becomes later as it passes through Nottingham and hurries to the Humber Estuary and the sea. We were into a rhythm now, the two of us, the way you get on the cut sometimes when you're working as a team, with each of you knowing your role and function and what you have to do next. Actually it was quite simple. All I had to do was steer the boat and keep myself cosy. Dave had to do everything else.

Stone was soon behind us and we passed into open countryside with only the distinctive black and white Trent and Mersey mileposts to track our progress south, like tiny chequered flags on the towpath marking off the distance to the inland port of Shardlow where the canal ends. We passed the small hamlet of Burston beyond the railway line that runs parallel to the canal, and soon we were in Weston upon Trent, an attractive village that straddles it and which – extraordinarily – was cited by the Russians in 1980 as a centre of anti-Soviet espionage.

Their allegations centred on an old World War Two military camp where the band leader Glenn Miller is reputed to have once performed. After 1945 it was taken over by the Ukrainian Youth Association and it subsequently became a cultural centre for expatriates – the sort of place, I suppose, where the kids could get together and play ping-pong while the old folk sipped vodka and waxed lyrical about the old country. According to the Soviets, though, the camp was being used by the CIA to train agents to discredit the Olympic Games, which were being held that year in Moscow.

And for all I know they might have been right. After finding a decommissioned nuclear bunker next to the cut in Shropshire I was ready to believe anything. OK, the idea of the CIA training anti-Olympic agents in this isolated village takes some swallowing. But so does accepting that there's a Ukrainian cultural centre in a place like this, miles from anywhere. I mean, it's hardly the last word in convenience, is it? Not the sort of place you'd use much if you lived in Manchester, say, or Glasgow. 'Nothing on the telly tonight. Why don't we pop out to the cultural centre in Weston?'

But I put all this to the back of my mind and pushed on through the driving rain, which hadn't eased since the morning. The miles passed; the deluge continued. It wasn't the intensity of the rain I minded, it was the malice with which it fell: every last drop determined to do what damage it could like some squadron of crazed kamikaze pilots going for the kill.

Poor Dave was soaked to the skin by now and as miserable as sin. There should be a word for this condition: it should be called 'skinsin'.

Eventually we arrived at the villages of Great Haywood and Little Haywood with which, as far as I know, I have absolutely no connection, despite sharing a name with them. Between the two is the splendid Shugborough Hall which we could just about make out across the fields through the thick mists now enveloping the valley. Shugborough is the ancestral home of the Anson family – the earls of Lichfield; the royal photographer Patrick Lichfield, the fifth earl, who died in 2005, is its most famous recent occupant. It's an imposing old pile, a bit like Huddersfield railway station except bigger and whiter as if it's just had a fresh coat of Sandtex.

And like the Ukrainian centre in Weston it's a bit odd, too. Or at least the garden is. Or at least that bit of the garden called the

Shepherd's Monument. This is a sandstone memorial in the shape of a blocked-off doorway with columns on either side, a decorative pediment over the top and a bas relief of Poussin's painting *The Shepherds of Arcadia* in the middle. Underneath is an inscription which has been described as one of the world's top uncracked cybertexts.

It has eight letters flanked by a further two on either side, separated and dropped slightly like this:

O U O S V A V V
D   M

Over the years the solution to this enigma has occupied the brain cells of some illustrious men. Charles Darwin is said to have had a go solving it, as did Charles Dickens and the potter Josiah Wedgwood. It still preoccupies people today; more than it ever did, in fact, since it's been suggested that it's a key clue to the whereabouts of the Holy Grail, the cup said to have been used by Christ at the Last Supper.

And ever since Dan Brown's *Da Vinci Code*, thousands of people have become obsessed by the topic, so that on any day of the week – even when the rain is belting down as it was when Dave and I passed – you'll be sure to find one or two devotees in Crocs and Black Sabbath T-shirts poring over the letters as if they were a religious text. Which, of course, to some people they are.

Even the professionals have got in on the act now. A few years back a married couple who used to work as government code breakers at Bletchley Park during World War Two attempted to solve the puzzle. He concluded it was a secret message from a heretical sect called the Priory of Sion and that it meant 'Jesus (as Deity) Defy'. She came to a different conclusion, though.

She thought it was a Latin poem to a departed loved one that translated as 'Best Wife, Best Sister, Widower Most Loving Vows Virtuously.'

Makes you wonder how we ever cracked the Enigma, doesn't it?

That night we moored in Rugeley, in the shadow of the cooling towers of the power station that dominate the skyline in that part of the world. As far as I know no one's ever accused Rugeley of harbouring CIA spies. Neither has it got any incomprehensible cyphers on its walls, unless you count some of the graffiti at the back of Morrisons. In other words, Rugeley is a normal place, or about as normal as you get in contemporary Britain. It's an old pit town and a bit rough around the edges, but at least you know where you stand with it. A few years back Em and I were having a drink in a local pub when a youth staggered through the bar with his eye hanging out. It says a lot for Rugeley that no one sitting around drinking that night seemed to think that this was particularly unusual. It says a lot, too, about our relationship to alcohol that we didn't react either. We sat and calmly finished our drinks and afterwards we'd probably have had another, except that a second youth steamed through the place with a knife looking for the first one. Presumably to finish him off we thought, though we didn't hang around long enough to find out.

Rugeley has a bit of a problem with murderers. It had a doctor in the 1850s called William Palmer, who was suspected of poisoning fourteen or fifteen people including his wife, his mother-in-law and his four kids; though in that fastidious way typical of the Victorians no one seemed inclined to do much about curtailing his hobby until he overstepped the mark and killed a man. Even so, as a member of the professional classes he'd have probably got away with that as well if there hadn't been money involved.

It came out in court that Palmer had been to Shrewsbury races with his victim who'd won a fortune of nearly £2,000, which the doctor attempted to collect from the bookmakers afterwards. This wasn't exactly a smart move for an educated man who should have known that bookies will do anything to avoid paying out. Eventually he was arrested, convicted at the Old Bailey and hanged in public in Stafford, a gesture doubtless intended as a deterrent to other doctors in the future although it obviously didn't work particularly well with Harold Shipman.

The most famous murder on the canals system happened in Rugeley too, in 1839, when thirty-seven-year-old Christina Collins was pulled from the cut dead after being brutally assaulted by the crew of a boat carrying her as a passenger to London. The story, transposed to the Oxford Canal, was adapted by detective writer Colin Dexter in his book *The Wench is Dead*, the plot of which has Inspector Morse solving the crime more than a century later from his hospital bed as he lies recovering from a perforated ulcer.

In reality, the contemporary police were onto this case fast enough not to need help from any source, let alone a twentieth-century fictional one; and two men were eventually hanged for the crime and a third transported for life. Collins herself is buried in the local St Augustine's churchyard, though her legacy continues in the folklore that surrounds her. Blood is said to still seep from the canalside steps she was carried up after being taken from the water, and accounts of this happening persist even though the actual steps have been replaced many times since.

I don't know if I believe in these sorts of things. Even so, I know I wouldn't want to put myself in the position of having to find out.

So, later that evening, as Dave prepared to leave for the train to take him back home, I said to him: 'I'm not walking up that towpath with you to the station, not for all the tea in China.'

'What about for a pint then?'

'Oh go on, if you insist,' I said. 'But you'll have to owe it me. I'm not drinking in Rugeley again. I think I'd rather meet the ghost.'

It was still bucketing down as we left the boat and there was a sharp wind coming down the canal, working the water up into wavelets which slapped noisily against the hull. The towpath was deserted and almost pitch black from the dark rainclouds hovering motionless above us like so many ghouls in billowing black capes.

'Are you sure you don't want to walk the street way?' I asked. 'There are lights on the streets.'

'The towpath's half the distance,' said Dave. 'Stop moaning, you soft jessie. The haunted steps are a mile away near the aqueduct. We're nowhere near them.'

'But she might wander further afield. She might come down this way on nights like this.'

'She doesn't come any way,' said Dave. 'She's a ghost. She's not real. And even if she was real, she's not a haunting ghost, she's an oozing ghost. It's just her blood people see on the steps, nothing more.' But then he went quiet. The wind seemed to have got up even more in the time we'd been walking. It was playing in the trees now, creating a low drone like the lament of a lost soul.

He suddenly stopped. 'What's that?'

'What?' My heart stopped with him. 'It's just the wind, isn't it?'

'No, not the wind. Over there.' He pointed towards a bush on the other side of the water.

'What do you think it is?'

'I think it's a bush,' he said. 'But we should be careful. It might be an ambush.'

And with that appalling apology for a joke, typical of him, he went tripping up the towpath cackling to himself.

After he'd got on the train I walked the long way back and got lost, so that I was still walking around the deserted streets of Rugeley half an hour later. This meant that at least I got a taste of what Dave had been putting up with all day. Without the protection of the boat, the poncho or the sou'wester, I got as soaked as he had, worse maybe because the rain seemed to be coming down more furiously with every hour that passed.

I wondered would it ever stop?

The cat loved the rain. She couldn't get enough of it. She'd sometimes be curled up asleep in the chair, lost in fireside dreams of bowls of biscuits and scurrying creatures and dark, secret woodland places where every fallen leaf promised a new delight. But then she'd hear the rain falling on the roof and her ear would cock up as if it was a radar mast grafted to her head; and before I knew it she'd be out on the deck biting at the drops; or lying on her back writhing about, letting them fall on her stomach; or just sitting there letting them encase her, behaving as you or I might do in a shower.

This caused problems. Normally she'd have come in from her night-time wanderings by the time I woke in the morning, or if not she'd come in as soon as she heard me when she knew there was a half-decent chance of getting the feeding bowl stocked up for the day. If it was raining, however, she was markedly reluctant to come in at all.

She'd sit on the deck trying to ignore me in the hopes I'd go away. Or she'd develop an acute interest in a berry that had dropped from an overhanging tree, or a twig that had been brought in by the wind. She'd swipe at it with her paw, or move it around the deck in intricate patterns, apparently fascinated with it. If I showed any intention of picking her up, though, she'd be off in a flash, aware of what I was doing even before I was.

All this was irritating enough, but more so in Rugeley where a few years back Em and I had lost another cat of ours for a couple of days while it went off looking for a bit of local rough. I was concerned about Kit doing the same thing. But I was concerned about her wasting my time, too. I was cruising to a schedule. I couldn't afford to mess about with cats.

The day after Dave left, I got up at first light. Still unable to move around normally with my ankle, I'd realised that I'd have to make up with steady endurance what I wasn't going to be able to do with athletic prowess. Travelling at standard canal speeds it would take about five or six days to get to Cropredy. But I was single-handing. And I was nursing the injury. If I was going to do it in that time I'd need to keep going longer. I'd have to cruise for twelve hours a day – more than that if I was to have proper rests.

What I didn't need was a cat holding me up. That morning, though, Kit was particularly uncooperative, probably because the rain was particularly heavy, which is the way she likes it.

So we started a sort of intricate dance in which we moved around each other but never got close. It was like the hokey-cokey, which my mum and dad used to do every Christmas after they'd run out of light ales and started on the snowballs. I put my left leg in and my left leg out; I put it in and out and I shook it all about. Then she'd run off. So I'd do the same with the right leg until she ran off again. Eventually I could have screamed with frustration. I mean, I don't mind a joke. But not the same joke. Not a joke played on me time and time again.

Eventually I realised that this wasn't going to get me anywhere and that I was going to have to be patient and let her do things at her own pace. But when was it ever any different with this cat? I had shopping to do, anyhow. I'd have another cup of tea and wait until the supermarket opened.

This was the moment at which she hopped back into the cabin.

She shook herself down as if making a point. Then, soaking wet, she jumped up on the table and began to butt my chin affectionately with her head.

Coming out of Rugeley the rain-drenched pigeons sat dripping on the telegraph wires like notes from the score of Handel's Water Music.

I passed through Armitage where they make toilet bowls and where there was once a tunnel which collapsed years ago, leaving for passage a long sandstone cutting no wider than a boat. The stone is red and damp and it feels like the edge of a matchbox, but looks like blood on your fingers. On the long cutting towards Fradley I saw a kingfisher flashing among the luxuriant birch trees along the edge of Ravenshaw Wood, the silver of the bark and the flash of autumn orange on its breast the only colour in the countryside on such a drab, unrelenting day. At Fradley itself I turned onto the Coventry Canal and that night I pulled up beyond the railway bridge at Huddlesford Junction, where the Wyrley and Essington Canal once used to emerge after its meandering journey from Birmingham.

No sooner had I turned off the engine than the rain stopped. It stopped suddenly, as if on cue. As if someone had blown a whistle or fired a gun. Or turned off the tap. The sun came out immediately afterwards, and when it set it bathed the countryside in the colour of the Armitage stone, although more luminous and incandescent.

Kit came out eventually. She looked around her and I could see she was sulking because it was dry. She had a disconsolate look on her face which I had learnt to read.

But then she spotted an inviting spinney nearby and she was off.

NINETEEN

Back on the Oxford Canal again

What was it I said about travelling on a narrowboat? About it being a philosophical thing? About the journey being more important than the arrival? Forget it. Forget every word. I was being pompous; I was talking nonsense. The idea of narrowboating as a leisure activity – drinks at the pub and barbies on the towpath, that sort of thing – all that's a modern concoction. It was certainly never like that when the canals were built. They were the motorways of their time; and narrowboats were like lorries banging up and down the cut loaded with coal and pig iron and anything else you'd need to make a backward agricultural country into the biggest powerhouse economy on the globe.

The canals can sometimes get you like that, though: they can lull you into a stupor so you forget you're in the present. Some boaters play along with it. A few play it up. They take it to extremes. They buy old working boats with voluminous holds and they sardine themselves into the tiny cabins at the back of them, reproducing the privations of the old boat people in the name of heritage. The women wear long Victorian dresses and the men tie red bandanas round their necks as if this were some sort of authentic waterways costume rather than a bit of fancy dress which someone knocked together a few years back for a laugh.

But you can't dispense with the present so easily, and certainly not by these cheap tricks. Canals are a great place to unwind – the fastest way of slowing down, as they say. But a narrowboat isn't the Tardis. It doesn't take you to other worlds, let alone other ages and if you think it does, sooner or later you're in for a shock.

I was in for a shock on this section of my journey. More than one, in fact.

I flew down the Coventry like Meat Loaf on a Harley. That night, after more than twelve hours on the go, I moored at the top of the flight of locks at Atherstone in Warwickshire. The night after that, with another ten hours' cruising under my belt, I stopped near the short tunnel at Newbold on Avon, where in the 1820s a modernisation programme aimed at cutting out time-consuming bends left two pubs beached on a small road which was once the canal.

The weather had improved since Dave had gone. The rain had finally eased off, and at last I felt confident putting away the poncho and hanging up the sou'wester. For periods the sun even revealed itself, peeking uncertainly through the clouds like someone stealing a glimpse of the morning through their bedroom curtains. Its appearance was enough to warm up the day and the fields soon began to steam gently in the heat, the atmosphere becoming humid. It was almost as if

I could taste the countryside in the dampness of the woods and the impenetrable green hedges along the towpaths which were thick with flowers: tall golden rod, purple wild basil and creeping bindweed, its blooms the shape of white wedding bells.

The corn was beginning to ripen in the fields and for the first time in weeks I began to remember that it was still summer. Until now I'd imagined that if I got to Cropredy at all it would be like so many English music festivals at this time of the year: washed out and knee-deep in mud. Now, for the first time, I allowed myself the indulgence of thinking more positively. Maybe – who knows? – it might even be dry. Maybe – whisper it softly – it could be warm.

At Hillmorton, near Rugby, where the canal edges around a plantation of radio masts, a young guy accosted me at the bottom of the locks. He was in his thirties, dressed in pressed slacks and trainers with a jacket tossed over his arm. A floppy lick of chestnut hair fell across his face giving him the look of Hugh Grant in a low-budget movie – though since all Hugh Grant's movies tend to be low budget that doesn't really say much.

'Are you that, you know, that guy?' he asked. 'You know, the one who writes. It's for a magazine, isn't it, you know? You write books as well, don't you?'

This was not great detective work on his part. My name, along with Em's, is painted in traditional fashion on the side of *Justice*. I am used to this level of recognition as people stare at it in a daze trying to work out where they've seen it before. This guy at least had gone a step further. He'd roughly identified what I did and it was enough for me to feel disproportionately flattered.

We chatted for a while, during which time he was unduly complimentary. I can't deny it; I found it gratifying, like Kit does when I tickle her stomach. I was at the stage she gets to with her legs waving in the air and her modesty compromised when he said, 'I know it's a bit cheeky of me to ask, but would you mind signing one of your books? I've got one at home if you wouldn't mind hanging on while I pop back and get it. I'll only be a few minutes…'

By now I was so pumped up with vanity I was like a balloon about to burst. I waited at the bottom for him, but when, after twenty minutes or so, he didn't show I went up the locks and waited for him at the top where it was more convenient to tie up.

There are three locks in the flight at Hillmorton and they're standard narrow width, though unusual in that they're doubled up in pairs which allow boats to move in both directions at the same time. They have wonderful paddle gear too. The paddle gear is the mechanism that allows you to control the water flow with your windlass or lock key, and the design is so commonplace that generally you hardly notice it. But at Hillmorton the old cast-iron cogs and ratchets look so crude but are so precisely made they could be exhibits in an industrial museum. They are greased to a satanic black and sit on their own pedestals like display stands, all the more beautiful for being entirely functional.

I must have waited around for another hour, but he didn't show, the bastard. He didn't show then and I doubt that if I'd have hung around for the rest of the day he'd have showed, either. In fact, I think if I was moored in Hillmorton now I'd still be waiting for him. As for his flattery, that was probably about as genuine as the book of mine he said he'd got at home. Then I thought of the bloke in Market Drayton who'd walked off to the lavatory and left me, too. What was it with this tendency of people to disappear in the middle of conversations with me? Was it something to do with my face? Or something in my manner? I was beginning to feel paranoid.

I rang Em hoping she'd reassure me. The reception on my mobile was bad; I could barely hear what she was saying. Eventually we were cut off. Or perhaps she hung up on me. She hadn't been too keen to talk in the first place, it was true. Something about a meeting. A report she had to write by the end of the day.

She may have said something too, about me needing to pull myself together. Though perhaps I got that wrong. Maybe she was just asking about the weather…

That night I stopped just outside of Braunston on that exquisite stretch of canal between the M45 and Willoughby, where the Northamptonshire fields are corrugated with the patterns of ancient strip farms that have never yielded to the plough. Once, one autumn many years ago, I passed here when mallards that had flown to Britain for the summer were gathering to migrate. A whole meadow of maybe ten or twelve acres was teeming. There were hundreds of them, perhaps as many as a thousand; and the sound of their raucous, boisterous squabbling was deafening.

Periodically a random group would suddenly take off as if at some prearranged signal and I'd watch them disappearing out of sight, evaporating into the skyline. Conversely every now and again a small group of four or five would fly in and circle once or twice overhead before landing in the canal, sliding into the water with grace and elegance the way ducks do. Though they can make a hash of it too, sometimes, especially landing on ice when they don't know it's there so that they go sliding across the surface rebounding off the banks in slapstick fashion like feathery curling stones. That day I stopped the boat mid-stream and spent half an hour or so watching them. They took absolutely no notice of me. Eventually I started up the engine and left. They took no notice of that, either. I felt very insignificant and overwhelmed by my insignificance.

We humans think we're very important in the scheme of things. We think we're above nature rather than a part of it. It disconcerts us when other creatures don't defer to our ascendancy.

The canal was frenetic the following day because it was that that time of the week when the hire boats head back to base. The period of the school holidays is the pinnacle of the hire season and this part of the Midlands is the most popular area in the country for cruising. There are about half a dozen companies nearby, and although they stagger their changeover day to minimise excessive congestion, it's not possible to avoid it completely, and things can get busy on Fridays and Saturdays when everyone's rushing to get home.

It can be scary having so many inexperienced boaters on the water at the same time. Most hire boat crews are perfectly competent, more competent than a lot of the crews of private craft, in fact; for whether you can afford a boat of your own has got nothing to do with how well you can handle one, and some of these folk have been renting for decades. But novice boaters – complete beginners – are a different matter. When they first go out, they know nothing, but they know they know nothing and they are cautious as a result. Now, after a week or two, they think they know everything there is to know about canals and boats and they get foolhardy. They're full of reckless confidence. They'll edge into narrow spaces which a few short days before would have terrified them. They'll effect manoeuvres of extravagant complexity which would had have panicked them at the start of their trip. They'll steer reading the paper or changing the baby. Sometimes they'll even let the baby steer. Changeover day can be a nightmare.

I was coming up the Napton flight and feeling cheerful because I realised that after a week of relentless travelling, early starts and late finishes, worrying every moment about my ankle and whether it would stay the course, I was now so close to Cropredy I could be confident I'd get there on time. It was a gorgeous day too, the first I'd had for weeks: the sun shining consistently rather than in bursts, the sky rained-out so there was barely a cloud to be seen. The steady stream of boats coming down the flight made it easier for me too, because we work to a one-up-one-down system on the cut, and as boats came out of locks I could move straight in without the bother of having to open the gates myself.

I'd just steered into one and was edging forward to kiss my bow against the top gates. This is a standard procedure going uphill in locks. You make contact and then increase the power of your engine to keep your boat stable against the surge created by the thousands of gallons of water which flood in once you've opened the paddles.

This time, though, it didn't happen in this way. This time it went horribly wrong. I was hardly in the lock before the gates I'd just passed through slammed shut behind me. Before I knew what was happening two teenage girls had opened the paddles above me and were releasing a torrent of water into the enclosed space. The boat heaved uncontrollably, rocking and bumping about until the suction of the surge began to suck it forward, accelerating it towards the top gates. A collision was a guaranteed certainty even at this stage. No engine can hold you against the power of that amount of water.

I clambered onto the boat roof as fast as I could and hauled myself up the lock ladder. What I saw there horrified me. On the end of the lock beam was a little girl, perhaps four years old. She was in her nightdress. She had pulled it down around her knees the way little girls do. She was cuddling a floppy rabbit.

Justice crashed against the front gate with the full weight of her twenty tons. There was the sickening sound of breaking glass and china from inside the cabin. At the same time the little girl was tossed in the air like a rag doll. Everything went into slow motion. She somersaulted like a gymnast, and seemed to hang in the air there for what felt like an eternity. As if she could fly. She seemed resistant to gravity. But then – suddenly – she dropped onto the brickwork below with a dull thud like a sack of cement falling off a lorry. Thank God, she landed on her shoulder rather than her head. She was hurt, but she wasn't badly injured. If she had landed on her head the impact might have killed her. If she'd landed on the raised brick footholds nearby, it definitely would have done.

Yet not one of the adults on the boat in charge of her was even in a position to see the accident, let alone prevent it happening. Even the two teenage girls who I took to be her sisters ran off, vaguely aware that they were the cause of whatever had occurred. So it was me who was left to comfort the girl. Me who had to take her back to her boat and tell her blithely unaware father that his daughter seemed fine, but that maybe to be on the safe side he ought to get her checked out by a doctor as soon as he could.

'A doctor?' he said. 'Has something happened?'

What can you do in circumstances like this when people are so unaware of how close a brush they have had with tragedy? If – God forbid – something more serious had happened to the girl, it would have been no comfort to me that technically I was blameless. After all, I'm an experienced boater. They're just hirers. Why should they know about the turbulent dangers lying just under the serene surface of canals?

The point was brought home to me with a vengeance the next day when I passed through the beautiful Varney's Lock on the approach to Cropredy. There I discovered that just twenty-four hours before a hirer had been dragged dead from the water after falling off her boat. Talk on the towpath was that the same thing which had happened to me had happened to her. Her crew had opened the lock paddles too fast, and as the boat had been sucked forward in the lock she'd slammed her engine into reverse and had gone crashing backwards against the bottom gate, throwing her into the water and under the propeller.

No one or nothing except ignorance was to blame for the incident, but all the same maybe those of us who are experienced boaters should take some measure of responsibility for it. After all, we know that canals can be dangerous places. We know it because we are aware of what hirers are not: that a significant number of us die on the canals each year. Sometimes it's incidents like this; sometimes drink is involved; sometimes our boats are badly maintained and we blow ourselves up or suffocate ourselves with carbon monoxide from our fires. But we don't like to talk about it, we feel uncomfortable. We don't want the health and safety police crawling all over the cut more than they already are, putting up fences and erecting unsightly signs all over the place. And we don't want to frighten ourselves more than we have to either, let alone unsettle hirers who are just out to have a good holiday.

So we stay silent while the most appalling things are happening in front of our eyes. Kids playing on the roof as boats approach bridges, young people dangling their legs over the bows, kids – like the ones I'd experienced – left unsupervised at locks. Is it our English reserve that prevents us from saying anything? Is it just our middle-class reticence?

After the Napton incident I witnessed another shocking episode as I came back through Fradley Junction on my way north again after the Cropredy Festival. A couple of teenagers, a boy and a girl, were messing around on the swing bridge there. Playing chicken as they slammed it open and shut. Daring each other to leave their legs in until the last moment.

Yet next to the bridge a boat was moored. And on the front deck the owners sat watching everything. 'Why didn't you stop them?' I asked as I went by. 'Why didn't you tell them to leave it alone?'

'Nothing to do with me,' the man replied. 'It's not my responsibility.'

His position was reinforced by his wife when she was challenged by someone in a following boat who, like me, had seen the incident and been horrified at their indifference to it.

'When I hear them scream, I'll call the ambulance,' she said.

TWENTY

The Cropredy Festival

Some things in this life you don't do a second time because once is more than enough, thank you very much. Think eating tripe. Think reading about George Michael's personal life. Some things, though, you don't do again because they were so perfect the first time round that they represent a highpoint in your life, and you know that however often you repeat the experience it can never be as good again. This is how it was with Em and me and the Cropredy Festival. Our last visit there – our only visit there – was unforgettable, a gilded milestone of our past. Why should we ever want to go again? Why should we want to compromise such precious memories? It had been in the 1980s: the grass was somehow greener then, the sun somehow brighter, the music somehow more compelling. We were young, of course – that's what it was. It could never be as good again because we'd never be as young again.

That year, when the festival was only a two- rather than a three-day affair, we cruised up Friday evening from Banbury with some friends on another boat; and as we came around the wide bend which skirts the hill after Slat Mill lock we could hear tantalising fragments of faraway music seeping from the stage, enticing us to the site. We felt like the sailors of classical myth must have felt hearing the Sirens, and like them we were compulsively drawn to the sound.

In those days it was no problem to moor in Cropredy during the festival; I doubt there were more than half a dozen boats there that year. The night was balmy, gently warm. We sat on the grass near the front and soon the dark evening began to envelop us, the light from the stage reflecting on our pale faces so that the black field became a dapple of ghosts in the gloom. John Martyn was playing. His voice was hypnotic, a strange and strangled instrument with the quality of another world about it. Sometimes it crackled like electricity on a power line; sometimes it was like a long, low lament of a lost soul in Hades. His lyrics were poetry: verbal honey on viscous waves of solid air. We were taking our time, we were walking the line. We didn't want to know about evil, we only wanted to know about love. The evening turned to night and then, somehow, almost without us having noticed, it was suddenly day again and the sun was shining once more and the music was still playing like I have never heard it play before or since.

'Are you really sure you want to go back?' I asked Em when she'd first suggested the idea. 'This is a fragile past you're reaching for; it may crumble in your hand.'

'I want to see Steve Winwood,' she said. 'I've never seen him play live.'

'Is it just that? Are you sure? It's not to do with getting old, is it?'

'I just want to go,' she said.

Although I couldn't stop adjacent to the festival site as I'd done the first time, I still managed to moor *Justice* close by – much closer than I'd have thought possible arriving so late. Em came up a couple of days later. It was a glorious, placid evening when she arrived, an unusual sunset saturating the sky with cloud strata of different hues, layered like a strudel. There wasn't a breath of wind in the air. The next day we met up with some friends who were to stay with us on board for the weekend. The weather had improved beyond my wildest imaginings. It had turned idyllic; as idyllic as it had been all those years ago. It was summer again. It was summer 1985.

At the festival site I was struck by the plethora of flags and food stalls all over the place. I was struck too, by the numbers of people sitting on collapsible canvas chairs. These hadn't been invented when Em and I were here before and no one would have been seen dead using them even if they had. The stage was much bigger than it used to be too. It had video screens and huge banks of speakers on either side so the crowds at the back could see and hear everything as clearly as those at the front. I guess this was a necessity because there were far more people than there'd been before – 15,000, maybe 20,000, perhaps more.

On one level it all seemed very different. But go to the front, closer to the performers as we did, lie back on the grass and squint against the glare of the sun, and not that much had really changed. The same sort of people who'd been around then were around now, though most of them were young people, certainly people younger than us, people not even born in the 1980s. Girls with braided, dyed hair in floaty dresses, or in combats and army fatigues or in tie-dyed skirts, sequined and bejewelled, their wrists heavy with bangles, their fingers creaking with rings. Blokes in top hats, in crochet hats, straw hats and felt hats; in T-shirts of every conceivable design, in shorts and jeans and some of them in fairy dresses too, with gossamer wings sprouting from their shoulders. There were hippies, goths and eco-warriors; bikers, folkies and punks. There were New Agers with their beards knotted and plaited and curled and back-combed; and even some other Old Agers like us, still tuning in and dropping out after all these years, still flying the flag (though not literally) for a world long past. It was a great car crash of contemporary style, a chaotic fusion of everything which is today.

And yet the most intriguing thing about the festival – and others which are like it, such as Glastonbury – is that although they mirror the present, and although the present is so unremittingly urban, they take place in the middle of the countryside which stamps them with their own particular character. Cropredy is not a festival that could take place in a city park or a suburb. It is in the countryside because it is of the countryside. The countryside's intrinsic to the way it feels and the way it looks. Beyond the press of the crowd and the prancing performers and the stage and the speakers and screens; beyond this one field lost and stranded in a shallow bowl of undulating Oxfordshire; beyond the tent villages which grow up in fields around the site, there are other fields for as far as the eye can see.

But then, it's funny like that isn't it, England? From the crashing coasts of Cornwall in the south to the windswept Northumberland beaches close to the Scottish border, fields are what this country is made of. Field upon field, endless ranks of them, one after the other. Fields which have seen all this festival nonsense and much more besides, fields which in their time have presided over moots and parliaments, over rites and rituals, battles and reconciliations, over myriad harvests and countless sunsets. It's the way this country is: a realm of Albion with its history layered, era upon era, each past the foundation for the next, each present superseded by another: a chaotic fusion of everything which was yesterday.

The crowd had thickened by the time Steve Winwood came on to play, so we had to stand for his set, though we were close enough to see him clearly. He was electrifying, his unmistakable voice as soulful as ever, barely changed in almost fifty years. Em was transfixed.

'I don't care about the rest of the festival,' she said. 'It was worth coming just for that.'

A couple of evenings later, as always, Fairport Convention closed proceedings with 'Meet on the Ledge', their lament to lost friends. We sang along to that, just as we had all those years ago at our first festival. It was more poignant now than it had been then, though. Then, young, I don't think we'd really understood the song. Now, older, we've lost too many friends ourselves and we're too close to being blown off the mountain with the wind not to take it personally.

Some people measure out their lives in coffee spoons; some measure them out in music festivals.

Cropredy transforms itself for three days every year but it very quickly gets back to being a normal country village again. By late Sunday afternoon all but a few stragglers wandering around lost clutching rucksacks had left for home, and we and our two friends sat on the deck in the sunshine over the remains of roast beef and summer pudding.

Suddenly there was a great splash in the water beside us, as if someone had thrown a brick in our direction. We all recoiled, then stared into the water puzzled at what it could have been.

As we watched, the water exploded once more and we glimpsed the flash of the tail fin of an enormous carp. In fact, there were three of them hanging around scavenging for food, huge brutes the size of legs of lamb.

I don't know if carp have got teeth, but I wouldn't have wanted to fall in and find out. Take it from me, those beasts in the canal at Cropredy that day didn't need teeth. They were so big they could have sucked you to death.

Dave came up later that evening on the second part of his mercy mission for my ankle. Actually, it hadn't been too bad for a day or two. At least it didn't hurt. Well, it didn't hurt until I put any weight on it. Then it hurt like hell. I was relieved to be leaving Cropredy though; I always am pleased to leave a place after mooring more than a few days. Kit was the same. She liked the canals but she liked them because of their tranquillity and remoteness. A music festival wasn't exactly her bowl of Whiskas. The noise was a cacophony to her ears; there were too many unhygienic long-hairs around, and as a long-hair herself she knew the importance of careful personal grooming.

We set out early the next morning for the slow climb out of the Thames valley, the next leg of my trip. It was a journey which would take me towards the Midlands and on to Stafford where I was scheduled to attend a rally being held by an Internet boating club I'm involved with.

No, you didn't read that wrongly: an Internet boating club. This fusion of canal cruising – a pastime rooted in an eighteenth-century transport system – and the world of cutting-edge twenty-first century IT, may at first glance seem improbable, but it's not as odd as it appears. Though we may give the impression of being essentially solitary sorts, easy with our own company, we narrowboaters are at heart a gregarious breed; and when we get together, released from the constraints of polite society, we like nothing better than indulging ourselves in boaty stuff.

We can bore for England talking about propeller sizes or engine oil-changing regimes; about the best routes through Birmingham or bridge numbers on the Coventry Canal. Trust me, trainspotters have nothing on us; stamp collectors are Renaissance men by comparison. Put a few of us in a room together and we'll chatter away for hours like a raucous flock of starlings. The Internet allows us to do all this 24/7, without actually being anywhere close to each other. It's a secret vice; something best done in private like watching Corrie or readjusting your underwear. I used to do it when I was at work but I got caught once. It could have been embarrassing until I told them I was surfing porn sites. It was a close shave though.

We live in our own world, we Internet narrowboaters, but that's OK because we know each other there. However once a year, just to make sure, we hold a convocation of the brotherhood at which we enact mystic rituals, indulge ourselves in dark arts and drink large quantities of beer. Even as Dave and I ploughed north, thousands of us were heading to Stafford from all points of the compass. Well, hundreds were. Well, OK, about fifteen of us were, maybe twenty – which isn't a bad turn-out for an event it might take you a couple of weeks to get to.

Later that day we reached the summit of the Oxford Canal: a twisting, turning, writhing, squirming pound of ten and a half isolated miles which is hauntingly beautiful in its seclusion, though it's tortuous going, especially in a boat like *Justice* which is too deep-drafted for the shallow water. The canal snakes around following the contours of the land, coiling one way and then the other in a series of blind bends on which there will invariably be a bridge where it's impossible for two boats to pass. They're hell to navigate, because by the time you've seen something coming your way it's too late to do anything except panic.

You have to wonder about these bridges. I know they're a remnant of a different world where meandering roads punctuated the English countryside, carefree in their abandon; but somehow I can't help thinking that their positioning at these inconvenient points on the cut is an ancient joke, the punchline of which stretches out to us across the centuries. I guess deciding the course of a canal could become as boring as any other job after a while. Why shouldn't surveyors have a laugh like everyone else? I can imagine them chuckling to themselves as they positioned bridges at spots where they were likely to cause maximum inconvenience. What a wheeze that must have been. What a way of making a dull Friday afternoon pass a tad quicker.

We came down Napton locks where recently I'd had such a scare with the young girl. The hire boats had thinned out by now; the season was getting later. We had the flight to ourselves and we made a steady descent in the shadow of the hilltop windmill that stands imperiously dominating the landscape.

They farm buffalo in this part of the world, presumably to make mozzarella cheese for pizzas. Half way down the flight there's a sizeable herd grazing very close to the locks.

'What's the difference between a buffalo and a bison?' Dave asked with the easy familiarity of someone you've known for years.

'They're different species,' I said. 'The American buffalo – the bison – isn't really a buffalo at all. There are only two types of real buffalo, the African and Asian water buffalo...'

'No,' he said, interrupting me. 'You can't wash your hands in a buffalo.'

Coming round Hawkesbury Junction on the outskirts of Coventry we decided to moor overnight, squeezing into a space before the turn next to a hippy boat. I call it that because of the psychedelic design of its paintwork, all purple whorls and *Magic Roundabout* flowers; but I could just as easily, and more rudely, have called it a squat boat. Its roof was covered in broken toys and pots full of scrubby herbs and branches of trees salvaged for the fire from the canal; and across its open back deck was a selection of rusty engine parts making it look like something that would have been more at home in a scrap yard than on a canal.

The crew, though, were a delight. There were two couples and five or six well-brought-up kids who may have been holidaying together, but who were just as likely to be living together in a commune. They came over and helped us get settled and we chatted for a while about where we were going and where we'd come from. Like us, they'd been at Cropredy for the festival.

It was an unusual set-up, even for the canals where unusual is often the norm. It was so alternative, so unorthodox, so... so 1960s. But what struck me most about them wasn't their lifestyle but their impeccable RP accent, which was like something out of a documentary about the House of Windsor. It was George Bernard Shaw who said that an Englishman had only to open his mouth to betray his class and background; and believe me, listening to this lot talk you weren't exactly reminded of backstreet Northern terraces and boiled black pudding.

They reminded me of a cricket team I used to play against in the 1970s. They all worked for a Marxist London bookshop and it was a match I always used to dread because I knew it would invariably be a hard-fought game with balls flying about all over the place at dangerous speeds. The bookshop team all had long hair and spouted revolution, but whenever they appeared at the crease it was impossible to say which was more impeccable: their whites or their blocking defence off the back foot, both the legacy of their public school past.

Dave left me at Nuneaton to go back to London. Or perhaps he left me at Atherstone or somewhere else. Maybe we'd arranged that he should; maybe he just got fed up with locking and slipped off the boat without me noticing, the bastard. Either way I was back to single-handing again, taking everything as steadily as I could to avoid my ankle giving up on me once more. It wasn't the potential pain which worried me, or even the inconvenience. It was just that I couldn't take another sanctimonious lecture from Em who, at the slightest suggestion of a twinge, would be sure to play her trump card and remind me that she'd told me so. The prospect made me proceed very carefully and my progress began to slow to a crawl, especially in locks when there was nothing I could do except hobble around like an invalid. At least in the open water I could travel at a normal speed.

Well, I could when there wasn't anyone delaying me. It was a different story when I encountered lamebrains like the Mr Bean I met near the Staffordshire village of Hopwas who held me up for nearly an hour pottering along at tickover and refusing to let me pass. I could have screamed. There are rules for these things; there's a protocol. If you want to travel slowly on a canal you don't hog the canal so boats can't get past you.

Well, this is the rule. But if Mr Bean that day knew it, he certainly wasn't letting on. He was travelling remarkably slowly, barely fast enough to control his boat. OK, the canal north of Hopwas is a charming stretch passing between the River Tame on one side and thick woodland on the other. With its ancient trees and mossy knolls tumbling down to water's edge I can't help thinking every time I pass how I would love to see it as a set for *A Midsummer Night's Dream*, though that might be a bit difficult unless you hired Quentin Tarantino to direct since it's used now as a military firing range.

Yes, it's a beautiful length of canal. Even so, no one's going to want to travel along it that slowly. Not unless they've got engine trouble. Or a personality disorder. I couldn't work out what the problem was with the guy in front. He wouldn't look at me. Not when I came close to him. Not when I shouted to him. Not when I sounded my horn. Eventually I concluded he was blanking me and eventually I lost patience and powered past.

Of course, immediately afterwards Sod's Law ensured that I got my propeller fouled so badly it stopped me dead in mid channel. Mr Bean went cruising by even more slowly than he'd been travelling before, a smile on his face so smug his ears wiggled. I finally managed to manoeuvre myself into the bank. That was Sod's Law, too. I finished up at a spot where only moments before an inconsiderate owner had allowed his dog to dump its still-steaming load. I carefully worked my way around it as I set about removing the obstruction which turned out to be some sort of silver sheet like a space blanket made out of hi-tech fabric which was as tough as cheap steak.

The upside of the delay was that it got me talking to another boater, a lively young woman who lived on the canals with her boyfriend. She joined me in a companionable moan about slow boaters, messy boaters and hire boaters. In short, about any other boaters who weren't us. She solved my problem too, about what to do with the silver space blanket once I'd got it off the propeller, which was a pig to do. She took it off my hands to cover her winter logs.

The downside was that I got so involved in chatting I forgot all about the dog shit and stepped back into it giving me further reason to curse the world and its perversity.

TWENTY-ONE
The Stafford Festival

I was on the cabin floor on my hands and knees. I'd been spending a lot of time on the cabin floor since Dave left. It was the cat's fault. She'd probably been waiting for him to go before she started showing off. Or maybe the hunting had improved since we'd turned from the Coventry Canal onto the Trent and Mersey. Either way, I was getting to know the floor very well as a result of the large quantity of corpses and body parts of our more common hedgerow mammals which she brought in and which I had to clear up. This last day or two, though, she'd changed tactics. Now she was bringing in her prey alive. Presumably this was so that she could torture it under controlled conditions. So it'd be fresh. Maybe it was because when she got bored she could let it go and catch it all over again.

That morning, stumbling half-asleep into the galley in my dressing gown to make tea, I trod on something squidgy and soft. Thank God I didn't put my weight on it. I knew what it was straight away and I grabbed a glass and dropped to my knees. I'd discovered that you could catch mice like you caught wasps. You just dropped the glass over them and slid a piece of cardboard underneath so you could pick them up and throw them out. The trouble is that mice like being picked up in a glass about as much as they like being terrorised by a cat, and it's no use telling them it's for their own good.

But it is for their own good. Stuck on a boat like this, with a hominid and a felis for company, my top tip to a young mouse would be to give yourself up to the big hairless one every time. At least that way you stand an odds-on chance.

I attempted to corner the mouse but it was having none of it and it darted away whenever I got close. It was far quicker than I was. I did get within arm's length at one point, but then Kit intervened and scared it off. She thought all this was a great wheeze, me and the mouse scrabbling around on the floor like this. I could almost hear her chuckling to herself in that discordant estuary English of hers which I was beginning to dislike so intensely. I could almost hear her urging me on. 'There it is, there! There! Cam' on, cam' on! Yer not tryin'.'

Finally I realised I had to be more astute. After all, I was the most advanced species of the three kicking around the cabin that morning. I was much further up the evolutionary chain. All I had to do was use my head.

So instead of pursuing the mouse and panicking it, I decided to adopt a more softly-softly approach. I leaned back against a chair, taking stock of the situation, waiting for it to make its next move. The cat sat back too, taking stock of me, waiting for me to make my next move. Unencumbered by predators for the moment, the mouse got cheeky. It perched on the edge of Kit's drinking bowl and took a long draught of water, its tiny nose twitching as it touched the surface, its whiskers quivering like reeds in the wind. This was all I needed and I pounced, glass at the ready. I was fast, but not that fast. Certainly not as fast as the mouse, and nowhere near as fast as Kit either. Before I was even aware of her moving she had it by the scruff of its neck and was carrying it across the room in her mouth as if it was one of her kittens.

A moment later it was dead, executed by a couple of neat tooth incisions in the back of its neck.

This wasn't funny. Clearing up after her nightly carnage was bad enough, as was groping around on the floor trying to liberate her intended victims before she butchered them. But having them put to death in front of me was a step too far. How was I supposed to ever see her in the same way again? How could she be my cuddly pet puss as she had been? How was I supposed to welcome her to my lap and tickle her tummy and scratch her behind her ears when her mask had slipped and I could see her for what she really was: just a domesticated wild animal, a killer capable of this sort of cruel excess?

My scruples obviously didn't worry her much. With the mouse lifeless, she lost interest and dropped it where she stood. She pecked at her tail for a few moments in an indifferent parody of grooming and then she strode from the boat with an hauteur which said more about what she thought of me than words ever could. What she thought of me, of course, was that I was an effete wuss, a namby-pamby with an excessively sentimental view of the world. I was like one of those committed carnivores who goes squeamish when they pass a butcher's shop, unable to bear the idea that civilisation's a veneer, and that everything in our world is just a trade-off between the savage and the sophisticated.

It troubled me, however; it put me in a mood. It wasn't a bad mood as such, though it certainly wasn't a good one, either. It was just that after what had happened something was gnawing away inside me as it does when you've been upset by a dream but can't quite remember why.

After breakfast I cruised up to Rugeley, which seemed a particularly appropriate place to be with Kit, given its association with murderers. I needed to stock up the larder for the Internet festival and it's got a busy centre with a good selection of shops. On the way to the supermarket I saw a bed store which I popped into with the intention of buying a mattress cover. I'd have done it too, if the salesman hadn't been so determined to sell me a completely new mattress and got stroppy with me when I wasn't interested. Then, in another shop, I saw a kitchen chair I'd been trying to find for a while. There were four of them for sale along with a table at £260. The bloke was willing to sell them separately but he wanted £180 a chair and he was completely deaf to any sort of negotiation on the price.

'One hundred and eighty, one hundred and eighty,' he kept repeating incessantly until I half expected Eric Bristow to come marching through the door carrying a dartboard under his arm.

'I'd like to say it's been a pleasure talking to you,' I said when I left the shop. 'Except it hasn't.'

As if the day wasn't turning out badly enough I got accosted outside Morrisons by the Cancer Research people who were running a competition to name a pink teddy bear, a fearsome thing 4 or 5 feet tall. I chucked a couple of quid into the tin but a woman came running after me thrusting a clipboard in my direction.

'You've got to write a name down,' she said, 'you've got to write it down.'

'That's OK, it's just a donation.'

But she insisted. 'You have to write it down,' she said. 'It doesn't count if you don't write it down.'

'I'm a bit pushed for time at the moment...'

'Then I'll write it down for you.'

'But I can't think of a name...'

'It doesn't matter, really. Any name will do.'

'Satan,' I said, my patience snapping.

And can you believe this, she did write it down.

I hope I didn't win the competition. I wouldn't like to think that thanks to me, there'd be a kid somewhere in the wilds of Staffordshire cuddling up in bed these long winter nights with a giant pink teddy named after the Prince of Darkness.

The incident with the mouse soured the relationship between Kit and me, there was no denying it. I knew that in Catworld having a mouse brought back for you was a sort of tribute, a high compliment indeed. Killing one in front of you was probably the equivalent of getting an MBE. Me though – call me old-fashioned – but if I had to have some token of the esteem in which I'm held, I'd have liked something a bit more traditional. A pair of socks maybe, a bottle of Scotch.

At first I found it difficult to treat her in the same way. Of course, I fed her and gave her water and even fussed her a bit in the mornings when I first got up – though this may have been less an expression of affection than relief that she hadn't brought in any more mice to tread on. But there wasn't that same easy intimacy between us now. I felt uncomfortable when she came close to me; I felt uncertain when she rolled onto her back inviting me to scratch her. I just couldn't help thinking of that mouse hanging from her mouth; I couldn't help thinking of that last fleeting glance she shot me before she killed it. Was I imagining that glance? It seemed so chilling now, looking back on it; but was it just one of her normal looks? Was it just me who'd invested it with such menace?

And why should it worry me, anyhow? I knew what cats were like and what they did – I'd had enough of them as pets over the years. And I wasn't stupid. *Justice* wasn't a mammalian equivalent of an elephant's graveyard. All those rodents I'd found dead on the boat hadn't come on board of their own accord. It hadn't been a party where someone had spiked the drinks. And all those odd heads and legs and tails I'd found kicking about underfoot, the mice and voles hadn't bitten them off themselves.

But knowing unpleasantness exists in this world is one thing; seeing it happen in front of your eyes is a different matter altogether.

The cat must have sensed the way I was feeling. She pressed herself on me less frequently, went out earlier in the evenings and stayed out later in the mornings. She was confused at my behaviour, I could see that. I'd become less her trusted companion, more just another of those incomprehensible bipeds with their funny ways.

One day I woke and she wasn't there. By now I'd learned not to worry about these non-appearances, but there were too many things about this one for me to relax. For a start it was raining, which she liked. And we were moored in the countryside adjacent to an overgrown coppice where there were a host of secret places to be explored. And then, of course, there was the question of our relationship, which seemed to be at its lowest ebb since I'd had her.

The thread between creatures of different species is always a fragile one; I couldn't help wondering if the one between her and me had snapped.

By lunchtime she still hadn't appeared and I was getting worried and exasperated too, impatient to get to Stafford where the festival would soon be starting. Eventually I decided to break my cardinal rule and go looking for her. On most occasions – as I'd learnt to my cost – this is a waste of time with cats. In the countryside they range far and wide, and even if you get close they'll go to ground if they don't want to be found. Shouting for them doesn't help either. It just warns them you're coming.

This time, though, I didn't have to search long. I found Kit 20 or 30 yards from the boat rooting around in last year's leaf fall. She came over to me as soon as she saw me, but when I bent to pick her up she ran off. Perhaps ill-advisedly in view of the fact that it was still raining and I was only wearing a pair of shorts and a T-shirt, I followed her, fighting my way through the undergrowth until I was soaked through and my legs and arms were torn to shreds by brambles and smarting from nettles. She let me get close to her once or twice, but this was more in the way of a personal entertainment for her, like switching on her iPod. If I got too close she ran away again, deeper and deeper into what was proving to be not so much a thicket as a substantial wood.

In the end I gave up. I wasn't dressed for this game and it bored me. I dropped onto a fallen tree trunk where I sat nursing my stings and lacerations. Within moments she jumped up on the other end, as cool as you like. She was close but not close enough for me to catch her. The rain continued to fall, hitting the trees with the sound of a gently steaming kettle. Kit began grooming the long tufts of hair between the pads on her feet, using her front teeth as a comb to untangle them.

I was at the end of my tether. 'Why do you do this to me?' I shouted. 'Why are you always making my life so bloody difficult?'

She cocked her head to one side and looked in my direction. She seemed puzzled, but I could have got that wrong: maybe what I saw in her face was just amusement.

'Do I ill-treat you?' I asked her. 'Do I starve you? Do I not give you cosy places to sleep and feed you delectable tit-bits? Did I not rescue you from the Celtic clutches of the fearsome woman from Cats Protection? Did I not take you home to love and cherish you? Why do you have to punish me like this? Why do you have to constantly make my life a misery?

'You get food, you get warmth, you get companionship,' I went on, exasperated. 'And what do I ask for in return? I ask that you don't shit in the house. I ask that you don't scratch me. I ask that you don't run off and that you don't commit gratuitous acts of cruelty in front of me...

'You've never mentioned that last one before,' she said. Or at least that's what I heard her say, though maybe she didn't say anything. Maybe it was me just thinking it.

I put this philosophical quibbling to one side. 'I've never mentioned that I don't want you to throw up on the kitchen table, either. I've never mentioned that I don't want you to rip up the carpets. Or tear up the curtains. For God's sake, I'm not writing a sodding book on feline etiquette.

'I've just had enough of you,' I screamed in frustration. 'I want no more of this running away, and no more mice on the boat or anywhere else for that matter, dead or alive. Anyhow, what do you see in it? Torturing little creatures like that? Brutalising yourself? You must be mad getting pleasure from it, completely mad.'

'Me mad? Me?' she said, shaking her head incredulously. 'Listen 'ere sunshine, I'm not the one talking to a cat...'

And at that she jumped down from the fallen tree trunk and ran off into the blackness of the undergrowth.

I didn't see her again for an hour or two. I went back to the boat and fell asleep reading in one of the armchairs in the cabin.

When I woke it was to find her on my chest, butting her face against mine and touching my nose with hers in that caricature of a kiss which had become part of her emotional stock in trade ever since I'd once done it to her. It was an attempt at reconciliation if ever I've seen one, and I'd be lying if I said I wasn't touched by her affection.

Until I noticed the biscuits in her feeding bowl were running low.

This reminded me of an essential truth of living with a cat, which every owner has to come to terms with sooner or later. Cats may appear to love and cherish you, they may seem to revere and esteem you; they may act as if their relationship with you is the single most important element of their existence. But this is all a front. The truth is that in the list of priorities that govern their lives you fall some way below a regular supply of food.

I cruised up to Great Haywood and turned into the junction with the Staffordshire and Worcestershire Canal, which goes to Wolverhampton and then onto the River Severn at Stourport. Soon after the turning you pass Tixall Wide where, as the name suggests, the narrow canal suddenly broadens into an expansive lake. This, it is said, was built as a condition of the canal being allowed to cross the lands of Thomas Clifford, one of the sons of Hugh Clifford, the Third Baron Clifford of Chudleigh, who saw an opportunity of getting an expensive water feature on the cheap. His nearby stately home, Tixall Hall, where Mary Queen of Scots had once been detained, was demolished in the 1920s and today just the old gatehouse remains overlooking the water. Mind you, this three-storey Tudor building with domed octagonal towers at each corner is itself as grand as a stately home; though it's stuck in the middle of a field without a garden or even a fence around it so that it looks misplaced and ill at ease.

It's a short hop along the canal from Tixall to Stafford and I'd have been there in no time if I hadn't got stuck for more than an hour just outside the town. The hold-up was caused by a traditional working boat which was wedged on something under a bridge. This is an occupational hazard for these craft which are deep-drafted and built for a different age when the cut was dredged to 5 and 6 feet and more, twice what you get today if you're lucky.

There must have been a queue of about a dozen of us hanging around in the rain while the crew laboriously hauled the working boat, inch by gruelling inch, over whatever obstruction was holding it up. Even after it had gone, getting under the bridge was difficult for the rest of us since work was being done on the brickwork and it was partly blocked by scaffolding poles. I thought I'd have trouble – *Justice* is deep-drafted too – but in the event I needn't have worried. As I'd been hanging around she'd drifted and found deep water, so that as soon as I engaged gear she slipped through without so much as a hiccup.

The crew of the traditional boat had moored on the other side to recover from their ordeal. They were drinking cups of well-deserved tea and they watched my progress with close interest. As I went by they were fulsome in their praise for my boat handling. This confirmed what I always think is the first rule of narrowboats: basically you just wait to see what they're going to do, then you look as if that's what you intended all along.

Once the rain had stopped, the weather held up for the festival weekend. During the day we all sat outside in the sunshine and ate and drank, and at night we went inside the clubhouse and did exactly the same, except, probably, more of the latter than the former, given the favourable prices being charged at the club bar. There was a lot of chat about inconsequential canally-type things, and a great deal of general banter about the state of our boats and the state of our livers. The women joined in all of this enthusiastically enough, though occasionally one of them would break away to do old-school housewifely tasks like baking cakes, which I suspected was just a way of reinforcing their femaleness against the weight of all the dominant testosterone.

Meanwhile, us men polished our boats and looked at each other's engines. On Saturday one of us set up a model steam railway around an old lock which has been rebuilt in the middle of the club grounds as a feature; and that evening Benny, who's a folk singer we all know, came and performed for us. On the Sunday morning we had an auction for a local kids' charity.

This caused me a bit of a problem. We were all supposed to bring something to be sold off for funds but I'd come unprepared. However – mindful of a six-figure product-placement deal which had only just been struck with an international jewellery company by the novelist Fay Weldon – I came up with the bright idea of auctioning a mention in this book. I had some notion that the successful bidder might be someone who wanted a dedication to his much-loved mother, or recently-graduated son, which I could somehow slip into the narrative.

In the event the winner turned out to be a company called Miracle Boat Products. They make cleaning stuff, apparently. Which is altogether more difficult for me to work in, given the state I'd let *Justice* get into for most of the summer.

Even so, I'm not knocking it. The sixty quid they shelled out might be a fraction of what you'd need to buy even the cheapest item sold by Fay Weldon's sponsoring company, but it'll still be useful introducing some of the poorer kids in Stafford to the waterways.

The festival at the Stafford Boat Club was a very English affair, redolent of 1950s church fetes and village galas; but Stafford Boat Club itself is a reminder of an older England when the Big Society wasn't just a political slogan but a reality in people's lives. The club was founded in 1964, a time when the waterways were in a parlous state: under-maintained, undervalued and under-used. The noble if rather hopeless aim of the club, which was encapsulated in its first constitution, was to promote canals and their restoration. This wasn't an easy task in those early years when canals were hardly rocking along with the Mersey sound as flavour of the month. Despite persuading Stafford Council to let them have use of a derelict brickyard adjacent to an abandoned arm off the main line, the sad situation was that by 1976 the club was almost on its last legs, with membership reduced to just three.

Having reached this Dunkirk, the indomitable trio made a last-ditch effort to save the club by using every strategy they could think of to drum up interest. They used the local media. They used personal contacts. They cajoled and they persuaded; they threatened and they sweet-talked. Finally, they arranged a Save Stafford Boat Club meeting, as a result of which they recruited enough new members to keep going. In time these new members recruited others who in turn recruited more people yet; and soon afterwards, by now a viable concern, the revitalised club managed to acquire the lease of the site from the council which allowed them to develop the infrastructure of the place. They created a marina and put in moorings, they put in a slipway, they landscaped the gardens and in the late

1980s they built an imposing clubhouse to replace the wooden hut which had sufficed for so many years.

This building stands on top of a steep slope commanding a fine view over the whole site. It's more like a yacht club than a boat club, more like something you'd see on a golf course than on the canals. But as impressive as the club and its facilities are, it's the manner of their construction that's most remarkable. For Stafford Boat Club has been built by its members – literally built by its members – brick on brick, using their own skills and collaborative working methods. When you join the club you don't just pay your fees. Unless you're incapacitated or exempted for other reasons, you're expected to join the regular work parties that not only maintain the place, but continue to improve it, making it an inspiring example of cooperative action and the benchmark to which other boat clubs across the country aspire.

I popped back to *Justice* after the auction; I wasn't sure I'd left the side porthole open for Kit and I didn't want to lock her in. When I got back to the clubhouse word had got out that I'd got a cat on board and the news excited a degree of interest among those who were cat lovers. Among these were Anne and Jez, who I happened to have been sitting with. Isn't it funny how you recognise cat people a mile off even though you might never talk to them about cats?

'What sort is she?' they asked.

'Nothing special. She's a rescue cat, black and white, a longhair – a bit of a weird creature, if I'm honest,' I said. I told them about her bushy tail and the ruff around her neck; I told them about her immensely hairy lynx-type ears; about her preference for bad weather, for rain and snow; and about the peculiarity of her swimming.

I could see them both glance at each other. They seemed very curious. Or perhaps I was mistaken. Perhaps they were just sceptical at what I was saying.

'Where is she now?' Anne asked. 'Could we see her?'

We walked back to the boat where Kit lay basking in a beam of sunlight shining through a porthole. She was stretched out on one of the cabin chairs and looked about twice her normal length. As soon as we came in it was as if she instinctively recognised Anne and Jez as kindred spirits. Within minutes she had them cooing over her as if she'd been a newborn baby. I saw them look at each other again with that same quizzical look in their eyes.

'She's rather beautiful, it's true,' said Jez.

'And very friendly,' said Anne.

'But a bit small,' added Jez.

Small. Small! What on earth were they talking about, small? That day, lying there in the sunshine, she looked enormous to me.

'I meant for a Maine Coon,' Jez said.

'A what?'

'A Maine Coon,' said Anne. 'An American breed from… er… Maine. She's a textbook example, really. The hair, the ears, the ruff, the fascination with water…'

'Except she's just not very big,' said Jez, interrupting. 'For a Maine Coon, I mean. Normally they're enormous, the size of small dogs. They can weigh up to thirty pounds.'

As soon as I got the opportunity I found a computer and looked up the breed on the Internet. I could see what they meant. Almost every characteristic of a Maine Coon was characteristic of Kit, even down to the tufts of hair between the pads on her feet. It was spooky. You couldn't come to any conclusion other than that she was a Maine Coon. I began to read about the history of the breed. It was fascinating. There's a story that Maine Coons originated after Marie 'Let them eat cake' Antoinette had attempted to flee to the United States to escape execution during the French Revolution. It's said she filled up a ship with her prized possessions, including six of her favourite Turkish Angora cats, but she was arrested and lost her head on the guillotine before she could make her getaway. Even so, though she may not have made it to the land of liberty, the cats did. And it's said they took a lot of liberties with the local American cat population as soon as they landed.

So now it seemed that rather than the rough-edged Sarf Lunnon street cat I thought I had, what I actually had was an 'aristocat' who could trace her lineage back to the royal courts of eighteenth-century Europe.

Back on the boat it took me a while to come to terms with this. I suppose for a start it explained why she was such a supercilious cat, a touch toffee-nosed if truth were told. It explained the mouse too, didn't it? A classy cat like her wasn't going to do whatever business she had with mice in public, was she? Things like that you did discreetly. You did them back in your private chambers, didn't you? It was understandable in the circumstances.

I sat in the cabin and looked at her, fascinated by every detail of her blue-blooded demeanour. She was lounging on the chair as she had been most of the day, apparently asleep. But cats never sleep. Not really sleep. Not the way you and I sleep. I could tell that she was awake enough to know that she was being watched. And I could tell that being watched unsettled her. Eventually she opened an exploratory eye and fixed it on me.

'So, you're a posh cat, eh?' I said. 'Who would have thought it?'

She opened her other eyed and yawned. 'You should never judge by appearances,' she replied. 'You English always do that.'

I felt uneasy as I always did when she got overly communicative like this. But this time it wasn't so much the fact that she seemed to be talking that so unsettled me. It was the accent in which she did it.

She had lost her estuary intonation completely. Now she spoke with a soft and mellifluous New England lilt, like a character out of a Henry James novel...

TWENTY-TWO
Burton-on-Trent

*B*efore I left Stafford I decided to take advantage of the concessionary prices the club charges for boat diesel, which I'd worked out would save me a lot of money.

'Fill her up,' I said to the bloke on the pump. 'As much as she'll take.

'Keep it coming,' I urged, spurring him on to greater effort when he looked as if he was flagging. 'There's room yet. We can get another twenty litres in there and no mistake.'

After a while he stopped the pump and came over to me. 'Are you sure it's not going into the canal?'

'Er, no, I've just got a big fuel tank,' I said. 'Traditional engine and all that…'

'Then why does it smell so much?'

This was a good point and a more difficult one to answer. On examination it seemed the stuff was somehow leaking. The boat was reeking like a garage forecourt. The engine room was particularly whiffy.

'Mmmmm, I guess it must be full,' I conceded. 'I suppose I should pay you…'

It wasn't a good start to the day. Diesel gets everywhere; it's a devil to get rid of and the stink of it hangs around for weeks. This was the beginning of a bad stage of the trip – I guess I was due one. Just because you're cruising on a canal boat and not having to go to work, which would be most people's idea of paradise, it's silly to pretend that everything's hunky-dory the whole time and that there aren't occasionally phases when everything you do goes pear-shaped and you feel like sitting in a dark room with your head in your hands.

It was already drizzling as I started out, but the worst was waiting for me. Once I was underway the rain began hammering down with the urgency of a bloke who's finally found the urinal after a night on the beer. The changeability of the weather from scorching hot to wet and soggy, and back again, was getting me down. It had been getting me down all summer. What is it with this God of ours that He does this to us? Has He got a downer on the English? Does He take some perverse deific pleasure in tormenting us like this? Does it give Him a bit of entertainment after a hard day managing celestial infinity?

I retraced my steps to Great Haywood along that bit of the canal that passes through the wide and marshy valley of the River Sow where the mainline Virgin trains roar by, at places so close to the water they travel alongside it on a series of parallel viaducts. I could glimpse the faces of passing travellers through the windows. I imagined them warm and dry, drinking their coffee and reading their newspapers. They must have wondered what on earth anyone was doing out in rain like this. I felt the same way myself.

It couldn't keep going on indefinitely, though. Not at that tempo. There just wasn't enough water in the sky to maintain it. At length it eased off, although the weather remained bleak and murky; and what scant pleasure I got cruising in those conditions was marred by the all-pervasive odour of diesel which was turning into more of a problem than I cared to admit.

I knew it was bad when I passed people on the towpath. They were out to get some fresh air before the rain started again. They were taking the kids out, or taking their dog for a walk, tripping along jauntily with a spring in their step. But I'd pass and they'd suddenly stand stock-still sniffing the air. They'd identified a smell but they couldn't place it. It was like a rattly old bus going by. Like a lorry on the motorway chucking out exhaust fumes. Like a traffic jam in town. Like anything except a canal on a grey August afternoon.

I felt as if I'd broken wind at a party. 'Good afternoon,' I'd say with an innocent smile.

'Good afternoon,' they'd reply, always cheerfully.

I was heading due south now on the route I'd taken earlier in the month on my dash to Cropredy. On that journey I'd swung east onto the Coventry Canal at Fradley Junction. Now my plan was to continue onwards down the Trent and Mersey past Burton-on-Trent and towards Red Hill on the River Soar where the Inland Waterways Association (IWA) was to hold its annual national festival. The National, as it's known to boaters, is the mother of all inland waterways festivals, the oldest and still the largest. It started life in the early 1950s when it was used as a powerful political tool to campaign against the threat of waterway closures. If any was so much as mooted – and many were, even in places like Stratford on Avon where the canal's now a centrepiece of the town – hundreds of boats from all points of the compass would descend to publicise the message that waterways were a valuable national asset, and that to lose even one of them was to strike at the very fabric of the system itself.

Little by little, by this strategy and others like it, the IWA began to change the prevalent view of canals as disease-ridden, dirty ditches which were better filled-in than left as places for kids to drown.

Today the waterways have secured their place in the country's psyche and the narrowboat has been promoted to the status of an icon of English life, like the English bobby, the English breakfast, and Alan Bennett. It's meant the National's had to adapt its role. Recently it's become less of a campaigning event and more a publicity and revenue raising opportunity for the IWA. These days it's as much a trade show as anything, and most visitors arrive not by boat but by car. Even so, it's a remarkably popular event, and the numbers of those attending have reached unprecedented levels, though the social cost of this has been that it's lost the cosy quality that once made it unmissable. Nowadays many complain that it's a soulless affair and that it has grown too big – which is impossible to dispute, since at some venues even if you come by boat you can be moored so far away from the central site you have to catch a bus to reach it. Even on smaller sites it can be impersonal if you go there on your own, knowing no one; or cliquey if you attend with friends or in a group.

All the same, if I was immersing myself in waterways festivals it was too important a date on the canal calendar to ignore.

I stopped that evening among the birch trees on the approach to Fradley and the first chance I had I went into the engine room to try to do something about the diesel stench which was now nauseous. The prognosis was worse than I imagined. I discovered the problem wasn't just spillage but a fracture from a pipe leading into the fuel tank. A certain amount of diesel had seeped out during refuelling at Stafford, but it had probably been leeching out for a while before that without me noticing. I patched it up as best I could, but the next day I had no choice but to take *Justice* into a boatyard to have the job done properly. Luckily one nearby could fit me in and I got away the next day without too much of a delay.

And that should have been the end of the matter, except that while I was showing a bloke at the boatyard what the problem was I got up without thinking and turned awkwardly on my ankle. As soon as I did it I felt a jolt up my leg as if I'd stuck my toe into a 240V socket. I could have screamed, and not just with the physical pain of it. The frustration was much worse. I realised this was a recurrence of the old injury that had been plaguing me throughout the summer and I knew that I'd be weeks getting over it. It was demoralising. What could I do with this bloody ankle? Would it ever sodding-well heal? Would I ever be able to use it again normally?

I'd rested it as the medics had instructed; I'd exercised it as they'd advised; I'd taken care of it as they'd recommended. Taken care of it? That was an understatement if ever there was one. Blimey, this ankle had been so well treated it'd get its own first class seat if it was flying. It had been pampered, cossetted and spoiled. It had been given VIP status, put on its own diet and tucked up at night with a big kiss. But it just wasn't reliable. And I doubted it ever would be now. I was finally beginning to accept that the ankle was like the rest of me and getting old.

And that, I can tell you, didn't make me feel a whole lot happier about myself.

I strapped it up with elasticated bandages and as soon as I felt confident it would take my weight I set out along what in my opinion is the nastiest stretch of canal in the whole country.

The Trent and Mersey's pleasant enough as it passes through Fradley, which is one of those cutesy canal junctions you see in books with a dreamy pub on one side, a swing bridge on the other and a flight of twee locks passing between the two. It's not too bad, either, through Alrewas, an attractive little village situated at a point where the Trent crosses the canal. But beyond that, it runs alongside the A38 which used to be the Roman Iknield Street; and the dreadful clamour of that four-lane highway to ears that have become accustomed to the placid sound of birdsong and the soothing melodies of water trickling from gently leaking lock gates is almost unbearable.

It's not just the noise that spoils the cruising here. On a wet and windy day like this, the traffic throws up a constant, filthy spray; and since you're too close to the road to avoid it, you get covered in the stuff. After half an hour I looked as if I'd been motor cycle scrambling. My clothes were caked in mud. My face was splattered with it. *Justice* looked as if she'd been painted with it. Further towards Burton, as if things aren't bad enough already, they get worse. Next to the canal there's a quarry where lorries laden with loads of dripping aggregate manoeuvre about with so much squealing of their brakes and so much beeping of their reverse warning lights that you feel like your head's going to explode.

That evening a bit of mine did. I'd tied up on visitors' moorings in the town and taken a hot shower to scour away the memory of the day. Afterwards, I was cleaning my teeth when the floss I was using caught against a cap on one of my back teeth and sent it catapulting out of my mouth, ricocheting around the bathroom like a pinball. After the weather, the diesel and the ankle this was just about the last straw. It was God conspiring against me again. I felt like banging my head against the cabin wall; I felt like tearing out my hair; I felt like kicking the cat except she could sense the mood I was in and had taken shelter under the coffee table.

For heaven's sake, I hadn't even known I'd got a cap on that tooth. In fact, I thought that was the only one of my teeth that hadn't got a cap. I was very proud of it. I'd entered it into competition for Teeth Over the Age of Sixty and I may have even won a prize or two. To discover the tooth was capped was bad enough. Losing the cap was one intimation of mortality too far.

I went to bed early but I didn't sleep thanks to a barn owl screeching away the whole night. A barn owl, for mercy's sake. A barn owl! What's a barn owl doing in the middle of Burton-on-Trent? Did it know I was coming? Had the bloody thing been waiting there just to irritate me?

It was still raining next morning. I heard it drumming on the roof as soon as I woke, and I lay in bed trying to summon up the enthusiasm to move. I really couldn't face any more canalling that day, so I made the decision to stay put. It suited my plans, anyhow, since I needed to see a dentist as soon as I could. After breakfast I hobbled into the town centre to arrange an appointment, leaving the side porthole open as usual for the cat. When I got back she was still in the boat. What's more it was clear that she hadn't left it while I'd been away.

Anne and Jez had told me in Stafford that Maine Coons had a top coat of fur which was water resistant, and in that Kit was an advert for the breed. But it seemed to me that during this current bout of heavy rain she'd lost confidence in her genetic inheritance. It could have been my imagination, but she seemed less keen to go out in heavy rain than she once had. In fact, she seemed less willing to go out in any rain at all. Water resistant fur may be a feature of thoroughbred Maine Coons, but who was to say she was a thoroughbred rather than just a cat whose mother had had some nooky up the alley? After all, I hadn't got a certificate to attest to her breeding. Or any paperwork about her at all except for a receipt from Cats Protection for the 'donation' I'd made to funds.

Kit certainly seemed to be less contented now when it rained. She acted more like a normal cat. Only the other day I'd caught her looking out of the door forlornly wondering when a downpour would stop. She hadn't noticed me but became embarrassed when she did, throwing back her head and chirruping at me in her hoity-toity New England way as if to say, 'Do not think I have not got a coat appropriate to these weather conditions if I wish to go out. It is just that at the moment I do not wish to go out...'

Burton-on-Trent is a surprisingly elegant town for one so industrial. But who's ever heard of a poor brewer? In its prosperous past it was said that a quarter of all beer drunk in Great Britain came from here and this has left it with a legacy of fine buildings. Some are the gracious brick-built wells and factories where beer was once brewed using the famous gypsum-rich waters found hereabouts; some are the grand houses of the brewmasters like the gated Tudor-style palace of William Bass, the founder of the Bass brewery, who for ten years from 1777 lived just a stone's throw from the current town centre.

Brewing is still a major industry in Burton, though the thirty or so independent breweries which once traded in the town have consolidated, and today the place is dominated by the multinational Coors company whose products litter the town slushing around in great corrugated stainless steel vats the size of four-storey houses. Coors describes itself as a 'global family brewer' which is as much an insult to the English language as some of its beers are to my taste buds. Most of them aren't beers anyhow, but fast-brewed 'lagers' – among them Carling, which is one of the world's most popular brands, one the company sells so much of it could probably fill up the Trent and Mersey Canal each year with its output. Which, in my opinion, would be a much better use for the stuff than drinking it.

Sadly, all this rationalisation of international beer production has left Burton with more than its fair share of pound shops and charity stores. Yet in a sense it only has itself to blame. Brewing in Britain used to be a cottage industry until William Bass upset the applecart by marketing his beers nationally. He branded them with the company's characteristic red triangle, Britain's first registered trademark, and transported them around the country on the rapidly expanding waterways network. In this way he laid the foundations for the structure of the modern industry which, if left to itself, would probably amalgamate into one mega-company somewhere in Milwaukee – which is the way things are going anyway, I guess.

Good beer's still to be had in Burton, mind you. A couple of small independent brewers survive and there are some decent pubs around town too, though you have to search them out. Em and I came across one a few years ago when we were walking back from town loaded with shopping and I was dying for a pee. Well, that was my story anyway. The Coopers Tavern was down an uninviting side street overshadowed by a dozen massive lager vats from a super-brewery opposite. It looked for all the world like a suburban Victorian villa, but it turned out to be a terrific pub, one of the best I've stumbled across in years, even though it was congested, cramped and without even an inside lavatory. But it was friendly and welcoming and it sold an impressive range of beers and ciders straight from the wood, not to mention a wide selection of fruit wines which Em jumped on with such gusto you'd have thought she'd got vitamin C deficiency.

And honestly, you'll have to take my word for this, the landlord hasn't bid a penny in a charity auction for me to say any of this.

I'd have dropped off for a pint there after the dentist except I was in the same crabby mood I'd been in all day, my disposition not helped by the fact that I'd been given an appointment which had been tacked onto the end of the working day when the dentist would have much rather been going home than seeing patients. Except he'd seen a mug coming and couldn't find it within himself to turn down the wedge he was intending to charge me. He advised me that I ought to get my cap replaced which – considering that I'd made the appointment to get my cap replaced – was rich. Well, he was rich, anyhow; I was a good deal poorer. Still, it's nice work if you can get it, eh? I should set up a business myself doing the same sort of thing. I could call it the Absolutely Bleeding Obvious Company and advise people whose cars had broken down that they needed repairing, or people who'd lost their way that they needed a map. The possibilities are endless.

Back at *Justice* I discovered I had neighbours. A small boat had moored a little way up the towpath and on board was a young couple who seemed to have a problem. I could see a man's head bobbing about underneath the stern deck; a woman stood above him holding a golfing umbrella, sheltering him from the rain which had been tipping down all day. Despite my ill humour I felt constrained to see if I could do anything to help. I expected to find the two of them as miserable as I was. Breaking down at any time is bad enough; breaking down in the rain is much worse.

In fact, I found them giggling to each other, having a laugh about the predicament they were in. It turned out they'd not long bought the boat and this current problem which was something to do with the electricity (what else?) was the latest in a series they'd had since taking it out on their maiden cruise.

'First of all there was the starting motor,' said Polly brightly. 'Then there was the alternator…'

'No! The water pump, the water pump was next. Don't forget the water pump,' said Peter.

'Yes, the water pump,' Polly agreed. 'Then it was the engine…'

'Yes, the gasket which went…'

'And then the propeller fell off…'

The two of them dissolved into helpless mirth.

'It sounds like a bit of a disaster all round,' I said, tempering my voice with what I judged to be a requisite amount of sympathy. This had the effect of sending them into fresh fits of laughter. They could hardly talk for it.

Eventually Peter took himself in hand. He pulled himself out from under the deck and stood under the umbrella, still spluttering as he spoke. 'Well, I suppose if you took it too seriously you might say that,' he agreed. He can't have been more than about twenty-three or four. He didn't look as if he'd taken anything too seriously his whole life which, in the mood I was, made me feel very old.

'It's all just a bit of fun, isn't it?' he went on. 'Boating, I mean. You can't take it seriously, can you? I know you've probably been doing it for years and you know everything there is to know. But for us it's all a great adventure, a sort of voyage of discovery. Like, you see places and things in a totally new way. It's exciting. And a bit amazing too, finding all these old waterways, like tucked away everywhere without anyone knowing they're there…'

The three of us had a cup of tea together on *Justice* and the whisky bottle soon came out. It was after midnight when they left.

That night the rain cleared and I woke the next morning with the sunshine shining into my eyes through the porthole in the bedroom cabin. Kit was out on the deck, enjoying the fine weather. She rolled over when she saw me, inviting me to play. I knew it was going to be a good day.

TWENTY-THREE
The National Festival

It was getting close to August bank holiday, and I was getting closer to Redhill where the National was scheduled to be held. For the first time I became aware of other boats heading in the same direction. Some of them I recognised; some recognised me. There was a lot of chat at lock sides and a sense of camaraderie in the air. School was out. Everyone was feeling lightheaded.

It was still, officially, summer; but somehow while I hadn't been looking, while I'd been messing around with my tooth or playing with the cat, the tenor of the world had changed entirely. A little while before – only a few days ago, it seemed – I'd been cruising up the Shropshire Union in a heat wave, the countryside a wash of greens adorned with blazes of bright flowers. Now it was turning autumnal before my eyes and the colours of the cut were of a more subtle hue: dark damasks and burgundies, magentas and deep, rich cherry reds. The hedgerows were thick with rose hips, hawthorn and blackberries and the violent, vibrant orange of rowanberries; and there were clutches of sin-dark elderberries bunched like tiny grapes, sloes and damsons as black as midnight. Fruit seemed suddenly to be everywhere, in the fields and along the towpath, in copses and thickets, and in the gardens of the houses I passed: pears, apples and plums in such abundance the trees were straining under their weight.

Following a period of sunshine the countryside had dried out and the farmers were back at work again gathering the last of the summer's crops. Around Weston Lock I watched as an immense combine harvester dragged itself laboriously up and down a field, shaving the edges off a swaying sea of wheat as if it were planing a piece of timber. As it moved it threw up great dust clouds which hung over it like smoke, so that when the sun caught its windows it looked as if it was ablaze.

After the horrors of the approach to Burton, the bottom end of the Trent and Mersey becomes pretty again and views open up across the broadening river to the low hills of the valley beyond. The river now toys with the canal in a graceful lover's dance, sometimes coming close, sometimes pirouetting away from it in lissom, flirtatious arcs. It's past its adolescence at this point, and with every passing mile it becomes more confident and self-assured. Meanwhile, the canal drops lower at every lock. Soon river and canal will be on the same level. Soon they'll join and be one.

The consummation happens a few miles beyond the inland port of Shardlow, where a four-storey mill built in 1780 welcomes you to the village. There's a sign emblazoned across its frontage in stylish white lettering – Navigation from the Trent to the Mersey – and its prominence is a mark of the pride which the canal builders took in their work. These were people who were not just building a waterway but constructing the future, putting together the transport arteries that would support Britain's industrial revolution. The Trent and Mersey Canal – the Grand Trunk as it was first known – was part of a larger scheme to link the four main rivers of England. This canal was to be followed by a connection south to the Thames and connections west to the Severn, creating a project known as the Grand Cross.

The mill at Shardlow is a pub-restaurant now, ponced up and pretty, but I remember it from the past when it used to be a chandlery and a bit of a shabby one if truth were told. In those days, when no one had really found a use for old industrial buildings and no one appreciated that sort of architecture anyhow, much of Shardlow was shabby. Today, the old warehouses on which the place once depended for its existence have been converted to posh apartments which command a premium price because they've got canal views. Canal views, can you believe it? In the past people would do anything to avoid a canal view. They'd build high fences and grow towering hedges. They'd block up their windows and put out their eyes. Nobody wanted to live close to a canal then. If you had one anywhere nearby it brought down the value of your house. Is it any surprise that those of us who liked them felt like outcasts?

I stopped for a cup of coffee just after Shardlow Lock and I stood drinking it on the towpath, enjoying the warm sunshine. Once I'd turned off the engine Kit came out onto the deck to see where we'd washed up; she was a naturally curious cat and often did this when I pulled up during the day.

At that moment a bloke happened to pass walking his dog. He was in his late sixties, not long retired, I guess; and he was full of his new freedom, striding along the towpath with his walking stick as if he was rambling across some upland moor, his head held high and his back as straight as a scaffolding pole. The dog trailing behind him wasn't half as happy. It probably walked this route twice a day every day; it looked as if it was bored by the whole process and would rather have been at home curled up in its basket. It was a sort of scrubby half-breed red setter and you could see just by looking that it wasn't in possession of the most intelligent strains of DNA ever to grace the canine world.

Even at their most intelligent, dogs rarely consider the implications of anything they do. This one certainly didn't. As it passed *Justice* it glanced at it, realised it was something new and without thinking it jumped on board to explore, sniffing about the deck oblivious to Kit's presence. When it finally saw her it stopped dead in its tracks. She froze too, and there was a brief hiatus as they took stock of each other, staring each other out as if locked together by their eyes. Kit ended the stand-off by bolting into the cabin, which the dog must have seen as a sort of territorial surrender since it hared off in pursuit.

The dog's owner and I glanced at each other horror-stricken, but before either of us could do anything there was a clatter of crockery crashing to the floor and a sound of terrible screeching, as if someone was having their toenails pulled out. It can only have lasted a second or two, but it seemed much longer. Then the dog came bolting out at such a speed you half expected to see a trail of high octane fuel jetting from its back end. Attached to it with all four sets of her claws embedded in its neck was Kit. She looked terrified but triumphant.

The dog bucked and reared while Kit hung on like a cowboy at a rodeo. This was probably no more than instinct on her part; but I like to think that with her genes steeped in the ranching tradition of America, it was inspired by the pioneering spirit of her forebears. Eventually, somehow, the dog managed to dislodge her and it went bolting down the towpath yelping in pain with its owner huffing and puffing behind it calling out its name, which I can't for the life of me remember except that I know it can't have been Champion.

Meanwhile, Kit had gone back to her original place on the deck and sat grooming herself, looking far too smug and self-satisfied to my mind, like a footballer at a press conference boasting about his new megabucks contract. I bent down to stroke her, but her adrenaline was running high and she growled at me in that throaty way that cats do, which reminds you that they have bigger and more ferocious relations prowling the savannah.

I decided to leave her be for the moment. You've got to be careful with these Americans. If you happen to catch them on the wrong day they can turn nasty. Just think how they reacted after a bit of extra tax on their tea.

A narrowboat moves differently on a river than on a canal. It's to do with depth. Canals are shallow even for boats with no draft; if you increase your engine speed they dig themselves into the bottom and all you finish up doing is churning up a lot of water to no purpose. On a river, however, a deep-drafted boat like *Justice* is liberated. Even with her engine in tickover she travels faster and sweeter in these open spaces than in the restricted channel of a canal. On a river she cuts through the water effortlessly, leaving just a gentle wash rippling behind her to show where she's been.

But rivers can be unsettling for someone used to the glassy stillness of canals. They're wide and can be fast-flowing after rain; they swirl about unpredictably and are a mass of dangerous eddies and currents. They rise and fall very quickly too depending on the conditions. The River Trent is particularly treacherous in this respect. I went to a school beside it and it was always flooding even then – and that was before we aggravated the problem by putting up housing estates on the surrounding water meadows.

Cruising alone in the past I used to be indifferent to the dangers of rivers; now age has made me cautious and I wear a lifejacket. Em had a bit to do with this, though. She pinned me against the living room wall one evening and said that if I didn't wear one she was going to knee me in the groin. Now I wear one of those flash designer-label sorts which are supposed to inflate when you hit the water. I am not sure how they do this, but then again I'm not sure how a jumbo jet stays in the air either and that doesn't stop me flying. Besides, I think it looks pretty cool when I'm wearing it. It makes me a look a few pounds lighter and a few years younger. Mine's in a particularly lurid shade of yellow, but they make them in a brassy fluorescent red as well. One day I'll buy myself one of those. It'll go much better with my skin colour.

Entering the Trent from the canal, the River Derwent is the first thing you see on your left-hand side. Rising in the high moorland of Bleaklow just north of Kinder Scout, it has along its course passed across the Chatsworth estate, home to the Dukes of Devonshire, as well as through the beautiful Peak District towns of Matlock and Matlock Bath. It arrives here, though, after a more recent detour through Derby and looks the worse for wear, as anyone who's ever been to Derby will understand. You can pass without even noticing it, but when it's high with a 'bit of fresh' in it (as us boaties say) it can be powerful enough to force you off course if you're not prepared.

Luckily, even with the rain we'd had recently, it was very tame that day. The Trent, however, was running much faster than normal and I skidded downriver through Sawley Lock to Trent

Junction where the Nottingham, Derby and Leicestershire borders meet and where the Erewash Canal, the River Soar and the Cranford Cut to Nottingham city centre converge in a confusing welter of water. Overlooking this complex junction is a railway viaduct carrying East Midlands trains. There's a dirty great weir here too, which runs furiously when the river's in flood, but which you really wouldn't want to go anywhere near in a boat even if it wasn't.

It's an intimidating stretch of water, Trent Junction; and you need to have your wits about you navigating it, especially in high summer when dinghies are buzzing about from a nearby sailing club and you have to weave all over the place to avoid them. I swung to the right up the mouth of the Soar in one of those manoeuvres you always execute perfectly when there's no one watching, but always balls up when someone is. Soon afterwards I was at Redhill under the shadow of the cooling towers of Ratcliffe power station and pulling into the mooring which was mine for the three days of the festival. It was against another boat, out from the bank, and it had a pleasant outlook over the water; though no sooner had I tied up than I became aware of covert mutterings of discontent which were threatening to turn into open rebellion.

My new neighbours, it seemed, were not as happy with their moorings as I was with mine. They were clustered around their tillers comparing notes on when they'd booked their places and how much they'd paid. Some had signed up at the end of last year's festival and they wanted to know why they hadn't been put closer to the site than people like me who'd only reserved a place a couple of months before. There were dark words whispered about favouritism; about how the organisers had nabbed the best places for their friends; about how these things were always a matter of who you knew.

To some extent you expect this. People always grumble about their moorings at the National – as they do at every other festival I've ever been to for that matter. It's a very English way to behave, and it's done for the same reason that the English on package tours always complain about their hotel rooms. It's this idea that other people have dropped luckier than you and that if you don't fight your corner you risk missing out.

In this case, however, they did have a point. The moorings weren't actually far from the site, but they were over the other side of the river, which meant that everyone was dependent on a ferry service that had been organised for the purpose. Unfortunately, at that early stage of the festival it hadn't got started properly and was operating erratically. This was unusual because although the National is run entirely by volunteers, it's generally organised down to the last detail. Just how organised became apparent to me watching how the ferry problem was resolved. News of the dissatisfaction had, I guess, filtered back to the festival managers; or maybe they'd been monitoring the problem themselves. Either way, the ferry timetable was rescheduled in no time and new, more frequent services were introduced. Soon a mood of harmony and reconciliation returned to the riverbank.

I went over to the site later that evening. The festival didn't open officially until the next day, but most of those who were attending in boats, and large numbers of those who'd come in cars with tents and caravans, had already arrived; the bar tent was doing brisk business. Next to it, like the encampment of some medieval army awaiting battle, trade stands and marquees resplendent with flags were laid out across the great, flat plain between the river and the power station, very close to the newly opened East Midlands Parkway railway station.

With planes regularly passing overhead from the East Midlands airport at nearby Castle Donnington, and with cars speeding up the adjacent A453 to the M1 just a few minutes' drive away, the organisers had decided, unsurprisingly, to make transport the theme of the event which was a bit dull. It undersold the festival and undersold the site too. A place like this bounded by roads and railways might sound a bit grim as a location for a bank holiday knees-up, far removed from most people's idea of what an idyllic narrowboat mooring should be. But in its own way, with the towers and turrets of the power station silhouetted against a sky broken by the glimmering light of overhead aircraft, Redhill was actually an impressive place, and unique.

Even so, to reduce a festival to the quality of the mooring is to miss the key point of occasions like this; for they're less dependent on location than they are on the enthusiasm of visitors determined to have a good time come what may. There's a fee to get in, but the festival's an open event and the public are encouraged to attend. Throughout the day there's a programme of organised entertainments – music, theatre groups, kids' stuff – the sort of thing you might get at any fete in England this time of the year. But running parallel is a separate festival which is in many ways more important and which takes place privately the whole weekend with boaters socialising among themselves. The beer and entertainments tents are a communal focus of this, for sure; but a lot of it takes place at parties and barbecues on boats as people who've met each other travelling along the system meet up again and renew their old acquaintance.

I spent a lot of time socialising with people I knew and some I didn't. I seemed to be at it from first light until the early hours when I collapsed into bed exhausted. Even Kit seemed to get in on the act. Once she'd explored the surrounding area and worked out which boats were cat-friendly, she was tarting about all over the place scavenging for titbits and affection, and we hardly saw each other for the duration. Time goes by very quickly in these circumstances. In fact, it doesn't so much go by as evaporate. Saturday quickly became Sunday, and Sunday became Monday, and soon the car parks were emptying and boats were moving off for home and the volunteer gangs were descending onto the site to dismantle it. I was one of the last to leave and I was astonished to see how quickly the whole thing disappeared as if it had never been there. One moment it was a vibrant town with people busily milling about all over the place; the next it was just an empty field again, fringed by a quiet river.

AUTUMN

TWENTY-FOUR

More Fun and Games at Barrow upon Soar

I feel a sense of proprietorship about the River Soar in a way that I don't about any other waterway. I consider it to be my river. This is because I was born in Loughborough which straddles it, brought up in a village which borders it, and because most of my formative experiences as a kid are somehow connected to it. When I travel along the Soar I don't so much make a journey along a river as take a trip into my own past. My grandfather used to live close to it – or at least close to the Loughborough Cut, which is the canalised bit of it which runs through the centre of town, while the river proper detours around the water meadows north of the A60 near the Brush Electrical – the Brush as everyone round there calls it.

My mother used to swim in the cut with her friends when she was at school because it was cheaper than the swimming baths. Later, when she left and went into the hosiery industry as a linker, like so many local girls did, gangs of them from the factory used to strip down to their bras and pants on hot summer days and take a dip in their lunch break. And woe betide any man bold enough to play the Peeping Tom. They were strong women, these; formidable in a way working class factory girls were in those days. You wouldn't have wanted to mess with them, let's put it that way. You wouldn't have wanted to mess with my mother, either.

As a youngster I gravitated towards the Soar myself, almost as soon as I was allowed to wander about freely on my own which must have been when I was about ten or eleven years old. This is something kids wouldn't be allowed to do nowadays, but because this was the countryside and there weren't the safety concerns for us then that there would be today, no one thought twice about it. Adults used to warn us to keep away from the river, though, and for good reason. One kid at the infant school I attended – Martin, was that his name? – drowned in it, and a few years later someone else from my class was dragged from it half-dead. Every year afterwards the teachers made the poor sod stand in front of the class and recount his experiences as a warning to the rest of us.

But young people love water, any water; me more than most. I remember long hours exploring the river from the towpath on my bike, and more than once falling in – once after I'd tried to cycle across a slippery weir channel near Kegworth. I fell into the mud at Barrow another time, when a gang of us were messing about on the rowing boats at Proctors Pleasure Park one winter. It was closed for the season and we'd got in by climbing over the gates. I thought I was a goner that day. I'd read about this sort of stuff in comics and I was convinced the mud was like quicksand and was going to suck me under, although in the event I only sunk up to my waist. It was a devil getting out, though, and no mistake. And I stank to high heaven for weeks afterwards.

I saw the river every single weekday of my life from the age of seven to eighteen as I travelled on the bus to and from various schools, and I observed it in all conditions: sweltering in the sunshine and swollen with floods; pelted with driving rain; and once, during the bitter winter of 1963, almost iced across but for a narrow channel running down the middle.

The river is a background to so many fragmentary memories of my childhood that when I cruise it I almost become a child again, watching myself through childish eyes as I skim stones across the mill lake at Cossington or launch a rickety old raft into the water at Sileby. The river had a sort of enchanted quality for me then; and it still has, despite the changes which the years have wrought on us both. Today the rebuilt A6 to Leicester thunders alongside the Soar for most of its length, even crossing it on a couple of occasions near Mountsorrel; yet for me it will always be hauntingly still and peaceful in a way I know bears no relation to reality, but which is somehow connected to those hot summer days I spent during the endless school holidays of my youth when I used to lounge on its banks squinting at the sun through my fingers.

If I'm honest, I felt somewhat piqued with all these other boats being around for the festival. It was as if they were encroaching on my private space, trespassing on it. I mean, how would you feel if someone tried to muscle in on your territory? If they turned up from nowhere and parked on your lawn for a long weekend acting as if it belonged to them? I think that's why I was one of the last people to leave the festival site: I wanted to give them all time to disperse so I could have my river back again. Not that many of them showed much sign of wanting to cruise it. I was heading upriver towards Leicester where I was to meet Em off the train for a week's holiday. It seemed to me that most boats at the festival – even if they were ultimately heading south – went north first to avoid passing through the city.

Leicester, you see, has 'a reputation'. Lots of places on the waterways have a reputation. Our home mooring, Banbury, had one once; Failsworth near Oldham still does. Even the delightful North Yorkshire town of Skipton, the 'Gateway to the Dales', has one, as do at least a dozen places I could mention up the Grand Union. What getting a reputation entails is difficult to say. Sometimes it's connected with teenagers and drink; sometimes stone-throwing is involved, sometimes jumping on boats at night. From time to time a place will earn a reputation because someone's had their mooring lines untied and they've found themselves floating in mid-stream the next morning. Or because they've had stuff taken off their roof and chucked in the water. Or – God forbid – because they've actually had stuff stolen.

A place can earn a reputation by any one of these means or a combination of them all. It can also earn one because someone in an adjoining house is playing loud music. Or because the local cycling club's gone by on the towpath too fast. Or because there's too much dog shit around or too much litter.

However a reputation is acquired and however trivial the basis for it, of one thing you can be certain: news about the place will spread along towpath telegraph faster than the squits at a dodgy restaurant.

A place may have had an unblemished reputation for generations as a superb mooring spot. It might be one of the most beautiful moorings in the country. The Teletubbies might even have lived there once, for all I know. But as soon as it's got a reputation people won't stop there any longer; and in some locations – in some towns and in some troublesome suburbs – as soon as boaters move out, rougher elements move in. In this way having 'a reputation' becomes a self-fulfilling prophecy.

In Leicester, the city council, British Waterways and the local Inland Waterways Association have made tremendous efforts to attract boaters, even to the extent of building a separate mooring jetty in the centre adjacent to Castle Gardens, a park which is locked at night to locals but which is accessible to boaters with a special key we carry. It must be one of the most secure and attractive city moorings in the whole country, but many boaters still won't stop there. Leicester, as I say, has a reputation. Twenty years ago some kids must have frightened the crew of a boat or something like that. Perhaps they were talking too loudly or laughing too much. Perhaps they let off a firework or had a party. Whatever. Since then the memory of the incident, whatever it was, has scoured the communal psyche of the boating fraternity who have never forgotten it and probably never will.

If I had my way, as soon as there was a report of any sort of incident on a towpath – any serious incident, I mean, not anything trivial – I'd conscript a fleet of boats to moor at the spot, and if there was further trouble I'd keep them there for weeks on end, months if necessary. This is a general point, as true for the streets of our cities as for the canals in our countryside: we can't continue to concede territory to the oiks. We can't just roll over and surrender. If we do, they'll soon have us cowering behind our front doors terrified to venture out. Lose one battle and we'll soon lose them all, I say. This sort of behaviour has to be confronted, but we're not very good at that, are we, us English? Confrontation is a real C-word for us. It sometimes seems we'd rather give up our old ways completely than go to the bother of fighting for them.

Cruising upriver to Barrow, I spent three or four days cycling around, visiting the old places and catching up with friends I'd lost contact with. I met one of them by coincidence on the towpath where I tripped over him. Literally tripped over him. He seemed a bit embarrassed to see me, but I put it down to the fact that he was sitting on the towpath fishing, and you can understand anyone being embarrassed fishing, can't you? Actually he felt like that because he knew I had a boat and such is the level of towpath fraternity between fishermen and boaters, he was worried one of his mates might catch him talking to me.

One day I went back to Rothley where I used to live and I had a drink in the pub which was once my local. But it had all changed. It had turned into a restaurant and nobody knew me there anyway so I didn't stay. Another day I went to Bradgate Park, a rocky 850-acre bracken heathland in the old Charnwood Forest area where deer still roam wild. Bradgate was once the home of Lady Jane Grey, The Nine Days' Queen who got caught up in Tudor politics and paid for it with her life. The remains of the family house lie in the park adjacent to the River Lin, a tributary of the Soar. Although it's ruined now and derelict, enough remains to see how grand it must have once been. It's a melancholy place, though – gloomy and morose, but I used to visit it a lot when I was a teenager and was gloomy and morose myself. I was drawn to Bradgate in those days; I was always there moping about and writing poetry, feeling sorry for myself and thinking about Virginia Smith who I had a crush on, though I never had enough bottle to ever ask her out. Virginia Smith, now there's a name to conjure with, a name I haven't thought of for years. I wonder what happened to her? Probably married somewhere and a grandmother. Probably dreaming of the old days like me.

I spent so long messing around at the bottom end of the river getting sentimental about the past that I didn't leave myself enough time to get to Leicester to meet Em, so I arranged instead for her to stay on the train an extra stop and meet me in Loughborough. Predictably, as soon as we'd agreed the arrangements for her to come up, the spell of half-decent weather which we'd had during the festival broke. It was September now and to be expected, I suppose. It turned grey and overcast. Soon it began raining and didn't stop.

On the day of her arrival I was still in Barrow and it was filthy. A storm had blown up overnight and the rain was pelting down accompanied by a raging gale. I could have kicked myself. If I'd taken any notice of the worsening conditions I could have moored beyond Pilling's Flood Lock which would have protected me from its worst effects. As it was, I'd stayed below Barrow Deep Lock and I was now in a bit of a pickle since the river had come up while I'd been asleep and it was now running dangerously fresh.

The Soar does this: it's notoriously unpredictable and goes up and down like a yo-yo. It's said that if you spit in it at Leicester it floods at Trent Junction. In villages like Barrow which lie alongside it, it breaks its banks and overflows across the road so often they've built raised pavements for pedestrians. There are even traffic lights at the locks to regulate boats. That morning they were on red. Under normal circumstances I wouldn't have even considered going on the river. But I wasn't going on the river. I was already on it and I only needed to get past Pilling's half a mile away to get to the canal where I'd have a safe trip into Loughborough.

Besides, what other choice did I have? The river was rising. If I didn't go on I'd have to go up the Deep Lock to get shelter, but that wouldn't have been easy. I was pointing the wrong way and I couldn't have risked turning round with the river as it was. Neither was my engine powerful enough to reverse me to safety in those conditions. In truth, I really didn't have a choice: it was do or die.

The problem was that between me and Pillings was Barrow Bridge, through which the water was already flowing treacherously fast. Getting under this is tricky enough at the best of times because it's on a bend with the river hitting you broadside when you come out of the lock channel. The difficulties increase the more water there is. Steering becomes challenging because against the force of a strong current your tiller is ineffective. The trick is to use the current. To ride it.

No one could say that I wasn't aware of the dangers. After all, I'd navigated this bridge in all manner of craft and all manner of conditions. I'd taken rowing boats through it a hundred times; I'd taken canoes through and rafts I'd made out of oil drums and pallets. I'd even gone through it in the dead of night with a mate on a pedallo we'd found floating in the water on our way back from a lock-in at the pub. I don't know who it belonged to, but I doubt they'd have wanted it back the state we left it in after ricocheting down the bank for half an hour in conditions which were no better than these.

I loosened off my lines and walked up to the bridge to inspect it more closely. You could almost see the level of the water rising as you watched; if it went up much more I wouldn't be able to get through at all. The rain was worsening too, bucketing down now. It was falling horizontally, propelled as much by the wind as by gravity. I decided it was now or never. It was no use procrastinating. If I delayed much longer it would too late.

I went straight back to the boat and fired up the engine. A bloke on the other side sheltering under the tree had been watching me.

'You're going for it then?' he asked, somewhat dubiously.

'I don't see I've got any other choice,' I said.

I wound up the throttle to full revs and headed straight for the brickwork on the left side of the centre arch. It was a precise manoeuvre and I had to judge it accurately. Get it wrong one way and I'd crash against the far side of the bridge; get it wrong the other and I'd be thrown by the current against the near side. I knew I had to hold my nerve. It was no use changing my mind half way.

I powered on, the rain driving into my eyes and the sound of the water on the bridge piers becoming deafening as I approached. The arch came closer and closer. I was a matter of a foot or two away now, so near that I could have counted the individual bricks. It was then I realised with horror that I'd misjudged the manoeuvre completely. I had chosen the wrong line and I was travelling far too fast. I was going to collide. I was bound to hit and I braced myself for the impact. But at the very last moment, just as my bow was about to ram the masonry, the current seemed to pick the boat up physically and throw it towards the other side of the arch with a roar like a wounded animal. Before I was aware of what was happening it had flushed me underneath and I was coursing down the river at an unprecedented pace with Barrow far behind.

After the furious sound of the water on the village side of the bridge, the river here seemed almost silent, just the faint hush of the rain kissing the surface to make you aware of its presence. But I had no time to relax, for as I rounded the next bend I saw that ahead of me the force of the water had uprooted a tree and brought it down across my path. I saw it coming towards me before I even recognised what it was through the murky miasma of the continuing rain. I swung my tiller a hard left to the far bank to avoid it, then swung it right again when it looked as if I was in danger of hitting the bank instead. This brought me back on a collision course with the tree and this time there was no avoiding it. I ploughed into the foliage with a volley of cracking branches and the low, guttural sound of scraping down my hull. But my speed and impetus carried me through and I emerged the other side, scratched and covered in leaves but otherwise undamaged.

As soon as I'd negotiated the flood lock I pulled up in a sheltered spot and went inside for a nip of Scotch to calm me down. My heart was beating against my ribcage; my legs had gone unaccountably shaky.

Kit, clearly, had hardly been incommoded by all this excitement. She lay in the cabin splayed on one of the easy chairs. I thought she was asleep until she opened one eye superciliously and focused on me as if querying the need for all these acrobatic Alton Towers japes which had presumably made it a little more difficult for her to get to the feeding bowl.

I felt like taking her back to the bridge, chucking her in and letting her see if she could do any better.

TWENTY-FIVE
Up the Erewash Canal

'So it was an OK trip then, no problems?' Em asked that evening, after I'd told her that I'd spent the previous night in Barrow and that I'd travelled down from Loughborough that morning.

'No, no problems at all,' I said. 'Just the rain, that's all. It was very wet. And it was a bit... well, a bit lively under the bridge. What are you having?'

We were in a pub queuing for a drink on our way back to the boat from the railway station where we'd met, and it had all been very relaxed so far. She'd had a difficult period at work and was pleased to be away for a week. I was fed up cruising on my own in the rain and was pleased to see her – as much to have another pair of hands on board as because I love her dearly and all that soppy stuff.

Either way, a white lie seemed a small price to pay for domestic harmony.

It was just that I was on very tricky ground with the bridge incident. I realised that much after I'd pulled up for a whisky after Pillings Lock. It was then it struck me that although I'd remembered enough from when I was a kid to get through the bridge in one piece – I'd remembered the right line to take, for instance, despite my last-minute uncertainties; and I'd remembered the correct speed for my approach, too – I nevertheless hadn't remembered everything.

For a start I hadn't remembered to put on my lifejacket before I'd set off. That wasn't only dangerous, it was crass. Frankly, I might as well have drowned because I knew that if ever Em found out what I'd done I'd be dead anyhow.

Discretion, I always feel in these circumstances, is the best strategy. What you don't know can't hurt you. Besides, who was it said that what makes for a successful marriage is not the things you tell your partner but the things you leave unsaid? Heather Mills McCartney? Ashley Cole? Whatever. It's best not to go there...

We set out the next morning after a leisurely breakfast. The rain had stopped overnight and the worst of the spate had cleared although the flow was still lively. Our plan was to head back to the mouth of the river at Trent Junction and from there to travel north on the Erewash Canal to Long Eaton where I was scheduled to give a talk that Sunday at the Long Eaton Festival. It was a pleasant enough day for cruising and if you hadn't known that the river had been running dangerously the day before... well, you simply wouldn't have known.

Em knew, though. Or at least she suspected. I sometimes forget she's been boating for as long as I have and that she reads the water just as well. Not that the messages it was sending out that morning were very subtle.

'It's running a bit fresh, isn't it?' she said after we'd gone skidding around Devil's Elbow on the approach to Kegworth, shaving off a chunk of bank in the process.

'No, no, it's just the way it is,' I protested. 'You've forgotten how fast-flowing the Soar is…'

She threw me a sceptical look and immediately I realised I'd made an appalling mistake. Oh my God! How could I have been so stupid? I could see what was going through her mind. I could read her like a book. She was thinking: 'If he's trying to tell me it's not running fresh when it obviously is, why's he doing it?' And then she thought: 'It's got to be something to do with Barrow Bridge, hasn't it? Otherwise he wouldn't have been so cagey about Barrow Bridge in the pub last night…'

Em knows Barrow Bridge. Not, perhaps, as well as I do, but she knows it all the same. By now she was imagining what the conditions would have been like there after heavy rain…

It was all up with me, I knew it. I was finished. It was game, set and match to her. Checkmate.

'Steve,' she said, fixing me severely in her gaze, 'have you been wearing your lifejacket…?'

It was about seven that evening before she spoke to me again. We'd got to Long Eaton by then and after a walk to stretch our legs we'd washed up in a pub which I won't identify because it was pants and obviously has enough trouble attracting customers without me making matters worse. Heaven knows why we went in there. It was about as cosy as the turbine hall of a power station and about as big too. It was cold as well, with only two or three people sitting around shivering over their pints. The only thing to commend it was that we could get a table.

And maybe that's why we went there: because Em wanted a table. We got our drinks and she led me to one. She sat down on one side and put me on the other. Then she looked at me in silence for a while. I felt like I'd been taken into the headmistress's office for a dressing down, which wasn't far wrong.

'Don't you ever do anything so stupid again, do you hear?' she said eventually. 'I want you to promise.'

I nodded my head.

'It was a senseless thing to do anyhow in those conditions, but to do it without a lifejacket was madness. Do you realise that?'

I nodded my head again.

'I can't imagine what you were thinking. Do you have some idea you're invulnerable – Mr Superboater or something? – just because you've been canalling a long time?'

I nodded my head once more but I could see by the look on her face that this was the wrong reaction, so I shook it instead which seemed to satisfy her. This went on for some time: criticism, question, head movement; criticism, question, head movement… Soon I didn't know where I was with it. Sometimes I nodded when I should have shaken; sometimes I shook when I ought to have been nodding. Finally I gave up trying to work it all out and I turned my attention to Sky Sports, which was on the telly on a wall behind me but which I could see reflected in a mirror above the bar.

After a while Em stretched across the table and kissed me on the cheek so I knew I'd been forgiven, even though I understood there'd be reparations to be paid in the future, whether by washing-up, tea-making or the like.

'Let's get out of here,' she said. 'For mercy's sake, let's find somewhere more cheerful.'

Long Eaton's not a bad place but like so many of these small East Midlands towns it's been through hard times, and it's only because of the pride and resourcefulness of its people they've kept going. We found a decent pub in the end and it had a DJ with a karaoke machine. There's nothing like karaoke for breaking the ice with people in a strange bar. After a few drinks everyone sounds as bad as everyone else trying to sing, so it's difficult to maintain any level of reserve the way you might in a quiet pub.

The real pleasure of karaoke, though, is having a laugh at the expense of those who are under the illusion that they have real talent as singers. It's like the early rounds of *The X Factor* in that respect. There was a would-be girl band that night that must have come from Planet Zog where they have different tonal scales. They obviously thought their version of the Spice Girls' 'Wannabe' was professional standard, whereas what I wanted, what I really, really wanted was just for it to be in tune.

One bloke who would never see fifty again made an impression too. He was dressed in a white diamante-encrusted suit with tight flared trousers, and he launched into a version of 'King of the Road' which, surely, is a song written so that it can be sung by a stone-deaf squirrel. I won't say much about his rendition beyond advising that if you're ever in Long Eaton in the autumn you should keep your eyes skinned. If you're lucky you might see Elvis dressed as he was in the Vegas years, jumping around in the trees collecting acorns.

Even I had to be restrained from taking the microphone at one stage approaching my third pint. Em threatened to walk out if I didn't sit down.

'You're giving a talk tomorrow. You can make a pilchard of yourself there if you want,' she said.

'But I've got a good voice.'

She shook her head disbelievingly. 'Dagenham,' she said. 'Dagenham.'

'Dagenham? What's Dagenham got to do with it?'

'The tube,' she said. 'District Line. Three stops past Barking.'

The weather next day was fine for the festival and I was pleased about that because events of this sort take a lot of effort to organise and they are important in the local calendar. With Em lending support, I did my gig at the library, a handsome building which sports the most wonderful Arts and Crafts-style stained glass window depicting the Muses of literature, poetry, painting and music. Afterwards we walked back to the festival field on the school grounds opposite the canal, where I got into the spirit of things. I ate some candy floss, I tried to win myself a prize at a hoopla stall and I held a hairy tarantula in the palm of my hand – much to the amusement of a gaggle of giggling girls who might have been practising for karaoke nights in the future given their delight at my discomfiture.

The Long Eaton Festival welcomes boats but it's not a boat festival as such, so apart from *Justice* there were only three other craft there, all of which I'd met at the National. One was a local boat but the other two were heading to their mooring about 12 miles away where the canal terminates at the grandly-named Great Northern Basin. They invited us to travel with them, which we were happy to do since everyone in the group had been involved for years with the canal association that had saved the Erewash from closure, and so it promised to be a more interesting trip as a result.

How this campaign succeeded is an engaging story of dedication and commitment, as well as a testimony to the stubborn pig-headedness of those waterway enthusiasts who have succeeded in rescuing so many of our English canals when, left to the intransigence of officialdom, many of them would have been closed and filled in years ago. This was the fate facing the Erewash Canal in the 1960s, when the newly formed British Waterways Board (BWB) was planning to abandon it and reduce it to a water-feeder. This would have been an ignominious end for the Erewash, which in its heyday had been one of the most commercially successful British canals of all time, one that had once paid an astonishing 78 per cent dividend to shareholders and had continued to return profits right up until it was absorbed into the Grand Union Canal in the 1930s.

Happily, the old girl was much loved locally and at this threat of closure civic pride kicked in. People already felt angry that the Derby Canal, which used to join the Erewash, had only recently been sold off and filled in, and they were determined this wouldn't happen a second time. Several public meetings were held and as a result the Erewash Canal Preservation & Development Association (ECP&DA) was formed. This group of enthusiasts spearheaded the battle by arranging working parties to keep the canal open. At the same time they leased and renovated the beautiful old lock cottage at the junction with the Derby Canal, which in an act of corporate vandalism BWB was intending to demolish. Today it's the association's HQ.

To encourage boaters to visit the canal, the group subsequently built a new terminus too, the original one having been filled in by BWB with its usual sensitive concern for the nation's heritage. That project involved enthusiasts digging out a derelict basin and clearing a lock into which someone had helpfully bulldozed the rather fine adjoining cottage, which should have been listed except that no one bothered about this sort of thing in those days.

Today the terminus is a pretty oasis of green parkland in an otherwise unprepossessing wasteland of industrial estates and retail parks. Then it was a real wasteland, derelict and overgrown.

There's a photograph of one of the working parties which managed to achieve such a startling transformation. It shows volunteers up to their knees in black, oily water, digging out centuries of accumulated coal slurry shovelful by shovelful.

But these aren't the sort of crazy obsessives the world imagines when it thinks of canal enthusiasts. They're just ordinary people, the sort you'd see on any street corner of any town in the country. There's a young guy with a beard, yes; and a bloke in wellies wearing dungarees and a beanie cap with his hands in his pocket like the foreman of a team of council road-diggers – typical stereotypes. But they're the exception. The majority of the men there look as if they push pens most of the week: they're wearing casual slacks and shirts with the sleeves rolled up and gloves to protect their hands because they're not used to physical labour. One of them has a panama hat on his head. There are women there too, almost as many as there are men. One is young and pretty and wearing her long hair in bunches. Another, an older woman, stands surveying events with a steely gaze, holding her shovel at the ready. You feel if she wasn't here she'd be at a school governors' meeting or chairing the local Townswomen's Guild.

Reading contemporary histories of the restoration of the waterways you'd wonder who isn't claiming credit for the revolution that's taken place these past thirty years. If it isn't this boating organisation it's that one; if it isn't Lord Something-or-other of Nowhere then it's the Right Honourable Sir Couldn't-care-less, MP for Wherever-you-want. Recently, as it begins to turn itself into a sort of National Trust for the waterways, even BWB – or British Waterways, as it's now called – is rewriting its own history in an attempt to distance itself from its disgraceful past.

But the people in the photograph are the real heroes and heroines of the restoration movement, the volunteers who put their muscle where their mouths were and rolled up their sleeves to fight for a little bit of England they weren't going to see destroyed, a little bit they cared about and loved.

We all owe them a great debt.

The next morning started badly. We'd travelled the few miles to adjoining Sandiacre the previous evening and had moored opposite Springfield Mill, a remarkably beautiful old lace factory which has been converted into flats. By any definition the place has a high wow factor. Built out of red brick and four storeys high, it must be 150 yards long, perhaps more, and it's in sections, divided by vertical turrets which make it look like the side of a great castle. With its black slate roof and its cast-iron windows it's got a grandeur that makes it seem even larger than it is; but it's also got some charming detailing too, with exquisite decorative brickwork under the eaves.

Impressive though this all is, it's set off by a tapered octagonal chimney which must be more than 100 feet high. This has a flared top and sits on a high pedestal in front of the building, ensuring that the whole complex stands out as a local landmark.

It's difficult not to find yourself distracted by the place. I must have been distracted by it and not really paying attention to what I was doing. Stupidly I started the engine in reverse gear. Before I realised what I'd done there was the agonising sound of steel grinding against stone as it hit the coping stones on the bank. But worse was to follow, for I soon discovered that the collision had knocked the tiller out of its housing and the only way I could move it now was by yanking it, or getting my back behind it and shoving it with my full weight. This had happened once before, years ago, just as Em and I were about to take *Justice* out into the Severn Estuary at Sharpness, probably the worst place on the whole waterways system to lose your steering. We discovered then that you can sometimes relocate it by lifting it up and dropping it in again; but it's a heavy and exhausting process – and this time we couldn't get it to work, anyhow.

Soon our travelling companions from the Erewash Association arrived to meet us as we'd arranged, and they lent a hand with the job too – though with no more success than we'd had on our own. Finally, with time getting on, we had to leave so there was nothing for it but to limp along as best we could. Maybe we could have another go at repairing it later. Maybe later it would just slip in again of its own accord.

The Erewash is a remarkably rural canal for one which was once so industrial. Looking from Pasture Lock across the fields to the hill on which Sandiacre church stands you can almost imagine yourself in the middle of the country. But the industrial side of the canal is just as impressive and all along the banks are the remains of the brickworks, collieries and iron factories that in the past made it so commercially successful.

Sad to say, this deters many people from exploring it. There's a type of boater who just doesn't like an urban landscape: they want canals as linear parks, not reminders of our sweaty past. A derelict factory or the back yards of a terraced row of houses puts them off. Or at least I think that's what puts them off – though I could be wrong. Maybe what actually puts them off the Erewash is a folk memory of the weed the canal once used to be plagued with. Or maybe it's the kids at Ilkestone, which I confess is not the most attractive of towns from the canal, especially around Barkers Lock where there's a hint of the gulags in the grey, breeze-block buildings, concrete walls and razor-wire fencing along the towpath.

All this means the Erewash is nowhere near as busy as it ought to be. On our trip it was evident we were the only boats moving on it, which – given the work it's taken to keep it open – is a disgraceful indictment of the waterways community.

At Eastwood Lock we ran into a couple of British Waterways men who were installing an anti-vandal lock to the paddle gear. This had been designed by one of the crew of the boats we were with, and it's a measure of the current level of cooperation between the Erewash Association and the authorities that this sort of thing happens regularly now. The BW guys were having a bit of trouble in that the rechargeable drills they were using had run out of power, but luckily we carry a generator on *Justice* which we were able to pull out to allow them to finish the job. In return, they gave us a hand trying to get our tiller back into its housing again. But the bloody thing was having none of it, and by the time we pulled into the canal terminus at the Great Northern Basin at Langley Mill it had all but seized up and was barcly uscable.

The Great Northern Basin could be a disappointment if you were expecting a massive dock along the lines of Bristol's Floating Harbour, which covers seventy-odd acres and was built for sea-going ships. The truth is it's only 30 or 40 yards across from one end to the other, so it's hardly a great basin at all. It's also not really a Northern one either – it's more in the Midlands, really. But the Quite Small Midlands Basin doesn't have quite the same ring to it, I grant you.

It's actually the junction of three canals, at the point where the Erewash meets the Nottingham and the Cromford Canals, both now abandoned – although the Cromford's under restoration and it does continue a couple of hundred yards further north, past a boatyard and a dry-dock where there are moorings. In the basin itself, apart from a small and rather delightful old toll office which the Erewash Association has lovingly restored to its original state, there's just a manually-operated swing bridge and space for about twenty or so boats against the side wall of a pub.

It was soon clear we were going to have to avail ourselves of the facilities on offer – and I don't just mean the pub. After a final futile session attempting to get the tiller back in its housing it became apparent that the only way we were going to solve the problem was by putting *Justice* in the hands of professionals at the boatyard and letting them take her out of the water. It wasn't a big job, but we'd have to wait for it to be done, and this effectively put pay to any more cruising for the moment. However, it didn't mean the end of Em's holiday, for Langley Mill is well-positioned as a base for visiting other places of interest and we quickly adjusted our plans.

It's on the edge of the beautiful Peak District; and only a step away from Eastwood, home of the writer D. H. Lawrence, whose birthplace is now a museum. The village of Cromford, where Richard Arkwright, the father of the factory system, established the world's first water-powered cotton-spinning mill in 1771, is only a short hop away on the bus, too; and before Em returned to London we set out early one morning on an expedition to explore the place.

Set among the lovely Derbyshire hills, the mill is actually a complex of three mills built at different times, and although it's an imposing memorial to our industrial past, it's like a prison and it reminded us too much of the price of progress for us to feel entirely comfortable walking around it as tourists. We were pleased to get away. Far more pleasant was to stroll from the mill along the top part of the Cromford Canal, which is one of the sections to have been restored. It's a glorious walk through a sylvan glade which leads to a small quay that was once a trans-shipment point for the old Cromford and High Peak Railway, now recently reinvented for ramblers as the High Peak Trail. It was a delicious day, so bright and cold and rich with the smells of autumn you could have put it on a stick and licked it.

Taking it steady to avoid aggravating my ankle, we climbed up the precipitous slope of what was once the old railway tramway; and at the top we walked through bosky, rock-lined cuttings which every now and again opened out to expose the landscape beyond stretching for miles in the distance. Close up, individual trees still seemed to be green; but looking down from this height, when you saw them together as woodland, you could see they'd already turned a faint mixture of brown and red, the colours smudged through the foliage like a subtle watercolour wash.

The summer was ending, that's what it was. You could feel it even if you didn't know it. The sun wasn't as warming anymore and when it went down at night it was suddenly bitterly cold. There was a dampness in the atmosphere too, a dampness which seemed to get into your bones; and there was a melancholy in the air as well which was difficult to define but which infected everything, my mood especially.

We sat on a bench and Em began to talk to me about my plans for coming home, a conversation I'd been anticipating, although not with the reluctance that I might have felt a week or two earlier. The fact was I was ready to go back now. I was beginning to feel that I'd done enough cruising for one year. If I'm honest, I had started to tire of it. I yearned to wake in the mornings not confused about where I was. I yearned not to have to worry about the basics of life, about having enough water or gas, or food. I yearned most of all to be static, to be able to just look at life without it passing me by, however gently or slowly.

Crazy, I know, but I'd begun to miss London as well. I craved to get back to the noise and the bustle and the clamour. I wanted to see the family and my friends again. I wanted to pick up the threads of my life.

Derbyshire seemed a long way away from anywhere.

TWENTY-SIX
To Leicester and Beyond

*J*ustice was in dry-dock a week longer than I thought she'd
be so I took the opportunity of working on her hull while
she was there, painting it with a layer of the thick tar bitumastic
which we narrowboaters slap below the waterline to protect
our boats from rust. Kit was confused by where we were and I
could understand why. She'd only just got used to the idea of
a boat being something that floated in water and moved. Now
she was being asked to accept that a boat could be static and
stand in a concrete chamber connected to the world only by
a narrow gang plank. At first she was hesitant to use this, but
then she became more confident, and finally so confident that
she didn't use it at all, but instead jumped from ship to shore
in a single fearless bound.

As she began to explore Langley Mill, the gang-plank became
a border post for her, the point at which the rest of the world
ended and home began. In her short stay she seemed to have
made the acquaintance of a lot of other cats, but she didn't

appear to get on too well with any of them. Every now and again, as I was working down in the dock, I'd hear her throw a hissy fit in the hedge and the next thing I knew she'd go sailing over my head escaping from them.

It's a strange thing to stand in a dry-dock and see a cat go over your head as if it's flying. But then it's a strange angle from which to see a cat at all. From her underside Kit was like some superhero, her front and back legs extended so that she lacked only a pair of tights and cape streaming from her collar to complete the look.

Now that I'd finally conceded that I'd had enough of boating and wanted to go home, I was keen to get back to Oxfordshire as quickly as possible and settle *Justice* in her winter moorings; so as soon as the tiller was repaired and she was back in the water I set off on my return journey which I estimated would take me a couple of weeks. My plan was to be in Banbury at the beginning of October in time for Banbury Canal Day, an event organised by the local authority and the last of the festivals I'd planned to attend when I'd sat down all those months ago in London and sketched out the plan of this cruise.

I'd probably have been better advised to delay my departure from Langley Mill until the following morning, for it was late in the day when I got off and I was soon cruising through the gloom of an approaching evening. No waterway anywhere feels entirely comfortable when you're navigating alone in gathering darkness, with every muffled noise on the towpath and every indistinct shadow in the hedgerow a potential threat, and the Erewash is no exception.

I moored that night just south of Ilkeston, which probably wasn't the cleverest thing I could have done, seeing as how everyone had warned me not to because of its reputation for attracting gangs of stone-throwing kids. But like most of these places along the canal with a bad name, their reputation never quite matches reality. I had a quiet night and the next day, with a weak sun filtering through the trees and everyone on the towpath wishing me a good morning as I passed, it was difficult to see what there could be to worry about. In no time at all I was back at Trent Junction and ploughing up the Soar again. There were no other boats around now and the river which so recently had been teeming with craft attending the National was deserted.

The following night I spent in Loughborough basin, where they've built a complex of student flats the colour of liquorice allsorts. I won't do that again. I was a student once; I should have known what students are like. They drink large amounts of alcohol and have parties all the time. Whatever made me think students today were any different to how I was? It was past 3 a.m. when I finally managed to get to sleep.

That Friday Em came up in the car for the weekend and we cruised to Mountsorrel, where we moored just up from the pub at the side of the lock. The weather was bright and clear, and I appreciated it because at this time of year every decent day you get is a bonus. I was impatient to be back to London, yes. But I wasn't that impatient. I knew I'd be away from the canals long enough over the winter. I knew the clocks would be going back soon, too. Autumn days like this when the light is so sharp you could cut yourself are what keep you going through those drab, damp months of winter when you close the curtains early and might as well hibernate for all the time you spend outside.

On the Saturday night a large party of us met up in Leicester for an Indian meal and the following day we hosted lunch on *Justice*, so it was late in the day before we had any time to ourselves.

We decided to go for a walk before it got dark. After I'd strapped up my ankle we set off up the steep outcrop of granite which overlooks Mountsorrel. Afterwards I led us by a back route I remembered alongside a quarry to the common, which as a kid I knew as well as my own back garden – better than my own back garden, in fact, since I used to keep away from that for fear of my dad conscripting me into weeding or some such abusive horror which the NSPCC probably campaigned to ban years ago.

The common, being a common, can't have been touched since I used to play there; but even so, it had changed beyond recognition and I couldn't understand why. Part of it, I guess, was the vegetation: the scrubby trees I recall from my youth had grown stouter over the years; the thin grassland, fed by decades of leaf-fall, had thickened. But this didn't account for it all. Everything seemed to be the wrong way round or in the wrong place; everything seemed familiar, yet I couldn't recognise any of it. It's strange, this process you go through as you get older of revisiting places you've known. What you remember is like the fading negative of a photograph through which you view the present, and you struggle to merge the two into a consistent image. But it's just not possible. Fragmentary though memory is, it's nevertheless resilient, hard-wired into who you are. It struggles for its right to exist and refuses to give ground even when confronted by the unassailable reality of the moment.

Things buzz around in your mind. You can't remember if they happened to you, someone you know or some character in a film you once saw.

'We just have to go through here,' I kept saying to Em. 'There'll be a path soon which will lead us back, I'm sure. Left here, left. It has to be a left. Then we have to go right...'

But there wasn't a path, and if there had been it wouldn't have led in the correct direction. And the left should have been a right, or the right a left. Or maybe we weren't where I thought we were at all and I didn't know where I was leading us.

Eventually Em saw a public footpath which I couldn't recollect ever having existed, and we were soon back at the boat.

'Don't worry about it,' she said. 'It happens to us all…'

'It's not happened to you yet.'

'It's not the same. I haven't got anything like the sort of connection you have with a place…'

'Then it hasn't happened to you,' I snapped. 'How can you know what I feel?'

My reaction stopped her in her tracks and for a moment or two she was silent. 'Perhaps you should explain it to me, then,' she said finally. 'Because from where I'm standing all that seems to have happened is that you lost your way on a walk.'

'It's not losing my way, that's not it,' I said. 'It's like losing my past. Like losing my mind. It's like… like a little bit of me is dying.'

'You're exaggerating. You're still a young man.'

'I'm in the autumn of my life – and you know what comes after autumn.'

'You're depressed,' she said. 'You've been travelling too long. You've been on your own too much. You should get out less.'

She drove back to London that evening and I left Mountsorrel at first light the next morning, untying my lines against the backdrop of a flaming sunrise which lit up the river all the way to Leicester. But I didn't want to stop in Leicester even though that's what I'd planned to do. Leicester was like Loughborough. It was like Barrow and Mountsorrel and Rothley. It was too burdened with memories for me to want to stay any longer, too heavy with the past for me to feel comfortable with it any more. A man can't live in the past forever. It's another country, isn't it? It's abroad.

So I moored at Castle Park for just long enough to pop down to the market; and that afternoon I pressed on into the suburbs, past Freeman's Meadow and the new Walkers Stadium, home of Leicester City Football Club. OK, I support City and so I'm bound to be biased, I suppose. All the same, I think the ground's rather elegant from this angle, seen across what could almost be a large ornamental lake which borders a huge weir adjoining a lock.

Apart from around the ground, I'm pained to confess that Leicester looked shabby. Limekiln Lock near Abbey Park was so squalid with rubbish I rang up to complain about it and found myself making headlines in the local paper. Even West Bridge – the jewel in the crown of the 'Mile Straight' which passes right through the centre of the city – was defaced with graffiti, as was every single lock as far as Newton Harcourt a few miles from where the half-mile Saddington Tunnel burrows under the hill towards Foxton. What is it about Leicester that prevents it caring for its canal better than this? What is it about Leicester people that they don't seem worried about the state it's in?

For heaven's sake, it's not as if it isn't used enough. There was a constant stream of people going up and down the towpath as I passed: kids, young couples, mums with pushchairs, people in wheelchairs, the elderly with walking sticks. It was like a moving walkway of every class and racial type which makes up Leicester's diverse social mix. Some of them stopped to chat as I went through the locks, yet they seemed to be unaware of the state of the canal, or disinclined to worry about it if they were. Eventually I began to wonder if it was me. If I was being too picky. Maybe a few tags on a bridge and a towpath scattered with Big Mac wrappers is part of the rich tapestry of the contemporary canal scene. Perhaps it's part of the rich tapestry of contemporary England, too. Perhaps people like me are just going to have to stop bellyaching and get used to it.

At Kilby Bridge I stopped to fill up with water and met a family out for the day on their bikes. There were four of them: Dad, his two lads and their mother, who was wearing a sari, which I wouldn't have believed possible on a bike, except I've seen it a lot in India.

'Going far?' I asked.

'To the end,' said Dad.

'The end?'

'The end of the canal.'

He was leaning against his bike and the two boys, who were as tall as he was, were behind him like a couple of minders trying to ensure he didn't embarrass them. Dads? Who needs them? Not these two lads. They were still wondering why he'd bothered coming along when they said they were going for a bike ride. And why he'd brought Mum with him when she hates bikes and had told him often enough.

I looked at them and then looked back at dad. The way he was dressed reminded me of my own father. He was wearing cavalry twill trousers and wool check jacket, and he had a collar and tie on as if he'd just left the office. His concept of the end of a canal intrigued me. Of course, there are ends of canals. The Great Northern Basin is an end of the Erewash; Whaley Bridge near Buxton is the end of the Peak Forest Canal. But these are exceptions. Mainly canals lead to other canals which in turn lead to others, a great looping 3,000-mile network of them which stretches from Bristol in the south to the Lake District in the north.

In this sense, there isn't such a thing as the end of the canal. Canals, like the universe itself, just go on for ever and ever, and when you're bored with them in this country you can cruise them in Ireland or the Low Countries, in France or in Germany, all the way to the Baltic. Then you can cruise them again in the opposite direction, when they look different. Or in the winter or the spring when they're different again.

I looked at the kids and they looked back at me suspiciously. They knew all this. They'd spent a lot of time messing about the canal on their bikes, and they'd learnt about them years ago in school as well. Something to do with history and all those dead people, and boring stuff like that. Certainly not as interesting as tracking up the towpath, racing each other; or exploring all the secret places you came across, wondering what you'd find around the next bend. They knew canals didn't end. They'd been telling their dad that for the last hour because they were fed up and wanted to go home now.

I turned my attention back to their father. I shrugged my shoulders and mumbled something about him being right because there wasn't a towpath through the tunnel, and he wouldn't want to go much further than that anyhow, not on an evening like this when it was getting dark and promising rain and none of them had got any lights.

I think they turned back after that, I couldn't be sure.

I went my way; they went theirs.

That's canals for you.

TWENTY-SEVEN
Back Home

I got back much faster than I thought I would. I knew on my own I'd be inclined to rush too much and I was aware that with my ankle in the state it was that could be a recipe for disaster. So I rang my friend Stephen who'd been angling for a trip for years and I threw myself on his mercy. He came up a couple of days later and in what seemed like no time at all we were tying up outside Castle Quay, Banbury's new canalside shopping centre.

The weather helped us make good time. There was the occasional shower, and it was chilly at nights, but on the whole it was fine and bright, the way Septembers have become recently.

We went up the famous flight of locks at Foxton which are actually two connected flights of five locks each. They're a 'staircase' design which means the back of one is the front of another, so that they rise steeply up the hillside like... well, like a staircase, really. They also have side ponds attached to each as a water-saving device which further complicates them. Getting us through safely was a baptism of fire for Stephen who'd never been on a narrowboat in his life, let alone negotiated a tricky set of locks like this. But he managed it well and even the lock-keeper was impressed.

The Foxton flight carries the canal 75 feet up the hill and at the top there's a magnificent view across the undulating Leicestershire plain, the fields at this time of the year a patchwork of green pasture and golden-yellow tracts of stubble where the corn had been harvested. From up here it seems a different world, a million miles away from the one we live in. The stretch of canal after the locks is like this too and particularly secluded. Even in the height of summer when it's at its busiest, it still seems somehow empty; but as we passed there was hardly a boat on it, and the few we saw were moored up and not looking as if they were likely to move any time soon. Their lines were tied tight; their fires already banked up, smoke gently curling from their chimneys in tribute to the changing season.

It was achingly quiet, just the occasional noisy V-shaped formation of geese flying overhead to fracture the silence. You didn't have to be a countryman to know that there was something in the air; you didn't have to be a meteorologist to know that it was probably winter. The clues were everywhere. In places a thick layer of fallen leaves lay across the surface of the canal; and some trees, like the horse chestnuts, were already bare and looking a little sad, with the glistening conkers they'd shed bobbing around in the water beneath them like discarded Christmas baubles. The hedgerows were quieter than they had been too, with fewer birds: just the odd magpie or two left cavorting in the fields, or the occasional murder of crows noisily squabbling with each other high in the trees.

And the gulls, of course.

As we crossed the county border into Northamptonshire, the hills enfolding us like sinuous rolls of soft flesh, the farmers were preparing the fields for the winter wheat; and in the thin sunshine of the autumn afternoon grey flocks of gulls shadowed the tractors as they scored the fields in lines so long and straight they could have been inscribed by a draughtsman. Occasionally they'd settle, apparently exhausted by their aerial acrobatics; but then at some perceived danger, real or imagined, they'd rise into the air again as if one, dipping and swooping in great arcs until they felt it safe to land once more.

After 20 miles and two tunnels, the canal drops down from the summit just behind the service station at Watford Gap on the M1. It's an abrupt return to the twenty-first century and a reminder that this country is no wilderness, and that you're never really far from things however much you kid yourself you are. As we approached Braunston, Stephen and I fell into conversation about the whimsical boat names chosen by couples who'd retired to the cut. They all seemed so melancholy and forlorn: *Last Chance, Autumn Mist, Close of the Day.* We entertained ourselves by seeing if we couldn't do better: *Graveside Dreams, On Our Way Out* or – Stephen's suggestion this, the best of the bunch – *Coffin Ready.*

We pressed on through what had now become a flat and featureless afternoon, and when next I noticed we were at the top of Napton flight gazing towards the windmill. When I looked again – just a moment or two later, it seemed – we were approaching Banbury and I could see the satanic chimney of the Kraft factory belching its usual noxious cloud of coffee-stained chemicals to welcome my return.

The Banbury Festival was an enjoyable enough day and it was pleasant to catch up with old friends and chat about our respective summer travels. But to be honest, I wasn't in the mood for it – and neither was Kit. She'd been listless since Em had left and the noise and commotion of the music and the crowds perturbed her. Me, I was feeling exhausted. A deep tiredness had set in. I was waking now dreaming of being at home.

And frankly, I'd seen enough bunting to last me a lifetime.

Once through the front door I stood in the hall, pleased to be home but feeling dazed, feeling somehow as if I'd never been away, as if I'd been standing in this same spot for months.

I opened Kit's travel basket and she emerged cautiously, sniffing the carpet and skirting-boards as if home was somewhere she didn't know any longer. Then she bolted into the kitchen and out of the cat flap and I didn't see her until Em got back from work. She went out again later for a couple of hours and the next day she was out pretty much from dawn till dusk.

The day after that she didn't come back at all.

'Oh, don't worry about it; she's probably just renewing acquaintance with some of her friends,' Em said when I first mentioned her absence. 'She'll be back soon enough.'

But she wasn't. She didn't come back that night or the night after, or the night after that. Soon she'd been gone a week and we began doing the sort of things you do when a cat disappears in a city. We knocked on the neighbours' doors to see if they could have inadvertently locked her in a shed; we pinned notices up on trees; we offered a reward for any information about her.

Mainly, we just prayed she'd return.

But she didn't return, and gradually it dawned on us that she never would.

I couldn't accept it at first. I couldn't understand why she'd just walk off like this so soon after getting home. Why she'd suddenly disappear at the very moment stability had returned to her life after months of not knowing where she was going to be from one day to the next.

I couldn't believe what a hole she'd left in my life, either. I don't think I'd noticed before how much she'd become a part of my life. It wasn't that at home she followed me around the whole time – though she did follow me more than any other of our other cats had done, and certainly far more than cats are supposed to – but she rarely wandered far away, either; whether at night, sleeping outside the bedroom door or waiting outside the dining room when friends came over. Alone with me, she'd always be interrupting whatever I was doing to check up on me. In the study she'd jump up on the desk and interpose herself between me and the computer, butting my chin with her head as if to demand my attention. Or in the garden, she'd bed herself in the compost I was using, or perch herself on the flower pots I was cleaning, meowing as if to announce that all this physical effort was a worthless waste of my life, and that what was really important – the only thing that mattered in this world – was paying her attention.

Even on the boat she'd never really left me alone. When I was steering I'd be aware of her coming out of the cabin to ensure that I was still there; and at nights while I was reading or cooking or tidying up, and she was supposed to be out, I'd still be conscious of her peeking through the porthole every now and again to reassure herself I was there.

Em was as upset as I was. She may not have wanted Kit as a pet in the first place – any more than Kit had wanted her as an owner. The two of them had gradually become attached to each other, though; they'd built up a mutual respect. Em, finally, had begun to appreciate Kit's appeal, and Kit, at last, had begun to understand Em's crucial role in the domestic set-up. Now none of it mattered. And all that emotional energy we'd invested in her seemed such a waste of time, such a dreadful, dreadful waste of time.

'It's not personal, you have to realise that,' Em said, trying to console me. 'She's not suddenly taken a dislike to you and decided to run off. Something's happened to her: someone's stolen her or… she's had an accident.'

'An accident?'

'A car. She's probably been hit by a car. That's what happens to a lot of town cats: it one of the biggest causes of death…'

Of course, I'd already thought of that myself, though I'd never allowed myself to believe it. I couldn't believe it even now – not really believe it. I took to walking around the streets at night calling for her in that demented way I did, choking her name out through my tears – though I did it more as a cry of anguish now than in any expectation she'd respond.

Em was right, she must have been hit by a car. I was just kidding myself after so long an absence to think anything else. But the idea of her mangled body in a gutter was too much to bear. The idea of her crawling off to die under some mangy hedge was just too painful.

But perhaps that's not how it had been. Perhaps what had happened is that, like Em and I and so many others before us, Kit had been bewitched by the magic of the canals and had grown to love them. Perhaps, like us, she had found herself inexorably drawn to them; and perhaps being taken away from them and brought back to London was too much for her to bear. Perhaps once she'd got back to London she'd had a nose around her old stomping grounds and realised that the canals were where she'd rather be.

And perhaps she'd gone off to find them again: a cat in pursuit of its dream, a cat chasing its destiny.

I don't know – who can ever know? Maybe, one day, I'll be pottering up the Grand Union on a sunny afternoon, or maybe trudging along the Shroppie again in a rainstorm, and I'll catch sight of her bushy tail in the hedge or see her long whiskers poking out from the grass. Maybe, one day, I'll be in Cropredy again, or Birmingham, or maybe on the hill above Foxton, or somewhere on the Oxford summit, and she'll be there like she always was, her lynx-like ears erect, her eyes bright and alert.

I'll know then that she made it, and that she's been waiting for me like I always knew she would.

POSTSCRIPT

She came back. Of course she came back. Didn't you realise that she would? Haven't you clocked the way she is by now? We were sitting over dinner one evening and she just walked in through the cat-flap as cool as you like, as if she'd never been away. Her biscuits were still in the bowl because Em had refused to give up hope she'd return and had never taken them away. But for once it wasn't food she wanted, it was us. She moved between us, coiling herself around our legs and jumping up into our laps, stroking herself against us, nuzzling us. I had never seen her more affectionate.

Whatever adventures she'd had seemed to have left her unharmed. She was in peak condition, well fed and well groomed. Perhaps Em had been right after all; not about her being hit by a car, but about her being stolen. Maybe she'd escaped. Or maybe whoever had her had got fed up and dumped her as she'd been dumped once before as a kitten. The truth is we can conjecture as much as we want but we'll never know.

A couple of months later, however, when Em was out for the evening I sat dozing in front of the TV with Kit at the side of me luxuriating on the sofa which she'd colonised since her return. She was asleep, or so I thought until she opened her eyes and smiled at me and spoke in that lazy New England drawl of hers, a cross between Katharine Hepburn and Isobel Archer in *Portrait of a Lady*. I wanted to ask her what had happened. I wanted her to tell me where she'd been.

But you know what dreams are like.

I think she said something about us humans not really getting it, and about what suckers we were, always falling for the same tricks time after time and never learning anything from our experiences. But that was probably just something on the telly I misheard.

After all, everyone knows cats can't talk.

THANKS

To everyone who made this trip possible. Especially Bob and Rosemary, Dave, Graham and Linda, Stephen and, of course, the people I met along the way.

And to everyone who made this book possible. Especially Miles for being such a consummate wordsmith and encouraging reader, and Moira for… well, for everything, really.

NARROWBOAT DREAMS

A Journey North by England's Waterways

 STEVE HAYWOOD

NARROWBOAT DREAMS

A Journey North by England's Waterways

Steve Haywood

ISBN: 978 1 84024 670 4   Paperback   £7.99

Steve Haywood has a problem. He doesn't know where he comes from. In the south, people think he's a northerner; in the north, they think he's from the south. Judged against global warming and the sad demise of *Celebrity Big Brother,* this hardly registers highly on the Richter scale of world disasters. But it's enough to worry Steve. And it's enough of an excuse for him to escape the routine of his life in London for a voyage of discovery along England's inland waterways.

Travelling by traditional narrowboat, he heads north from Banbury in deepest Oxfordshire, through the former industrial wastelands of the the now vibrantly modern Manchester, to the trendy affluence of Hebden Bridge at the centre of West Yorkshire's ciabatta belt. With irrepressible humour he describes the history of the canals, his encounters with characters along the way, and the magic that makes England's waterways so appealing.

'Haywood imprints his inimitable humour on his descriptions of the people and places he meets along the way' BBC COUNTRY FILE

'... an enjoyable, moreish read, and one of the better British canal travelogues of recent years'   WATERWAYS WORLD

ONE MAN
– AND A –
NARROWBOAT

*Slowing down time
on England's
waterways*

STEVE
HAYWOOD

ONE MAN AND A NARROWBOAT

Slowing Down Time on England's Waterways

Steve Haywood

ISBN: 978 1 84024 736 7   Paperback   £8.99

'If I'd really been serious about getting to grips with my mid-life crisis, then I'd have been better opting for a course of therapy than going off travelling. Or if I had to travel, I'd have been better opting for somewhere warm with a beach…'

In an attempt to get to grips with a BIG birthday, Steve sets out from Oxford to explore what makes the English… well, so English. His quirky humour is inspired by Tom Rolt, who took to the canals on a similar journey immortalised in the book *Narrow Boat*, kick-starting the revival of Britain's waterways. Prepare for a generous helping of mayhem, mishaps and the staple of every English summer: torrential rain.

'entertaining travelogue' THE INDEPENDENT ON SUNDAY

'a great read… earns its place in the canal book canon'
GRANNYBUTTONS.COM

TO HULL AND BACK

ON HOLIDAY IN UNSUNG BRITAIN

TOM CHESSHYRE

TO HULL AND BACK

On Holiday in Unsung Britain

Tom Chesshyre

ISBN: 978 1 84953 060 6   Paperback   £8.99

As staff travel writer on *The Times* since 1997, Tom Chesshyre had visited over 80 countries on assignment, and wondered: what is left to be discovered?

He realised that the answer might be very close to home. In a mad adventure that took him from Hull to Hell (actually a rather nice holiday location in the Isles of Scilly), Tom visited secret spots of Unsung Britain in search of the least likely holiday destinations. He got to know the real Coronation Street in Salford, explored *Blade Runner* Britain in Port Talbot, discovered that everything's quite green in Milton Keynes, met real-life superheroes and many a suspicious landlady, and watched a football match with celebrity chef Delia Smith in Norwich.

With a light and edgy writing style Tom peels back the skin of the unfashionable underbelly of Britain, and embraces it all with the spirit of discovery.

'... *serendipitous encounters with locals from Hull to Hell (Isles of Scilly) work well as a book. They might do even better on Radio 4.*'

THE TIMES

Have you enjoyed this book? If so, why not write a review
on your favourite website?

Thanks very much for buying this Summersdale book.

www.summersdale.com